SOLDIERS FOR SALE

Jean-Pierre Wilhelmy

SOLDIERS FOR SALE

German "Mercenaries" with the British in
Canada during the American Revolution (1776-83)

Baraka
Books
Montréal

We acknowledge the support of the Canada Council for the Arts which last year invested $20.1 million in writing and publishing throughout Canada.

Original title: *Les mercenaries allemands au Québec*
Copyright © 2009 by Les éditions du Septentrion
Publié avec l'autorisation des Éditions du Septentrion, Québec (Québec)

Copyright © Baraka Books

Published by Baraka Books of Montreal.
6977, rue Lacroix
Montréal, Québec H4E 2V4
Telephone: 514-808-8504
info@barakabooks.com
www.barakabooks.com

Book design and cover by Folio infographie

Cover illustration by Jean-Pierre Wilhelmy based on *Lossing's History of the United States* by F.O.C. Darley

Printed and bound in Quebec
ISBN 978-1-926824-12-3

Legal Deposit, 4th quarter, 2011
Bibliothèque et Archives nationales du Québec
Library and Archives Canada

Trade Distribution & Returns
Canada
LitDistCo
1-800-591-6250; orders@litdisctco.ca

United States
Independent Publishers Group
1-800-888-4741; orders@ipgbook.com

NOTES

Note 1:
The term "mercenary" did not, at the time of the American Revolution, have the pejorative connotation prevailing today. In Europe, only after the event of the Nation-State did the mercenary trade become considered as something shameful, and only after the institution of general conscription did the expression "mercenary" become outmoded.[1]

Note 2:
The Province of Quebec, the large tract of land cut through from northwest to northeast by the St. Lawrence River, *is called Canada* by the English who possess it.[2]

Note 3:
The *Canadiens* or *Canadians* originally described the French-speaking people born in "Canada," which was part of New France. After the British conquest and the Treaty of Versailles (1863), the terms *Canadiens* or *Canadians* continued to refer to the French-speaking population concentrated on the St. Lawrence River Valley but with settler communities scattered throughout the Great Lakes and what is now the United States Midwest. The terms were used to distinguish them from the Englishmen who chose to live in Canada. Not before the 1830s did *Canadians* come to include sometimes the English-speaking population of Canada. The term *French-Canadian* then took root to distinguish between the two peoples of Canada.[3]

1. Anthony Mockler.
2. *Journal of Du Roi the Elder, p.66.*
3. Lacoursière, Jacques and Philpot, Robin, *A People's History of Quebec,* Baraka Books, 2009, p. 78.

TABLE OF CONTENTS

To my wife and three children,
Martin, Karine, and Mylène.

PREFACE BY
VIRGINIA EASLEY DEMARCE, PH.D.

In the modern world, the term "mercenaries" brings to mind individuals who as that—as individuals—contract to serve in the military forces of a country not their own.

A few of the "mercenaries" who served in the forces of the various German principalities on behalf of England during the American Revolution met that criterion, although not in regard to England (it should be noted that England had some recruiting stations in the German principalities, and those Germans who were recruited to serve in English regiments can be regarded as "mercenaries" in the first sense). Rather, if they were men contracted to fight on behalf of a "foreign" ruler, that ruler was the German sovereign who contracted with the English government for the use of his troops.

Some of the regiments that served in Canada—that from Anhalt-Zerbst comes to mind first—did have significant numbers of enlistees who were not the subject of the prince who negotiated their service with England. Others—such as Hesse-Hanau—consisted almost entirely of subjects of the ruler whose policies sent them to Canada.

However these soldiers were recruited, until the work of Jean-Pierre Wilhelmy, they were largely ignored by historians. They did receive some attention from individual genealogists whose assumptions about being "French-Canadian" became bewildered as they struggled through the permutations of their ancestral surnames from something arguably French in the late nineteenth century back to something very different, and clearly German, in the last quarter of the eighteenth century.

The publication of Wilhelmy's study in English translation is very welcome and should be of great significance in making this group of eighteenth century immigrant soldiers better known.

Virginia EASLEY DeMARCE, Ph.D.
Past President, National Genealogical Society

PREFACE BY
THE LATE MARCEL TRUDEL

In Canada today there are about seven million French Canadians. But how many of them can honestly claim to have pure French blood on both sides of their family tree? For three centuries the population of North America was formed by people of many different ethnic origins who were recruited during immigration drives or who came here to escape economic crises at home. A certain amount of intermarriage was inevitable.

Since the time of the French regime, In fact, people from many countries have lived among us, intermarried and left descendants—Englishmen from New England, Scottish Catholics who first sought refuge in France before coming to Canada, immigrants from Portugal, Spain, Italy, Switzerland, and Germany. And we must not forget the many marriages between Canadians and Aboriginal people which at one time were actively encouraged by both Church and States, and which were only natural given the close proximity of tribes like the Montagnais and Abenakis, and others like the Aboriginal slaves.

New blood was added to this mixture after the British conquest, and again in the nineteenth century with the massive influx of Irish immigrants. In the twentieth century, our society opened its doors fully to the rest of the world, and the process is now complete. When tracing our roots today, we can no longer end our search once we determine from which French province certain of our ancestors immigrated—we must also try to find out which other European country or countries contributed branches to our famlly tree. It is not the number, large or small, of immigrants which matters, moreover, but the number of their descendants.

Jean-Pierre Wilhelmy is a French Canadian like the rest of us, except that, like his compatriots with surnames like Pozer, Ebacher, Dickner, Molleur (formerly Müller) and Caux, he can trace his German descent. Hence his interest in discovering more about the German branch of our communal family tree. Mr. Wilhelmy focuses his research on the mercenary troops which Germany provided to England at the time of the American Revolution. According to his calculations, some thirty thousand Germans came to America between 1776 and 1783. One third of them lived in the French Canadian community for seven years; two or three thousand remained in Canada at the end of the war. Mr. Wilhelmy relates the arrival of these eighteenth century German immigrants, and describes their settlement here and their contribution to the population—a contribution which is often difficult to trace because patronyms have been altered over the years. What we need now is a wide-ranging study of the present proportion of French Canadians with German ancestry. Once we know that, we could ask the same question about the descendants of immigrants from many other countries.

Marcel TRUDEL O.C., D. Ps L.

Professor Emeritus at the University of Ottawa (1984)

FOREWORD

Growing up with the name Jean-Pierre Wilhelmy in Quebec sparked curiosity. While most people had names like Tremblay, Gagnon, and Bouchard with easily identifiable French background, that was not the case with Wilhelmy. What's more, our family oral tradition was of no help. My own genealogy opened up a vast area of research. Never had I expected to devote seven years to intensive research that would result in a book and even recognition by the Canadian Government of a national historical event.

As I followed my paternal lineage back, I came across a document in which it was written: "sergeant-major in the Hesse-Hanau troops." That took me to the Canadian archives in Ottawa where I was told that the regiment was not known but that it surely must be recorded in the documents covering the English period of the archives.

I consulted hundreds and hundreds of pages in a variety of collections. What a surprise it was to find a vast correspondence between the governors of the period and German officers. Even more surprising was the fact that eighty-five percent of the correspondence was in French, ten percent in English, and the rest in German. I was also told that nobody had ever consulted the correspondence in depth. My own personal genealogical research thus came to an end. But research into what appeared to me to be of much greater interest, namely our own understanding of ourselves in Quebec, then began.

The correspondence led me to a series of original muster rolls and to the reconstruction of the massive puzzle that the German army of 1776-83 represented. After consulting the British, German, and American archives, I discovered several very enlightening diaries written by German officers.

Having completed the initial research, it appeared necessary to consult some professional historians at the Université de Montréal, thinking that they might grasp the importance of this discovery. The reception was little more than polite, cool even, and I was made to understand that there was really very little interest in what I had discovered. This did not discourage me, since my profession at the time (i.e., expressway interchange technologist for Transport Québec) demanded that calculations and design be verified many times over in order to convince decision-makers that a project was well founded. Moreover, I had no doubt about the significance of my findings.

I then began searching for someone who might listen to me and above all understand the importance of the work. A few weeks later, I called Marcel Trudel, Emeritus Professor of History at the University of Ottawa, who already had experience fighting to have his theories accepted. Quite naively, I asked very direct questions of this highly respected specialist in Canadian history. Did you know that German soldiers…? Did you know that they played a major role in Canadian history and that they made an important contribution demographically, culturally, and economically?

Intrigued, Professor Trudel agreed to read the hundreds of pages I had written. A few months later, he returned my manuscript with a note saying that I had indeed found a very interesting subject and that he agreed to help me. Thus began four years of intensive work with the Emeritus Professor of History from the University of Ottawa, who acted somewhat like a thesis director. He then suggested that I publish an article so as to protect my subject, which I did and even won a research fellowship for it.

Before I had even thought of contacting a publisher, I received an offer from a publisher who followed Marcel Trudel's work closely. We quickly reached an agreement, which was a particularly gratifying milestone.

Thanks to Marcel Trudel's legendary professionalism and generosity—he agreed to preface my book—the first edition appeared in 1984. Two new editions came out (1997 and 2009) as well as three books of historical fiction in French. (*La guerre des autres, De père en fille* and *Charlotte et la mémoire du cœur* respectively in 1987, 1989, and 1999.) Historical fiction allows one to use more of the information gathered during the years of research and to cover other aspects of a story that deserves to be known.

An historical plaque is unveiled on August 29, 2009. From left to right: Mr. Jean Dorval, President of the Quebec Historical Society; Mr. Jean-Pierre Wilhelmy, historian and writer; Dr. Aylmer Baker President of the Ebacher Baker Family Association.

It is hoped that with this book, finally available in English, Quebecers, Canadians, and many Americans, particularly those of German background, will discover a forgotten page of our common history. For example, a German-Canadian association showed their recognition by giving me an award in 1989 at the Roy Thompson Hall in Toronto and by submitting my name for a Canada-wide award granted by the Secretariat of State for Multiculturalism to honour a historian's contribution to a cultural community in Canada. What a surprise again to be chosen from among twelve finalists for the Secretariat of State's first prize.

The greatest honour, however, was the erection and unveiling of commemorative plaque on the Plain of Abraham on August 29, 2009 highlighting the contribution of the German troops to the defense of Canada during the American War of Independence (1776-83) and making it into a national historical event.

Jean-Pierre WILHELMY
August 29, 2011

Commemorative plaque unveiled at Garrison Club in Quebec City August 28, 2009

ACKNOWLEDGEMENTS

I wish to thank the following people for their help and encouragement in this project:

Marcel Trudel, O.C., D. ès L., the late Canadian historian and professor Emeritus in the Department of History at the University of Ottawa, without whom this book would probably never been published.

Karin, R Gürttler, Ph.D., Professor Emeritus from l'Université de Montréal for her corrections and encouragement.

Lent, Dr., Niedersächsisches Staatsarchiv, Archivoberrat, Wolfenbüttel, Germany.

Klubendorf, Dr., Niedersächsisches Staatsarchiv, Archivoberrat, Marburg, Germany.

Late Father Julien Déziel, o.f.m., Ex-president of the Genealogical Society of French Canada who was the first to give me an opportunity to make Brunswickers known to the public.

Bruce Wilson and Brian Driscoll, respectively Acting Chief, section of the Public Archives of Canada, and archivist at the same institution, for their generous help.

Virginia Easley DeMarce, Ph.D., Stanford University, U.S.A., for her preface, the translation of the poems of Gottfried Seume, and her great kindness.

Pierre Heynemand and Hrant Khandjian, for their many translations from German.

Daniel Olivier et Normand Cormier, respectively librarians at Montreal's Central Library (in charge of the Gagnon Room at the time) and at the Bibliothèque nationale du Québec.

Joachim Brabander, Dr. and his son Richard G. R. Brabander, Ad Hoc Advisory Committee of the German-speaking community in Montreal, former president (1985-87) of the German Society of Montreal, for their great implication in the recognition of the contribution of German troops.

Thérèse Fortin, for her exceptional contribution in reedited French version.

Karine Wilhelmy, my daughter, for her corrections, typing, and her support in this English adaptation.

Daniel Lavoie, for his technical assistance on drawings of German troops in Canada from 1776 to 1783.

Paul Fortin, who initiated the proposed designation of German mercenaries as a national event.

Aylmer Baker, president of the association of Ebacher-Baker families, for his great implication in obtaining recognition of the contribution of German troops.

And last but not least, my wife and three children from whom I borrowed many leisure hours, at very low rates...

Jean-Pierre Wilhelmy, September 2011

INTRODUCTION

Founded between 1607 and 1733 by people with widely diverse backgrounds, the Thirteen English Colonies in North America had very different political and religions traditions. The North's social and economic structure closely resembled England's own, but was unmistakably marked with the stamp of Puritanism; the cosmopolitan society of the Middle Colonies' large cities was in marked contrast to the middleclass South of small plantation owners. The only common goal for all these people was their desire for independence.

After the French defeat of 1760, the northern colonies were finally free of the ever-present threat posed by the French and Indians in the North; but the cost of their freedom was very high. The national debt had increased considerably since the last war, and the mother country no longer had the means to carry it. Most Englishmen thought the American colonies should share the costs of the war, a view the Americans rejected.

Over the next few years, the British Parliament passed a series of tax laws aimed at raising the revenue the government felt justified in demanding from the colonies. Each new law caused more unhappiness than the previous one until there was widespread discontent throughout the colonies. This led to the First Continental Congress in Philadelphia on September 4, 1774. The result was Thomas Jefferson's *A Summary View of the Rights of British America* which denied all power of Parliament over the colonies. The rallying cry was "No taxation without representation." Although the logic of Jefferson's argument pointed to independence, Congress offered to negotiate with the Crown one last time. George III's pride far outstripped his reason, and the angry monarch decided to subdue the rebels by force. A small army under General Gage was therefore sent to patrol the streets of Boston.

Since Congress hoped that the Canadians, who had only recently been conquered by the English, would join their cause, they decided to send them an official request, the final wording of which was approved on October 26, 1774. This message urged Canadians to "seize the opportunity presented by Providence itself. You have been conquered into liberty if you act as you ought." They were invited to win freedom and gain representative government by entering into a union with the other colonies, and to "take a noble chance for emerging from a humiliating subjection under Governors, Intendants, and Military Tyrants, into the firm rank and condition of free English citizens...." Furthermore, the Americans stated, "That we should consider the violation of your rights... as a violation of our own..." [1] Heady stuff, and an offer one would think the Canadians could not refuse.

American anger however had recently been raised to great heights by the passing of the Quebec Act, designed to maintain Quebec's loyalty towards Britain. To the British authorities this appeared to be a particularly prudent move in the face of the rumbling discontent in the Thirteen Colonies. But to the Americans it was a red flag to a bull. The Quebec Act "recognized and guaranteed the position of the Roman Catholic Church in the colony and legalized its right to collect tithes from its member." It extended the boundaries of the colony to include the rich fur-trading territory between the Ohio and upper Mississippi rivers, which had formerly been part of the French empire. But it "denied the new colony an elective assembly, one of the traditional features of British colonial government." [2] Angry American patriots denounced the Act "as being designed to do injustice to them by preventing the spread of American settlement and American liberties over the whole of the American continent," [3] and lashed out at the recognition granted to the Catholic Church. This anger spilled over into the letter they wrote to the Canadians offering them fellowship in the cause of freedom. It concluded with a barely-veiled threat: "You are a small people, compared to those who with open arms invite you into a fellowship. A moment's reflection should convince you which will be most for your interest and happiness, to have all the rest of North America your unalterable friends, or you inveterate enemies." [4]

The letter was translated, and French and English copies were distributed and widely read throughout the province. It angered the nobility and clergy, as was to have been expected, since the Quebec Act suited them very well. The tone was another source of anger. Renowned nineteenth-century French-Canadian historian François-Xavier Garneau wrote, "If the authors of this letter had been serious, their language would merely have been fanatical; but coming from men who wanted the Canadians to embrace their cause, it was foolish and childish."

The *habitants*, as they were known, were caught in the middle. To some extent they sympathized with the American rebels, because they "had no greater affection for tithes or feudal obligations than the American had for taxes, and all this talk of liberty from over the frontier was pretty warming stuff."[5] On the other hand, Bishop Briand sternly told them, "Your oaths, your religion, lay upon you the unavoidable duty of defending your country and your king with all the strength you possess."[6] In the end, most Canadians remained neutral. They had no wish to fight for their British conquerors, nor could they forget "that for more than a century they had fought and competed with the same Americans to the south who were now claiming to be their friends."[7] So for the most part, they did nothing.

One group which might have joined the American cause were the Quebec merchants, most of whom were English. They were angry at not being given a voice in government, since the Quebec Act denied the colony an elective assembly. But they were also angered by the worthless money paid by the Americans for goods bought in Canada; and they ultimately realized that Britain was "the source of their economic strength and prosperity."[8] In the end, they remained "passively loyal."

The War of Independence was declared throughout the Thirteen Colonies on April 19, 1775, after the first rounds of fire were exchanged. The next day, sixteen thousand men besieged Boston. While the British soldiers stationed in Boston posed little threat to the rebels, the rumours of an attack by an English army from Canada were of far greater concern. Benedict Arnold[9] and Ethan Allen[10] resolved, independently of one another, to block the British by capturing Fort

Ticonderoga[11] where they knew weapons were stockpiled from the time of the French and Indian War. On May 10 the two rebels unwillingly joined forces for a dawn attack. What followed was comedy —and victory.

Embarrassed by the actions of Arnold and Allen—never authorized by Congress—Congress sent off a second letter to the Canadians, urging them to join the struggle for a "common liberty." But this letter was no better received than the preceding one, despite its threatening tone. On June 27, 1775, Congress adopted Arnold's proposition to invade Canada. The siege of Quebec began on December 6. The night of December 30 saw a double American attack in which the rebels lost their leader, General Richard Montgomery, in the first round of fire. Despite a leg wound, Arnold was able to carry on with the siege, thanks in part to Governor Carleton's passivity.

The England of Hanover

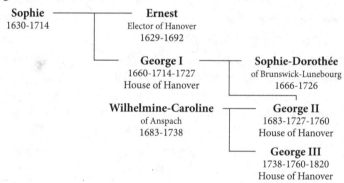

Sophie	Ernest
1630-1714	Elector of Hanover
	1629-1692

George I	Sophie-Dorothée
1660-1714-1727	of Brunswick-Lunebourg
House of Hanover	1666-1726

Wilhelmine-Caroline	George II
of Anspach	1683-1727-1760
1683-1738	House of Hanover

	George III
	1738-1760-1820
	House of Hanover

Filiation of the Dukes of Brunswick

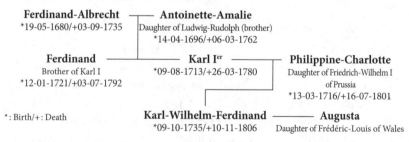

Ferdinand-Albrecht	Antoinette-Amalie
*19-05-1680/+03-09-1735	Daughter of Ludwig-Rudolph (brother)
	*14-04-1696/+06-03-1762

Ferdinand	Karl Ier	Philippine-Charlotte
Brother of Karl I	*09-08-1713/+26-03-1780	Daughter of Friedrich-Wilhelm I
*12-01-1721/+03-07-1792		of Prussia
		*13-03-1716/+16-07-1801

*: Birth/+: Death

Karl-Wilhelm-Ferdinand	Augusta
*09-10-1735/+10-11-1806	Daughter of Frédéric-Louis of Wales

Notes

1. George F.G. Stanley, *Canada Invaded, 1775-1776*, Toronto: Hakkert, 1973, 18.
2. Ramsay Cook with John T. Saywell and John C. Ricker, *Canada: A Modern Study*, *Toronto, Vancouver: Clarke, Irwin & Co., 1963*, 6-8.
3. Stanley, 17.
4. Quoted in Stanley, 18.
5. Stanley, 19.
6. Cook, 11.
7. Cook, 12.
8. *Ibid.*
9. Benedict Arnold was a prosperous New Haven merchant of drugs, books, and horses. When he learned of the fighting in Massachusetts, he hastily gathered some men together and volunteered to serve the "patriots" there. He was commissioned a colonel by the provincial Congress and was also given funds and the authorization to attack British forts on Lake Champlain. He defected to the British in September 1780, and in the United States his name is synonymous now with traitor or turncoat.
10. Colonel Ethan Allen was the very popular commander of the Green Mountain Boys of Vermont who waged a war of terror against the inhabitants of upper-state New York, a region claimed by both New Hampshire and New York. (It later became the State of Vermont.) The Green Mountain Boys were a band of undisciplined adventurers and outlaws, just what the Connecticut authorities wanted in order to combat the English. Thus Allen was authorized by Connecticut to attack Ticonderoga.
11. "Both Ticonderoga and Crown Point, known in Canadian history as Carillon and St.-Frédéric, had been built by the French as the outer works of Canada's defence system, and even though the official boundary line had been moved north by George III in 1763, the two forts were still the outer guardians of Canada's military security." (Stanley, p. 23)

Quebec Act of 1774

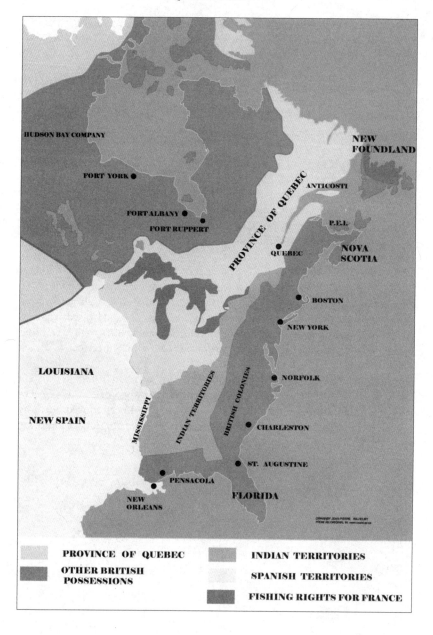

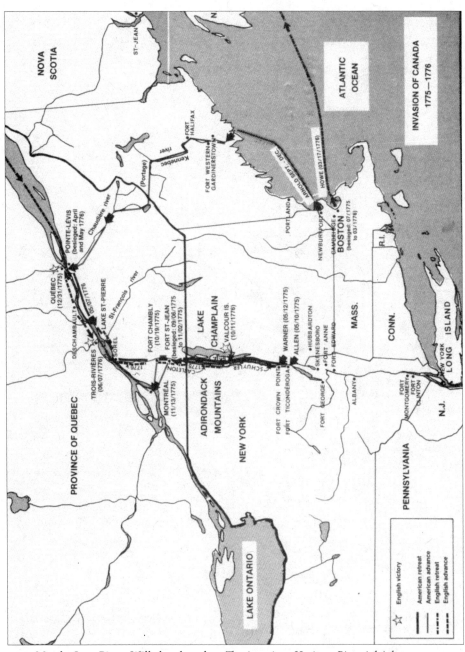

Map by Jean-Pierre Wilhelmy based on *The American Heritage Pictorial Atlas of U.S. History.*

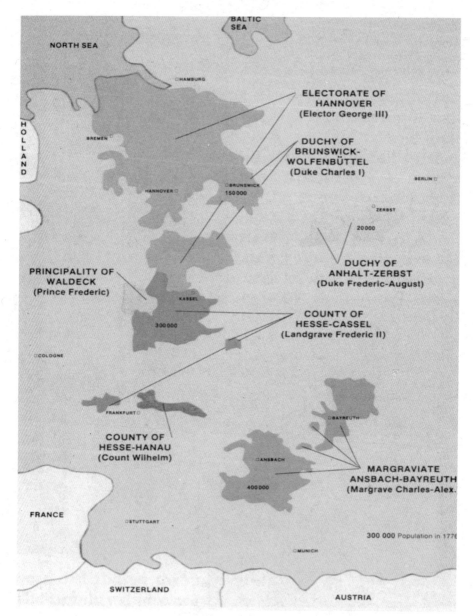

States of the German Empire at the time of the American Revolution. Map by Jean-Pierre Wilhelmy based on *Hessian View of America, 1776-1783*, Kipping.

Location of British Soldiers in 1775

Country	Infantry Reg.	Soldiers	Cavalry Reg.	Soldiers	Total
England	19	11,396	16	4,151	15,547
Scotland	1	474	—	—	474
Isle of Man	3	142	—	—	142
Ireland	21	9,815	12	2,718	12,533
Minorca	5	2,385	—	—	2,385
Gibraltar	7	3,339	—	—	3,339
India	3	1,909	—	—	1,909
America	18	8,580	—	—	8,580
Africa	1	214	—	—	214
Total		**38,254**		**6,869**	**45,123**

Chapter I

ENGLAND'S SEARCH FOR MERCENARIES

"England will never give up its colonies,"[1] George III had pro-claimed, anxious to maintain control over the Empire. The strength of his army would command respect, he had added. However, despite the king's brave words, England did not possess the armed might she was supposed to have. Little more than 45,000 men scattered around the world constituted the entire British army in 1775. (See Fig.1.)[2] In America, reports from Major-General Guy Carleton indicated that he was in charge of a mere 850 men. General Thomas Gage in Boston reported that he could command only 8,000 soldiers in circumstances calling for 25,000.[3]

King George III of England was the great-grandson of the German Protestant king, George I, who had succeeded Anne Stuart through the Act of Settlement;[4] he was also Elector[5] of Hanover, one of the numerous German states which made up the Holy Roman Empire. He was thus able to send five Hanoverian regiments to Minorca and Gibraltar, i.e., 2365 soldiers, to relieve some of his regular English troops. Subsequently, he tried to recruit 4000 new Hanoverian soldiers; the results proved unsatisfactory, however, as a mere 250 men answered his appeal.[6] Given the situation in the American colonies at the time, this number seemed paltry indeed. But there was no question of trying to attract new English recruits, as London deemed such a procedure too costly and difficult, as well as too time-consuming. It was also well known that many Englishmen found the idea of fighting their American cousins to be repugnant, so that conscription was likely to cause serious internal problems. England had to seek help elsewhere, as she had already done successfully in the past.[7]

The following summer, an unusual event marked English history. The British Ambassador to Moscow, a certain Colonel Gunning, was invited by the Russian Prime Minister, Nikita Panin, to discuss the evolution of the rebellion in the southern colonies. Gunning seized the opportunity to enquire as to Russia's response to a possible request from England for help. Panin's reply evoked Catherine the Great's affection for the English, which George III's ambassador took to mean that Russia was now morally committed to England's cause. In the days to come, this false assumption was to dampen relations between the two powers.

The Russian Empress, influenced by new ideas and by men such as Vergennes and Frederick of Prussia, soon sent the English king an elegantly sarcastic missive: "I have barely begun to enjoy our present state of peace, and Your Majesty is surely aware that my Empire is in great need of rest. It would be unseemly to employ an army of that size in another hemisphere, under the command of another power of which it knows almost nothing. Moreover, I cannot help but reflect upon the effects on our dignity, on our monarchies and on our two nations were we to join forces with the sole aim of subduing a rebellion which receives no foreign support."[9] Catherine the Great's rebuff was soon the talk of all of England, to the great displeasure of its leaders.

Musketeer with the Anhalt-Zerbst infantry regiment. (By Jean-Pierre Wilhelmy, based on Embleton/Osprey.)

Allies willing to hire out mercenaries were becoming scarcer. George III turned next to Holland, since that country was already under moral obligation to England, as the

Ambassador to The Hague, Joseph Yorke, pointed out. But the Dutch were scarcely more sympathetic to the cause of King George than the Russians. Even the most illustrious Dutch statesman of the time, Baron von der Capellan, the Overrijsel delegate, insisted, "A republic should never assist in making war on a free people."[10]

Holland had no wish to offend the English king, however, so it slyly offered one brigade on the condition that it not serve outside of Europe. The king refused.[11]

England finally had no choice but to listen to the German princes, even if negotiations threatened to be long and difficult because of the number of treaties which had to be concluded. Four German princes had already offered—not without self-interest—"the ardour and blood of their subjects"[12] in the aftermath of the battles of Breed's Hill and Bunker Hill. The four in question were Count Wilhelm of Hesse-Hanau, George III's cousin; the Margrave of Ansbach-Bayreuth, Karl Alexander, nephew of Frederick the Great of Prussia; Prince Frederick of Waldeck; and Prince Frederick Augustus of Anhalt-Zerbst, brother of Catherine the Great of Russia, whose generous offer would be scrupulously studied.

By November 1775, after an exhaustive study of the situation, the English cabinet decided to begin negotiations[13] with a view to putting an end to the American rebellion as quickly as possible. The Secretary of State, Lord Suffolk, asked Colonel William Faucitt to reach a rapid agreement with the German princes while incurring as small a debt as possible, since it was imperative that more men be found.[14] Colonel Faucitt had recently concluded successful negotiations for troops from Hanover. A few days later he set out for the Holy Roman Empire, forerunner to Germany, on his new mission.

At the time of the American Revolution, the Empire comprised about three hundred fifty states, varying greatly in size and population and, depending on the title of their leaders, labelled variously as principalities, electorates, duchies, margravates, landgravates, bishoprics, abbeys, seigniories or free cities ruled by secular or ecclesiastic Protestants or Catholics. The interests of each member state were discussed in the Diet, an assembly of all the states headed by the Emperor,[15] who was chosen by nine Electors. Each state, however tiny, was free to form alliances, to establish embassies, and even to wage war—as long as there was no conflict of interest with the Empire, naturally.[16]

The Empire's population numbered a little more than twenty million, divided equally, at least in the German sector, between the many cities and the rural areas. The German church was not as well organized as its French counterpart, owing to the many sects that flourished there. Religious divisions were very complex since it was up to each sovereign to decide how his subjects would worship. The Catholic clergy, wealthy and numerous, did not limit their activities to religious matters. On the contrary, many of them were heads of state far more concerned with material than with spiritual affairs.

There were two categories of nobles in eighteenth-century Germany. The first consisted of minor heads of state or knights with limited material resources who might be found in the service of the Emperor or a wealthy prince. The second included nobles who gravitated towards state rulers whom they served as ministers, diplomats or courtiers. Their fortunes were closely linked to the extravagance of their masters, many of whom delighted in a lavish lifestyle similar to that of the French aristocracy.[17] The many cities in the Empire differed widely in mentality. Some were the modern seats of princely residences, with progressive outlooks, and were often used as state capitals. Others were more conservative, with populations whose mentality revealed their peasant roots. These cities usually had old quarters, indicative of the strength of tradition.

About thirty percent of the Empire's population were peasants. In the west and south they lived like their French counterparts, with a large share of their revenue going to their lord as rent or in payment of his seigniorial rights. The peasants in the east and north lived like serfs in the Middle Ages. Personally and materially, they depended entirely on their lord. No matter where they lived, however, the peasants' education was minimal and their preoccupations limited to relations with their lord and harvest fluctuations. Religious faith was very strong in the country, and the piety of the peasants was often much more sincere than that of the clergy who guided them.[18]

The princely courts of the 1770s formed a closed world but were nonetheless influenced by the Enlightenment and a transformation that was felt throughout German society. Virtue triumphed, etiquette was relaxed, and poets reigned as kings. Long convinced of their natural superiority, the German princes had imposed their absolute power over less fortunate souls born beyond the pale of nobility. By the end of the century, however, several staid chamberlains and ministers had relinquished their positions in favour of poets and learned men in courts like that of Weimar.[19] This represented a mere crack in the social structure, for despite the new ideas shaking the foundations of the old Germany, the princes had difficulty accepting the loss, partial or complete, of their absolute powers. Their states were often poor and badly administered; but when seized with a sudden impulse to try some new pleasure, few rulers were willing to forego such self-indulgence for the sake of new ideas.[20]

The correspondence between Landgrave Frederick II of Hesse-Cassel and one of his officers in America, Baron von Hogendorff, gives ample proof of how few new ideas had been adopted by this prince. Here is what he wrote in 1777:

> Baron von Hogendorff, I cannot find words to tell you how overjoyed I was by your report of my brave Hessians, who sacrificed their lives so heroically for a foreign cause, which confirms my faith in their bravery and justifies my belief in their devotion to my interests, but I cannot forgive the English chroniclers for lowering the death toll so greatly, why not admit honestly that instead of 900 we lost 1700! To tell the truth, I am not satisfied with this number and can only attribute it to very selfish motives on their part.
>
> Do these gentlemen really believe that 30 guineas more or less mean nothing to me? Particularly after my latest expensive journey during which I contracted many new debts. No, dear friend, let your zeal for my interests as well as your own make you redouble your efforts on every occasion when you can inspire my loyal subjects to sacrifice their lives. To the last man. In order to satisfy legitimate, as well as necessary, aims.
>
> Would you please convey to Colonel M... my displeasure at his conduct to date. The only one of all our corps that has lost only one soldier, this is cause for shame and pains me greatly; signora F., whom I have just engaged in Italy, will cost me more than 500 guineas a year and then these blasted Englishmen want to quibble over wounded and disabled men, well no they will pay me at the same rate that we agreed upon for

men killed, or else, I would prefer that they follow the example of the ones who surrendered at Trenton, yes indeed, of what use would these wretches be to me! Here? Moreover they're not good for anything any more, those damned rebels who always shoot so low have probably made them impotent but as for that, the Jesuits whom I would like to invite to my states will take charge of that thousands of times better and will soon compensate for the depopulation which is already far too evident, this is an expedient which Cardinal T. gave me in Rome, promising to arrange this matter with all the dexterity one could wish: "You would not believe (he told me) how much the sight of so many fine guineas can restore a man's strength." Well, whatever happens, let us enjoy the present and not concern ourselves with the rest; with this, I pray God to keep Baron von Hogendorff safe and well. Cassel 1777.[21]

On January 9, 1776, barely a month after his arrival in Brunswick, William Faucitt concluded a treaty with Baron Feronce von Rotenkreuz, representative of Duke Karl. Power in Brunswick was shared by Karl I and his son, Prince Karl Wilhelm Ferdinand, who was also the brother-in-law of George III. Ferdinand[22] was a brilliant administrator who had established a lottery, run by a Minister of State, to help off-set the deficits caused by his father's extravagance. For Karl, like most of these little German potentates, liked to spend lavishly.

By the terms of the treaty,[23] the duke was to provide 3964 foot soldiers and 336 dragoons, or light cavalry, who would serve temporarily in the infantry until such time as horses could be provided for them. These men would be equipped by the duke, and would swear allegiance to the British crown, in return for which they would receive the same treatment as British soldiers. Because they would have to march from Brunswick to the ports of embarkation, George III would be responsible for preventing any desertions while they crossed his Hanoverian territories. Salaries would be paid through the duke at first and then directly to the soldiers once they reached America. Sick and wounded Brunswick soldiers would be treated in English hospitals, and those unable to continue fighting would be sent back to Brunswick at the expense of the British crown.

The treaty also stipulated that trained and fully equipped replacements would be provided as the need arose. As for any soldiers who died during transportation, in sieges, or from epidemics or contagious diseases, England agreed, in accordance with the treaty of 1702,[24] to defray the costs of their replacements until the latter arrived in America. But the duke reserved the right to fill vacancies and to choose his own officers, as well as to maintain jurisdiction over his soldiers. As for the monetary arrangements, England agreed to pay the sum of £7, 4s, 4½d (about $35.00 in 1884 or about $7,800 in 2010, using the nominal GDP per capita) for each soldier, as well as bonuses throughout their stay in America and for two years after their return home.

In addition, for each soldier killed, the duke would receive the sum of £7, 4s, 4½d, and the same amount for every three soldiers incapacitated. This last clause outraged some people, who denounced the negotiations as man-traffic and the prince as a seller of souls.

When Duke Karl I died in 1780, his son Wilhelm Ferdinand took the throne and became the only one of the six princes to reach an agreement with England to order those of his soldiers who were guilty of committing crimes or bad conduct, or those whose wounds made them unable to continue serving in his army, to stay in America.[25] All told, 5723 officers and soldiers were sent overseas from Brunswick, of whom only 2708 returned to Germany.[26]

The most important of the six German leaders who eventually concluded treaties with England was the Landgrave of Hesse-Cassel, Frederick II.[27] (not to be confused with Frederick the Great of Prussia). Frederick II ruled over a mainly Protestant population of 300,000 and allowed no one to dictate his behaviour. He had recently converted to Roman Catholicism, which so displeased his first wife, Princess Mary (a daughter of George II), that she decided to leave him after fourteen years of marriage. She took her three sons and went to live in Hanau. Along with herself, her eldest son thus became both the legitimate heir to Hesse-Cassel and the independent count of the tiny principality of Hesse-Hanau. It would seem that Frederick quickly consoled himself for the loss of his family, and bragged to anyone who would listen about the large number of children he had sired.

At the start of the American Revolution, Frederick II of Cassel was about sixty years old, living in peace and prosperity with his second wife. He was an excellent administrator, as the state of his treasury attests. Although his subjects lived in misery, his court rivalled the French for luxury. It had its own theatre, opera, and French ballet company; and since the language of Molière was in fashion, princes and diplomats often spoke French. Frederick's army was his pride and joy. Modeled along Prussian lines, it was one of the best in Europe.

The treaty[28] signed on January 15, 1777 by Frederick's Minister of State, General Baron Ernst von Schlieffen, was the most favourable of the treaties concluded by the German princes. The reason was simply that Cassel could afford to wait, while London could not. Schlieffen easily took advantage of the situation, and made England pay back £40,000 which she had borrowed from Frederick during the Seven Years' War. In general, this treaty resembled the one signed by the Duke of Brunswick with the following exceptions: the controversial clause (reimbursement for every soldier killed or his equivalent) was rejected; England agreed to come to the aid of Cassel should his state be attacked on European soil; and wounded Hessian soldiers were to be treated by doctors from Hesse in Hessian hospitals. Finally, the most important clause in the treaty, from Frederick's point of view, gave him twice as much money per soldier as the amount paid to the Duke of Brunswick. By this treaty, 12,500 soldiers from Hesse-Cassel, divided into fifteen regiments of five companies each, departed for America with the first convoy of German mercenaries. Altogether, Frederick II sent the most soldiers overseas of all the German princes. Of the 16,992 soldiers who left, 6,500 did not return to Germany. This was Cassel's sixth agreement with a foreign power in the space of a century; no less than four of these were with England.[29]

The heir to the throne of Hesse-Cassel, Count Wilhelm of Hesse-Hanau,[30] had lived in the tiny principality of Hesse-Hanau since his father's conversion to Catholicism. This county extended about 45 to 55 miles from east to west, although it was barely five miles wide in some places. Despite Wilhelm's claim to the throne of Cassel, his court did not enjoy cordial relations with that of his father. Hesse-Cassel would create problems for him, moreover, when his troops left for America. A true son of the landgrave, Wilhelm followed the family tradition of renting troops, and after 1775 he did not hesitate to offer his cousin George III the services of his loyal subjects.

> Sire, the present situation, which the problems created by Your Majesty's subjects in another part of the world have engendered, rekindles the zeal and the loyalty of all those who, knowing your goodness, Sire, long ardently for the happiness and peace of the best of kings. Moved by those feelings which my humble respect and my inviolable attachment to your person dictate, I beg you to consider, at a time when Your Majesty seems to wish for German troops, my unconditional offer of my infantry regiment, consisting of 500 men to do with as you will, all children of the land which Your Majesty's protection guarantees to me alone, and all ready to sacrifice as I am their lives and their blood in Your Majesty's service. I pray you will pardon the liberty I am taking and consider my intention and not the thing itself. Were I to have twenty thousand men to offer Your Majesty it would be with the same eagerness. May it please you therefore to dispose of my regiment entirely, at whatever time and place you command. It will be ready at the first sign you are kind enough to bestow upon me.[31]

Prince Wilhelm's lifestyle closely resembled that of his father, with whom he shared a fondness for expensive things and costly buildings; in short, for money and pleasure. But, to their credit, Frederick and Wilhelm were the only princes who lowered the taxes of any of their subjects who were closely related to a mercenary soldier rented to the English king from one of their two states.[32]

Despite Wilhelm's hasty offer of August 1775 to his English cousin, his emissary, Baron Friedrich von Malsbourg, only signed a treaty[33] with Colonel Faucitt on February 5, 1776. Its basic terms resembled those of the two preceding treaties. Hanau was to lend England 668 infantrymen as well as an artillery company of 120 soldiers. Following the example of the Duke of Brunswick, Wilhelm ratified the disputed clause. By the end of the hostilities, Hanau had furnished England with 2422 soldiers of whom only 1400 returned to Germany.[34]

Next on the agenda for Colonel William Faucitt was the small principality of Waldeck,[35] on Hesse-Cassel's western border. As was so often the case at the time, this small state had a tradition of supplying mercenaries to other nations. Since 1775, moreover, its people suffered under a decree whereby all male citizens of an age to go to war, with the exception of university students, were conscripted. Waldeck's warmongering prince upheld the tradition gladly, turning his little state into a veritable reservoir of mercenaries. At the time of the American Revolution, Waldeck's principal client, Holland, had two of its regiments on Dutch soil. Like the Count of Hesse-Hanau, Frederick of Waldeck smelled the money. In November 1775, he wrote Lord Suffolk to offer him a 600-man regiment. Imagine the surprise of the quartermaster when he discovered, on arriving in Waldeck, that a mere 200 men constituted the entire potential military reserves of the principality. In order to receive his share of the spoils, Frederick drew on the two regiments stationed in Holland to create what would henceforth be known as the third Waldeck regiment of German mercenaries.

The treaty,[36] signed at Arolsen in the principality of Waldeck on April 20, 1776, required Frederick to provide the English king with a company of 134 grenadiers, four companies of musketeers (130 men per company), fourteen artillery as well as sixteen staff officers, for a total of 684 officers and men. By the end of the war, 1225 officers and soldiers had been sent to America from Waldeck; only 505 returned to Germany.[37]

Next on Colonel Faucitt's journey lay the principality of Ansbach-Bayreuth, which had been formed in 1769 by the union of the independent territories of Ansbach and Bayreuth, under the rule of the margrave Karl Alexander.[38] Karl's father was a murderer; he once had a man put to death for not feeding his dogs properly. Fortunately for his subjects, the son was far more humane than the father. Like the landgrave of Hesse-Cassel, Karl Alexander did not endorse the disputed clause in his treaty with England. Still, burdened by debts contracted for the most part by his predecessors, the margrave thought to use his little army to his advantage, like the other princes. The treaty was duly signed on January 14, 1777, stipulating the loan of two regiments of 570 men each, 101 chasseurs as well as 44 artillery, for a total of 1285 officers and men. Nonetheless, the opportunity offered by his agreement with the British crown was a mere stop-gap. In 1791, Karl Alexander was forced to sell his lands to Prussia in return for a small pension. As for the men he hired out to the English king, by the end of the fighting their numbers had reached 2353, of whom 1183 returned to Germany.[39]

The final treaty was concluded with Prince Frederick Augustus of Anhalt-Zerbst.[40] Brother of Catherine the Great of Russia, Frederick Augustus can hardly be said to have ruled his 20,000 subjects, since for more than thirty years he had been living in various places—anywhere but in his own land—delegating his powers to secret or privy counsellors. The population of Anhalt-Zerbst lived in abject misery, suffering in addition from all kinds of calamities (famine, plague, etc.) which made it one of the poorest, if not the poorest, of all the states in the Holy Roman Empire.

Although the half-mad[41] Frederick Augustus had already offered the English king the services of his soldiers in 1775, his approach was so clumsy that support was needed from the courts of Brunswick and Hanau and even from the English ambassador to Holland before George III's emissary was authorized, on April 29, 1777, to begin negotiations.[42] The treaty was signed that October and, in the following years, 1160 mercenaries from Anhalt-Zerbst served in America. Of this number, 984 soldiers and officers returned home.[43]

Other negotiations were begun at the request of the Elector of Bavaria and the Duke of Wurtemberg; but they failed, partly because of the poor condition of the troops and their equipment, but mainly because of Frederick the Great's harassment whenever any soldiers tried to cross his territory.[44]

It is difficult to determine the exact amounts paid to the German princes during the course of the war and even, in a few cases, in subsequent years, because certain details were kept secret. The sums granted annually by the British parliament give us a good idea.[45]

An annual average amount of £850,000 was paid to the German princes for their soldiers. A few of them, like the Landgrave of Hesse-Cassel and his son William of Hesse-Hanau, received higher payments than the others.[46] Thus, in 1776 nearly 20,000 German mercenaries joined forces with the English troops, their number throughout the War of Independence equalling that of the English soldiers in America.

The British crown had, by its own powers, concluded costly treaties with the German princes for the services of their soldiers. The neces-

German States	Years of service	Sums
Hesse-Cassel	8	£ 2,959 800
Brunswick	8	£ 750 000
Hesse-Hanau	8	£ 343 000
Waldeck	8	£ 140 000
Ansbach-Bayreuth	7	£ 282 000
Anhalt-Zerbst	6	£ 109 120
Total amount received after the war		£ 1,150 000
Bonuses for 20,000 men at £ 6		£ 120 000
Total amount received as supplements for artillery		£ 28 000
Total amount received for the annual maintenance ofthe artillery		£ 70 000

sary funds however required the consent of the House of Commons which alone had the power to authorize spending. A Parliamentary Committee therefore had to ratify the treaty.

In February the fourteenth British Parliament resumed after the holiday break. On February 29, Lord North initiated discussions in the Commons, trying to convince the Opposition of the urgency and soundness of the treaties and explaining their implications. Hiring troops in this manner, he said, would cost the government less than trying to raise its own army. He concluded that because of their numbers and skills, the German mercenaries would quickly put down this incipient rebellion, perhaps even without bloodshed. To support Lord North's arguments, a Mr. Cornwall, a former payroll clerk who had been in charge of paying the German auxiliaries in the last war, explained to Parliament that the government was getting a real bargain with these treaties, since the German officers were unanimous in declaring that the terms did not favour their rulers. The next speaker, Lord Germain, reminded the Opposition that England had already had recourse to such measures before. As for Lord Barrington, while he did not really think the government was getting a bargain, he could not conceive what else it could do under the present circumstances. The Opposition remained deaf to these arguments, and through the Whig party leader, David Hartley, declared that the treaties represented a kind of alliance with detestable little princes. Moreover, even though England was bound by only one treaty to defend the territory of a single German state, how could she stand by and watch the invasion of any of these states, should it occur, when their armies were supporting the English cause in America? The Whig leader also deplored the use of force instead of negotiation in America, since this would indubitably lead to the escalation of an already unfortunate situation.[47]

Another Opposition member pointed out that there were already 150,000 Germans living in the colonies of the south. He feared that they might be inspired by a burst of patriotism to join the rebels if they learned that their former fellow countrymen were trying to reduce them to slavery. This could lead to a war between brothers, he declared, and it would be hard to predict the outcome of such a catastrophe. It was easy to imagine how many mercenaries would desert or even change sides completely. Lord Irnham declared that he did not trust the little German princes to keep their promises anyway, since they failed notably to respect their own Emperor. He compared them with Sancho Panza who, had he been king, would have wanted all his subjects to be black so that he could sell them and convert them into hard cash. A last argument by Alderman Bull closed the debate: "Let not the historian be obliged to say that the Russian and the German slave was hired to subdue the sons of Englishmen and of freedom..."[48] Despite these arguments, the House of Commons approved the motion by a vote of 242 to 88.[49]

On March 5, the debate went to the House of Lords, where the Duke of Richmond presented an address to His Majesty the King, begging him not to have recourse to foreign troops and pleading with him to put an end to the dispute with the Americans, pointing out the dangers of intervening in the colonies' affairs and the risk run by England of setting off a European conflict. The bill's advocates then presented their arguments contradicting the former points. Like the House of Commons a few days earlier, the House of Lords approved the motion by a vote of 100 to 32.[50]

Notes

1. Time-Life film on the American Revolution, produced by B.B.C. London and shown on Radio-Québec during the programme *America, America* on January 31, 1981.
2. Edward J. Curtis, *The Organization of the British Army in the American Revolution*, 3.
3. John Fortescue, *The Correspondence of King George the Third*, Vol. III, 214-215.
4. *Act of Settlement*: the act of succession whereby the British crown passed to Sophia and her descendants after the death of Anne Stuart. Sophia was the grand-daughter of James I; she had married the Prince-Elector of Hanover who, like her-self, was a Protestant.
5. Elector: prince or bishop entitled to elect the Emperor of the Holy Roman Empire.
6. Major Baurmeister, *Confidential Letters and Journals, 1776-1784 of Adjutant General Major Baurmeister of the Hessian Forces,* translated from the German by Bernhard A. Uhlendorf, 4. Henceforth, *Confidential Letters and Journals.*
7. Edward Jackson Lowell, *The Hessians and other German Auxiliaries of Great Britain in the Revolutionary War*, 2. Henceforth, *The Hessians.*
8. Anthony Mockler, *Histoire des mercenaires*, 108-109.
9. *Ibid.*, 110. Letter from Catherine the Great of Russia to George III.
10. Time-Life film on the American Revolution, produced by B.B.C. London and shown on Radio-Québec during the programme *America, America* on January 31, 1981.
11. Anthony Mockler, *Histoire des mercenaires*, 114-115.
12. Freidrich Kapp, *Der Soldatenhandel Deutscher Fürsten Nach Amerika*, 243. Letter from Prince Wilhelm of Hesse-Hanau to George III, on August 19, 1775, State Papers Office, Holland, vol. 592.
13. John Fortescue, *The Correspondence of King George the Third*, vol. III, 289-290. Letter from Lord North to King George III, dated November 12, 1775.
14. Bodham W. Donne, *The Correspondence of King George the Third with Lord North from 1768 to 1783*, vol. I, 294.
15. The Holy Roman Emperor at this time was Joseph II (1741-1790), who reigned from 1765 to 1790. The son of Francis I and Maria-Theresa of Austria, he is con-sidered to have been an enlightened despot.
16. Encyclopedia Universalis, 718, no. 1, *Le dernier visage du Premier Reich 1648-1806.*
17. *Ibid.*, 718-721.
18. *Op. cit.*
19. Pierre Lafue, *La vie quotidienne des cours allemandes au XVIIIe siècle* 165-185.
20. *Op. cit.*
21. Friedrich Kapp, *Der Soldatenhandel Deutscher Fürsten Nach Amerika*, 255. The style of the original has been preserved.
22. Edward Jackson Lowell, *The Hessians*, 8.
23. *Parlimentary Register,* first series, vol. III.

24. Major Baurmeister, *Confidential Letters and Journals*, 5.

25. Friedrich Kapp, *Der Soldatenhandel Deutscher Fürsten Nach* America, 254. Letter from Feronce to Faucitt, dated December 23, 1777, State Papers Office, German States, vol. 10.

26. Major Baurmeister, *Confidential Letters and Journals*, 5.

27. Edward Jackson Lowell, *The Hessians*, 5-6.

28. *Parliamentary Register*, first series, vol. III.

29. Major Baurmeister, *Condential Letters and Journals*, 6-7.

30. Edward Jackson Lowell, *The Hessians*, 5-6.

31. Friedrich Kapp, *Der Soldatenhandel Deutscher Fürsten Nach* America, 243. Letter from the prince of Hesse-Hanau to his cousin George III, dated August 19, 1775, State Papers office, Holland, vol. 592. The style of the original has been preserved

32. Major Baurmeister, *Confidential Letters and Journals*, 8.

33. *Parliamentary Register*, first series, vol. III.

34. Major Baurmeister *op. cit.*, 8.

35. Edward Jackson Lowell, *The Hessians*, 12.

36. *Parliamentary Register*, first series, vol. III.

37. Friedrich Kapp, *op. cit.*, 210.

38. Edward Jackson Lowell, *op. cit.*, 8-12.

39. Friedrich Kapp, *op. cit.*, 209.

40. Edward Jackson Lowell, *op cit.*, 12-13.

41. On April 29, 1777, he wrote: "Four brothers in Dessau housed with the burgess of Dessau. A fine garrison! At the first crack of a whip or call of a hunting horn, this rabble would assemble like troops at the sound of the drum. Hell! if we could make the Americans run like that, it wouldn't be bad." Friedrich Kapp, *op. cit.*, 250. State Papers Office, Holland, vol. 601.

42. Major Baurmeister, *op. cit.*, 10.

43. Kapp, *op. cit.*, 210.

44. Baurmeister, *op. cit.*, 10-11.

45. Max von Eelking, *The German Allied Troops*, 18.

46. *Ibid.*

47. W. Cobbett and J. Wright, *The Parliamentary, History, of England from the Earliest Period to the Year1803*, vol. XVIII.

48. *Ibid.*

49. *Ibid.*

50. *Op. cit*

Chapter II

RECRUITING THE GERMAN MERCENARIES

M uch has been written over the past two hundred years concerning England's hiring of German troops. From these writings two schools of thought emerge. The first, led by historians like Lossing, Lowell, Kapp, and Kipping, insists that the true "mercenaries" were the princes, not the ordinary soldiers who were merely victims of the man-traffic, almost slaves to their despotic rulers. The second, whose most ardent spokesman is Max von Eelking, holds that their situation was simply the result of the times in which they lived. Since objectivity is of prime importance in history, both arguments deserve a longer look.

According to the first school, once the treaties were signed, the princes launched a massive recruitment drive. Several rulers who had pledged their men to England began by ensuring the neighbouring heads of state would close theirs eyes to forays across their borders by recruiting officers in search of men. Next, as in Hesse-Cassel, the country was "cut up into districts, each of which was to furnish a given number of recruits to a certain regiment."[1] The War Department established district offices commanded by dragoon officers with instructions "to bring as many foreigners as possible into the service, in order to spare their own districts, whose inhabitants would always be at hand, to be called in case of need. (...) Forcible recruiting was forbidden; but this rule was probably intended to apply only to natives."[2] Despite this injunction, the recruiting officers resorted to various ploys to gather men, from getting them drunk to abducting them outright. The victims of these abductions tended to be marginal elements of society: political agitators, religious zealots, drunkards, in short, anyone who could be accused of causing trouble. Since payment was directly proportional to the number of new recruits, these "troublemakers" bore the cost of these transactions.[3] Historian Benson J. Lossing indignantly condemns these abductions as "a crime against humanity." "Laborers," he added, "were seized in the fields, mechanics in the workshops and worshippers in the churches, and hurried to the barracks without being allowed a parting embrace with their families."[4]

The ordinary soldier unfortunately had very little education, like the majority of his fellow Germans. For this reason, he left little in the way of letters or diaries. The first school cites the case of Johann Gottfield Seume[5] as a notable exception. Seume was a young poet who later achieved some recognition as a writer. His accounts give us an entirely different picture of events from that presented by the privileged class of German officers and generals in their writings. Seume was an avant-garde theology student at the University of Leipzig whose modern ideas were causing his friends some embarrassment. As a result, he decided to leave Leipzig and go to Paris. He set forth on foot, carrying a sword, a few shirts, and some books, with no idea that he was destined for America instead. Some time later he wrote:

> The third night I spent at Bach, and here the Landgrave of Cassel, the great broker of men of the time, undertook through his recruiting officers, and in spite of my protestations, the care of my future quarters on the road to Ziegenhayn,[6] to Cassel, and thence to the New World.
>
> I was brought under arrest to Ziegenhayn, where I found many companions in misfortune from all parts of the country. There we waited to be sent to America in the spring, after Faucitt should have inspected us. I gave myself up to my fate, and tried to make the best of it, bad as it might be. We stayed a long time at Ziegenhayn before the necessary number of recruits was brought together from the plough, the highways, and the recruiting stations. The story of those times is well known. No one was safe from the grip of the seller of souls. Persuasion, cunning, deception, force—all served. No one asked what means were used to the damnable end. Strangers of all kinds were arrested, imprisoned, sent off. They tore up my academic matriculation papers, as being the only instrument by which I could prove my identity. At last I fretted no more. One can live anywhere. You can stand what so many do. The idea of crossing the ocean was inviting enough to a young fellow: and there were things worth seeing on the other side. So I reflected. While we were at

Ziegenhayn old General Gore[7] employed me in writing, and treated me very kindly. Here was an indescribable lot of human beings brought together, good and bad, and others that were both by turns. My comrades were a runaway son of the Muses from Jena, a bankrupt tradesman from Vienna, a fringemaker from Hanover, a discharged secretary of the post-office from Gotha, a monk from Würzburg, an upper steward from Meinungen, a Prussian sergeant of hussars, a cashiered Hessian major from the fortress itself, and others of like stamp. You can imagine that there was entertainment enough, and a mere sketch of the lives of these gentry would make amusing and instructive reading.[8]

Although they differed in many ways, the men shared a single fixed idea: to escape from the camp and from the "grip of the seller of souls." Together they devised a plan whereby under cover of darkness they would overcome the guards, disarm them and kill any who resisted. They would lock the officers in their headquarters, spike the mouths of the cannons and flee, fifteen hundred strong, towards the border which lay a few miles away from camp. A leader was needed to put the plan into action, and Seume was offered the position. Luckily, at the entreaty of an old sergeant-major, he declined the offer, thereby saving his life; for the plot was discovered and the leaders, arrested. As an accomplice, Seume was arrested as well but was subsequently released because of the large number of accused. "The trial went on," Seume wrote; "two were condemned to the gallows, as I should certainly have been, had not the old Prussian sergeant-major saved me. The remainder had to run the gantlet a great many times, from thirty-six down to twelve.[9] It was a terrible butchery. The candidates for the gallows were pardoned, after suffering the fear of death under that instrument, but had to run the gantlet thirty-six times, and were sent to Cassel to be kept in irons at the mercy of the prince. 'For an indefinite time' and 'at mercy' were then equivalent expressions, and meant 'forever, without release.' At least, the mercy of the prince was an affair that no one wanted to have anything to do with. More than thirty were terribly treated in this way, and many, of whom I was one, were let off only because too many of the accomplices would have had to be punished. Some came out of prison when we marched away, for reasons which were easy to understand: for a fellow that is in irons at Cassel is not paid for by the British."[10]

Since new recruits could quite easily desert in small states where the borders were nearby, the authorities took every precaution to minimize the inherent loss of revenue. The people sympathized with the fleeing soldiers, despite the threat of harsh reprisals. One stratagem consisted in blocking off all access to a town in which a deserter was known to be hiding. If he did not surrender or was not turned in after a certain length of time, a townsman of approximately the same size as the deserter would be forced to take his place. Frequently it was the son of one of the town's notables who was chosen. The people were warned of the risks they took in helping deserters; every month a proclamation to this effect was read to them in the public square. Among other things, they could lose their civil rights and be sent to prison or condemned to hard labour. In Cassel, the law was softened somewhat by the offer of a reward to anyone giving information which would lead to the recapture of a deserter. However, the village was held responsible for any deserter who managed to escape. The law stipulated that anyone meeting a soldier more than a mile from his barracks must ask to see his pass.[11]

Life was difficult for the recruits but it was no less so for lower-grade and non-commissioned officers who were responsible for bringing batches of new recruits from the neighbouring states to the barracks. In many cases they had to cover fairly long distances which offered many opportunities to would-be deserters. In the course of research, German historian Friedrich Kapp was fortunate enough to discover a contemporary instruction manual[12] advising the officers in charge of these marches on ways to avoid problems. The officer or NCO was to be armed with a sword and pistol. While on a march, recruits had to precede them; no one but an officer must ever close the column. Cities or other hiding places were to be avoided. Recruits were not to come near an officer, even if their life were in danger. If the journey took longer than a single day, care was to be taken that the innkeeper shared the officer's views and not those of the recruits. Recruits and NCOs had to undress and give their clothes to the inn-keeper for safekeeping in a secret place. The inn where the recruits spent the night was to have separate rooms for this occasion and, if possible, barred windows on the upper floor. A candle was to remain lit all night. The NCO was to hand his sword to the innkeeper for safekeeping, lest the recruits capture it and use it against him. He was to rise before the recruits in the morning and be fully dressed by the time they were awakened and given back their clothes. A recruit was always to enter a room or a house first, and leave last. During meals, recruits were to be seated against a wall, and if any showed signs of rebellion for any reason, their belts and buttons holding up their trousers were to be cut so that they would have to hold them up with their hands. Use of a trained dog was strongly recommended. If by chance the NCO was forced to kill a deserter, he was to take all relevant documents to the local magistrate.

According to the first school of historians, recruiting grew more and more difficult as the war progressed due to the way recruits were treated. As a result, officers began recruiting cripples and old men. Several good examples of this practice are provided by Ernst Kipping: "For example, the Landgrave had to order the discharge of a 63-year-old man who could not walk erect; another he found 'completely lame and limping' because one of his legs was some inches shorter than the other."[13] To avoid this kind of situation, an age limit of forty was set for recruits.

To reduce the number of possible defections to the rebel cause, the wives and children of many mercenaries were allowed to accompany them. The presence of families, however, often posed problems, such as in this sad case reported by Colonel Johann August von Loos: "The wife of a soldier of one of my companies became ill this morning; an hour later she gave birth to a girl. (Since this child was born on English soil, she is more or less naturalized.) The military child bed lacks the arts of our modern doctors, and a simple company surgeon had to replace Dr. Stein. All our petted beauties of Cassel would be touched if they could see this poor creature. Instead of having nourishing broth, essences, and other needed things, she lies in a dark place, stretched on a mat; a mouthful of brandy, warm beer, and pepper were her only sustenance."[14]

The argument of the first school concludes that since the quality of recruits kept declining as the war went on, the English authorities had to make them undergo thorough examinations before leaving for

America to ensure that the terms of the contracts were met. As for the German officers, this school of thought insists that they were prepared for their role in America by a few ignorant Frenchmen with no idea of the causes and effects of the war. Moreover, all too often anti-revolutionary newspapers completed an education[15] which owed more to military pride than to a proper understanding of their actions.

For the second school and its strong proponents, nineteenth-century historians Max von Eelking[16] and William L. Stone,[17] it is unthinkable to compare their period to that of the American Revolution. According to Eelking in his 1856 book, the hundred years between the war and his own day had brought about "a great change, not only in the realm of principles and ideas, but in that of actions."[18] The military had also been affected by these changes, and despite the claim of some people that the army had always been conservative, the facts constituted an irrefutable proof of its evolution.

As for the term "mercenaries," this school feels that at the time of the American Revolution it did not have the pejorative connotation which it has since acquired, because in the eighteenth century the concept of a "fatherland" was less rigorously defined than in subsequent ages. According to Max von Eelking, until the end of the eighteenth century, most European governments found it increasingly necessary to recruit soldiers because, as he points out, armies were indispensable and no other method of raising them had been devised.

This school believes that recruiting was carried out in the following way: some men enlisted for a fixed number of years and for a salary; others, like the marginal elements who were a burden both to society and to their families, were simply forced to join the regular army, according to the ways of the time. Raids were permitted, and barely half the troops were actually citizens of the state. The others came from other principalities and countries. This use of force may appear unacceptable today, say the historians of this school—although the practice was still in existence in the maritime states in their own country as late as 1868—but it was very common at the time.

Life was particularly hard for everyone at the time of the American Revolution, and recruiting was universally practiced. Everyone was used to it and had learned to deal with it. Once in the army, a soldier owed complete allegiance to his sovereign. Nationless and with all close ties severed, he became an object which his new master could dispose of at will. Still, for regular soldiers, there was doubtless some excitement at the thought of escaping the endless round of boring daily duties in the barracks, no matter the destination or the reasons for being sent there. Military life was wretched for these men. Is it any wonder, asks Eelking, that they leaped at the chance to escape the routine by waging a military campaign for their sovereign? They also knew that death of many of their superiors from wounds and epidemics would open the door to career advancement for themselves.

As for Johann Seume, the Eelking school finds nothing unusual in the way he was captured and conscripted. Things were done like that in those days. Only Seume's later renown distinguished him from any other Hessian citizen, they say. Eelking argues that when Seume was picked up, just after leaving the University of Leipzig for ideological reasons, he looked more like a tramp than a travelling student. He points out that Seume himself wrote an amusing account of his arrest in his autobiography[19] and later spoke in favourable terms of the opportunity he was given to cross the ocean. When Seume was finally able to return to Europe at last, he was not overly enthusiastic: "The news of peace was not very welcome, because young people, desirous of signalizing themselves in battle, did not like to see their career thus brought to an end. They had flattered me with the prospect of becoming an officer, in which event a new career might have opened for me; but with peace all this vanished." Eelking asks, "Does this sound like disgust or dissatisfaction with his situation? If the sending of soldiers to the American war by German princes was as dishonorable as many represent it at the present day, the service, certainly, would not have contained so many thorough and honorable men who went with the troops as officers."[20]

Historians of the second school refer to only two of the princes who signed treaties with George III, Frederick II, Landgrave of Hesse-Cassel, and Duke Karl I of Brunswick. They mention the criticism levied against Frederick, maintaining that it is difficult to judge his actions since he was forced to participate in the war. A confidential letter from the heir to the throne of Brunswick reveals that: "The landgrave will very likely... furnish all or part of his troops. Otherwise he might get into difficulty with both sides; for he is not strong enough to remain neutral, as his funds would soon be seized, and a lack of everything would soon be felt."[21]

Convinced that sooner or later the hostilities would be carried over onto the soil of England and then to Germany, Frederick II had no choice but to sign an agreement with the English king, who guaranteed in return to come to Hesse's defence in time of need. Indeed, this school recognizes the enviable state of Frederick II's treasury at this time, acknowledging that the English subsidiary money helped to swell his coffers even more. Nonetheless, writes Eelking, "it should not be forgotten that with this surplus, structures were erected, which to this day are an ornament to the land, and also that the state received its share of that sum."[22] Upon his death, moreover, Frederick willed his personal share of the benefits to the state.

As for Brunswick's motives in sending troops to America, this school stresses that they were entirely different and that in peacetime, an army quickly racks up debts. At the time of the American Revolution, Brunswick had just ended its involvement in the Seven Years' War. Since England needed men and since the Duke of Brunswick had to replenish his coffers, the historians of this school consider it perfectly natural that mutual satisfaction should quickly have been reached.

Because of varying distances to the port of embarkation, all these soldiers followed different routes and thus had to overcome different problems, sometimes extremely difficult. Whereas the troops from Waldeck, Brunswick, and Hesse-Cassel met relatively few obstacles, the men from the other three states, because of the geographical location of their homes, were forced to cross territories whose rulers were not always sympathetic to their cause.

As we have seen, the courts of Hanau and Cassel did not enjoy cordial relations, even though Count Wilhelm of Hesse-Hanau was also the legitimate heir of Hesse-Cassel. In fact, relations between the two were so strained that Wilhelm had to consider using the Rhine to avoid his father's territories. This solution was far from ideal, however, as the proposed route meant crossing many small states whose leaders might, at any time, impede their progress. Knowing the risk, Wilhelm still considered this to be the best solution under the circumstances, and agreed to the alternate route. Fortunately for the Count, no serious problems arose. Occasionally minor difficulties arose. On March 8, 1777, for instance, the Archbishop of Mainz[23] held up the march by demanding the return of eight of Prince Wilhelm's chasseurs, alleging that they were deserters who had illegally joined Hanau's forces. On another occasion, on March 25, 1777,[24] Wilhelm lost several men in Holland when local citizens helped them desert. Apart from a few incidents such as these, Wilhelm of Hanau's men managed fairly well.

While all this was going on for Wilhelm, the Margrave of Ansbach-Bayreuth, Karl Alexander, faced much more serious problems. Two regiments, one each from Ansbach and Bayreuth, which had left Ansbach on March 7, 1777[25] along with 101 chasseurs and 44 artillery, marched into Ochsenfurth-am-Main, about 140 kilometres from the town of Hanau. The new recruits were not used to being packed like sardines onto the smelly decks of smelly ships which made them sick. That evening, while at anchor in the harbour, they suddenly mutinied in a spontaneous and wholly unexpected surge towards freedom. They had neither a plan nor a leader. The chasseurs of Ansbach-Bayreuth managed to put down the mutiny from the neighbouring hilltops with the help of some hussars and dragoons sent by the Bishop of Würzburg, the local head of state. Because of the size of the rebellion, however, the margrave had to be sent for. Karl Alexander addressed his men at the site of the mutiny, informing them in no uncertain terms that their families and property would be the objects of reprisals. Thus threatened, the rebels quietly returned to their quarters, and there the matter ended.

The margrave had more problems to deal with. In the autumn of 1777, Karl Alexander wrote to his uncle, Frederick the Great of Prussia, requesting permission for his men to cross Prussian territory on their journey to England. The margrave was so sure of Frederick's support that he had already given his soldiers their marching orders. Karl Alexander obviously did not know his uncle very well. When his troops were only a few kilometres from the Prussian border, he received the following unexpected reply to his letter, dated October 24, 1777:

To my Nephew!

I must admit to Your Royal Highness that I never think of the present war in America without being struck by the haste shown by a few German princes in sacrificing their troops for a cause which has nothing whatsoever to do with them. My astonishment increases all the more when I consider ancient history and our ancestors' wise and wide-spread disinclination to shed German blood to defend the rights of foreigners.

But my patriotism is carrying me away here! And it is Your Royal Highness' letter of the 14th which has revived it so strongly. You request free passage for your troops on their way to serve Great Britain, and I take the liberty of pointing out to Your Royal Highness that, if you want to march your men to England, there are shorter routes to the crossing point which would not encroach upon my territories. I put this suggestion to Your Royal Highness' judgement, and close with all the affection owing to my nephew from Your Royal Highness' fond uncle.

Frederick[26]

Since it was already too late to recall his troops, Charles Alexander could only hope that his uncle would eventually change his mind. Surely it was only a matter of time! But several weeks went by, with no change in Frederick's stance. Finally the margrave ordered his troops to retreat to Hanau where they would spend the winter. After several months' delay, but with the addition of new recruits from Hesse-Hanau, the Ansbach-Bayreuth forces finally reached the ports of embarkation, and left for England in April 1778.[27]

Because of Frederick the Great's refusal to allow German troops to cross his territories on their way to England, the men from Anhalt-Zerbst were forced to cross no fewer than seven territories and free cities. This circuitous route caused several problems for Prince Frederick Augustus' troops.

One day, for instance, in the village of Zeulenrode,[28] a corporal in hot pursuit of a deserter saw his quarry disappear into an inn. The innkeeper's wife was quietly eating her dinner inside when she was suddenly killed by a bullet to the brain. The panic-stricken corporal had fired in the direction where he thought he had seen the fugitive, without even giving him a chance to surrender, accidentally killing the poor woman instead. A few moments later, some villagers who had witnessed the incident gathered at the inn, along with others who had heard the noise of the gunshot. A riot ensued during which a lieutenant was killed.

Another time, Prussian recruiting officers managed in ten days to persuade 334 recruits to desert, leaving the Prince of Anhalt-Zerbst with a paltry 494 soldiers for the ports of embarkation. However, the prince's officers were able to find more than one hundred new recruits along the way, so that in the end, 627 men embarked at Stade on April 22, 1778.[29]

Frederick the Great's harassment continued at Magdebourg and Minden, as well as in the lower Rhine region. Benson J. Lossing says that he "took every occasion to express his contempt for the scandalous man-traffic of his neighbours. Whenever any of these troops were compelled to pass through any part of his dominions, he claimed the usual toll for so many heads of cattle, since, as he said, they had been sold as such."[30] Later, in his memoirs,[31] Frederick was to criticize George III for instigating this traffic together with the German courts, whose collaboration meant that the Empire would be left defenceless in the event of a European conflict. According to Lowell, Frederick's attitude stemmed partly from a desire for revenge because of England's reaction to the events surrounding the port and city of Dantzig.[32] As for delays caused by Frederick's tactics, historian Friedrich Kapp believes this may well be why Sir William Howe failed to defeat Washington's army at Valley Forge, since his reinforcements arrived late, and he did not know if more would be coming.

Though he belongs to the same school as Kapp, Lowell does not share this view. "But such a consequence of the delay in receiving fifteen hundred men, and of the abandonment of a scheme for obtaining a few thousands more from Würtemberg, seems to me too remote for serious consideration." And he adds, "Is there any reason to suppose that Sir William would have made a better use of the fifteen hundred German soldiers he expected than of the twelve or fifteen thousand he had already?"[33]

Ansbach-Bayreuth Regimental Colours. Courtesy of West Point
Museum Collections.

Frederick the Great's acts of reprisal against the British crown
ceased after 1778 when his business sense resurfaced and took precedence over his emotions.

The troops from Brunswick, Hesse-Cassel, and Waldeck faced far
fewer difficulties, since they had only to cross their own territories or
those of the English king. Despite this, the chaplain Father Melsheimer
reported in his journal that the troops from Brunswick had a long
and difficult march to the port of embarkation.[34]

The commander of the first German troops to leave for America
was Major General Friedrich Adolphus von Riedesel,[35] a brilliant soldier and a man of great culture and refinement. He was born on June
3, 1738 into the great baronial family of Rhenish Hesse. Under pressure from his father, he studied law at Marburg at the age of fifteen.
One day, as he was watching the manoeuvres of a Hessian infantry

battalion, he was tricked into joining it by a wily major who was anxious to get his hands on a new recruit and who persuaded the young man that his father approved. Riedesel quickly realized how the major had deceived him when he received a disapproving letter from his father, who cut off his allowance as a sign of his anger. This stern attitude soon softened, and Friedrich was back in his father's good graces by the time he joined the landgrave's regiments destined for London. When the Seven Years' War broke out he was recalled to Germany where he began his spectacular career. First, he left the Hessian army to join the Brunswick forces; with his tact and his connections he soon joined the staff at Ferdinand of Brunswick's headquarters. In no time he became the favourite of the prince, who made him first a lieutenant-colonel in command of the regiment. In December 1762, while billeted for the winter in Wolfenbüttel, he married Friederike von Massow, daughter of Frederick the Great's quartermaster general. A few years later, in 1772, Riedesel became a full colonel and on the evening of February 22, 1776, while en route to the New World, he learned that he had been promoted to Major General.

Riedesel was an excellent soldier as well as a devoted husband and father. On February 22, 1776, during the army's first halt at Leifert, he wrote to his wife:

Dearest Wife:

Never have I suffered more than upon my departure this morning. My heart was broken; and could I have gone back who knows what I might have done. But, my darling, God has placed me in my present calling, and I must follow it. Duty and honor force me to this decision, and we must be comforted by this reflection and nor murmur. Indeed, my chief solicitude arises from the state of your own health, in view of your approaching confinement. The care of our dear daughters, also, gives me anxiety. Guard most preciously the dear ones. I love them most fondly.

I am thus far on my journey without accident and in good health, although very tired in consequence of my anxiety of mind the past few days. I am hoping, however, for a refreshing sleep, and trust that you may be blessed in a similar manner.

I have this evening been raised to the rank of major-general. Therefore, my own Mrs. General, take good care of your health, in order that you may follow me as quickly as possible after your happy delivery.[36]

Thanks to the memoirs, letters, and journals of the baroness and her husband, several Canadian historians have been able to provide us with a wealth of details concerning the lives and customs of Quebecers' ancestors, about whom we would otherwise have no knowledge.

Riedesel left Brunswick on February 22, 1776, heading for Stade where, sometime between March 12 and 17, he embarked with 2282 men from the first Brunswick division and 77 wives. Five days later, they were at sea, reaching Portsmouth on March 28. The 2018 men of the second Brunswick division left Stade during the last week of May 1776. Thus the two divisions under Riedesel's command totalled 4300 German soldiers. The Hessian troops were also divided into two divisions; the first left Cassel at the beginning of March, embarking from Bremerlehe, and the second followed suit in June. The 668 men of a Hesse-Hanau regiment[37] were added to the Brunswick troops. On April 6, 1776, on board the *Pallas,* Riedesel wrote to his wife that they were able to depart sooner than hoped and that on April 4, under favourable winds, a fleet of thirty ships had set sail for America with the 3000 Brunswickers[38] of this first division.

The crossing was difficult, reminding the men of the hardships they had endured even before leaving German soil. Riedesel's and Captain Georg Pausch's journals provide daily details of the journey. It should be remembered that their point of view was vastly different from that of the common soldier whose problems were of another order entirely. For instance, Captain Pausch described the fittings of his cabin as follows: "My three officers and myself have a pretty large cabin, the wainscoting, upholstering and table of which are very neatly finished in Mahogany."[39]

Johann Gottfried Seume, the young poet in captivity, has fortunately left us a description of the quite different way in which he and his fellow soldiers—the vast majority—were billeted. In *The Hessians,* Jackson summarizes Seume's observations:

> The men were packed like herring. A tall man could not stand upright between decks, nor sit up straight in his berth. To every such berth six men were allotted, but as there was room for only four, the last two had to squeeze in as best they might. 'This was not cool in warm weather,' says Seume. Thus the men lay in what boys call 'spoon fashion,' and

when they were tired on one side, the man on the right would call 'about face,' and the whole file would turn over at once; then, when they were tired again, the man on the left would give the same order, and they would turn back on to the first side. The food was on a par with the lodging. Pork and pease were the chief of their diet. The pork seemed to be four or five years old. It was streaked with black towards the outside, and was yellow farther in, with a little white in the middle. The salt beef was in much the same condition. The ship biscuit was often full of maggots. 'We had to eat them for a relish,' says Seume, 'not to reduce our slender rations too much.' This biscuit was so hard that they sometimes broke it up with a cannon-ball, and the story ran that it had been taken from the French in the Seven Years' War, and lain in Portsmouth ever since. The English had kept it twenty years or so, and 'were now feeding the Germans with it, that these might, if it were God's will, destroy Rochambeau and Lafayette. It does not seem to have been God's will, exactly.' Sometimes they had groats and barley, or, by way of a treat, a pudding made of flour mixed half with salt water and half with fresh water, and with old, old mutton fat. The water was all spoiled. When a cask was opened, 'it stank between decks like Styx, Phlegethon, and Cocytus all together.' It was thick with filaments as long as your finger, and they had to filter it through a cloth before they could drink it. They held their noses while they drank, and yet it was so scarce that they fought to get it. Rum, and sometimes a little strong beer, completed their fare.[40]

Names of the transport Ships	Number of Tons	Names of Captains	Names of the Officers on Each Ship	Number of Soldiers	Names of the Companies	Regiments
Pallas	344	Captain Bell	Général von Riedesel, captain Fricke et Gerlach, Lieuts. Cleve, O.F.C. Gœdecke, régiment Langemeyer, captain Foy.		General-Major von Riedesel Esquadron.	Prince Ludwig Dragoner embark 13 March 1776 at Stade.
Minerve	311		Lieut-Col. Baum Rittm. Reineking, Cornet Graefe Stuzzer, Chaplain Melsheimer, Auditor Thomas, Surgeon Vorbrodt.		Leib Esquadron et Obstl. Baum.	Prince Ludwig Dragoner embark 13 March 1776 at Stade.
Minerve	261		May von Meybom, Rittmstr. von Schlagenteufel sen. and jun., lieutenant von Sommerlatte, Bothmar Bornemann, captain Schönewald.		Leib Esquadron Major von Meyboom.	Prince Ludwig Dragoner embark 13 March 1776 at Stade.
James and John	356	Captain Watson	Obstl. Breymann, captain von Hambach, lieutenant Uhlig, Gebhard Rudolphi, Mutzel, Wwinteschmidt, Reg-feldsch. Henkel		Obstl. Breymann prince Friedrich Regiment.	Grenadier Bataillon embark 13 March 1776 at Stade.
Laurie	380		Captain von Baertling, senior, lieutenant Helmcke, von Wallmoden, Mayer.		Captain von Baertling, Regiment von Rhetz.	Grenadier Bataillon embark 13 March 1776 at Stade.
Royal Briton	303		Captain von Löhneissen, lieutenant Trott, Blacke, lieutenant von Cramm.		Captain von Löhneissen, Captain von Morgenstern, Regiment von Riedesel.	Grenadier Bataillon embark 13 March 1776 at Stade.
Apollo	361		Captain von Schik, lieutenant von Mayer d'Anières jun... embark 13 March 1776 at Stade.		Captain von Shick,	Grenadier Bataillon régiment Specht.
Prince of Wales	447	Captain George Prissick	Obstl. Praetorius, captain von Thunderfeldt et von Zielberg, Lieut. Hartz, du Roi et von König. F. Sternberg, Audit Wolpers, (Régiments-Feldscheer) Berns.	213	Obstl. Praetorius and captain Tunderfeld.	Prince Friedrich (Durchl.) Embark 13 March 1776 at Stade.

Names of the transport Ships	Number of Tons	Names of Captains	Names of the Officers on Each Ship	Number of Soldiers	Names of the Companies	Regiments
Providence	366	Captain Watson	Major von Hille, captain Sander, lieut. Wolgast, Burghoff, F. Kotte, lieut. Schröder.	170	Major von Hille and captain von Tunderfeldt.	Prince Friedrich (Durchl.) Embark 13 March 1776 at Stade.
Lord Sandwich	317	Captain Devonsh	Captain Rosenberg, lieutenant Volkmar, F. Reinerding, F. von Adelsheim, Feldsch, Fugerer.	146	General-Major von Steimer et captain von Tunderfeldt.	Prince Friedrich (Durchl.) Embark 13 March 1776 at Stade.
Peggy	360	Captain Wilson	Captain Diterichs, lieut. von d. Knesebeck. von Reitzen stein, F. Langerjaan.	149	Captain Diterichs, captain von Tunderfeldt, captain Morgenstern.	Prince Friedrich (Durchl.) Embark 13 March 1776 at Stade.
Harmonie	449		Obstl. von Speth, captain Morgenstern, von Baertling junior, lieut. Morgenstern, von Burgsdorf von Meyern, F. von Meybom.		Obstl. von Speth et captain Morgenstern.	Prince Friedrich (Durchl.) Embark 13 March 1776 at Stade.
Nancy	304	Captain Wilson	Major von Mengen, captain von Girsewald, lieut. Hoyer, F. Hauberlin, Feldschr., Mylius. Stade.		Major von Mengen et captain Morgenstern.	General-Major von Riedesel embark 15 March 1776 at
Polly	309		Captain Harbord, lieut. Reincking, von Pincier; F. Unverzagt, Aud. Zink.		General-Major von Riedesel et captain Morgenstern.	General-Major von Riedesel embark 15 March 1776 at Stade.

Notes

1. Edward Jackson Lowell, *The Hessians*, 37.
2. *Ibid.*
3. Ernst Kipping, *The Hessian View of America, 1776-1783*, 6.
4. Benson J. Lossing, *Lossings History of the United States*, vol. III, 848.
5. For more on Johann Gottfried Seume, see:
   a) *Mein Leben* (autobiography), Prosaschriften. Darmstadt: Melzer Verlag, 1974, 51-154.
   b) *Schreiben aus Amerika nach Deutschland* (Halifax, 1782) Neue Litteratur und Völkerkun. Für das Jahr 1789, 2Bd. Herausgegeben von J.W. v. Archhenholtz, 362-381. Leipzig, 1789. Translated by Michael Wolfe.
   c) *Some Unpublished Poems of J.G. Seume*, by Bernhard A.Uhlendorf: A contribution to the Washington Bicentennial "The Germanic Review", vol. VII, 320-329. Translated for the author from the original German by Dr. Virginia DeMarce.
6. Ziegenhayn was a noxious Hessian camp where new recruits for America were assembled.
7. Von Gohr, like many German names, appears under different spellings according to the whim of the writer.
8. Edward Jackson Lowell, *The Hessians*, 38-40.
9. The "gantlet" (not to be confused with "gauntlet," was a form of military punishment in which the offender ran between two lines of men armed with clubs, who struck him as he passed.
10. Edward Jackson Lowell, *The Hessians*, 40-42.
11. *Ibid.*
12. Friedrich Kapp, *Der Soldatenhandel Deutscher Fürsten Nach* America, 13-18. Although this manual was not published in Berlin until 1805, it presents an accurate picture of the challenges faced by the recruiting officers and NCOs .
13. Ernst Kipping, *The Hessian View of America*, 1776-1783, 7.
14. *Ibid.* About 2000 women were at one time or another under the command of General Burgoyne. However, only about 300 seem to have been recorded in the returns. Marvin L. Brown Jr., *Baroness von Riedesel and the American Revolution*, *XXII.*
15. Edward Jackson Lowell, *The Hessians*, 44-45.
16. Max von Eelking is the author of *Leben und Wirken Herzoglich Braunschweig'schen General-LieutenantFriedrich Adolph von Riedesel*, Leipzig, 1856, 3 volumes.
17. William L. Stone translated, in two volumes, Eelking's *Leben und Wirken*, Leipzig, 1856, under the title: *Memoirs and letters and Journals of Major von Riedesel*, 1866-1868. Henceforth, *Memoirs and Letters and Journals.*
18. Max von Eelking, *Memoirs and Letters and Journals*, tr. by Wm. L. Stone, vol. I, 19-20.
19. J.G. Seume, *Mein Leben*, Prosaschriften. Darmstadt: Melzer Verlag, 1974, 51-154.
20. Max von Eelking, *Memoirs and Letters and Journals*, vol. 1.
21. *Ibid.*, 21-22.

22. *Ibid.*, 22.
23. Edward Lowell Jackson, *The Hessians,* 47.
24. *Ibid.*
25. *Ibid.,48.*
26. Friedrich Kapp, *Der Soldatenhandel Deutscher Fürsten Nach* America 259, letter XXIII. Anspacher Manual - Akten I, p.190.
27. Edward Lowell Jackson, *The Hessians,* 52.
28. *Ibid.*
29. *Ibid,* 5-6.
30. Benson J. Lossing, *Lossings History of the United States* vol. III, 848.
31. Memoirs, in *Oeuvres de Frédéric le Grand*, vol. VI, 117.
32. Dantzig: today the Polish city of Gdansk. In the eighteenth century it was an important port, controlling most of Poland's foreign trade. In 1772 Frederick the Great succeeded in annexing the vital area of Poland in which Dantzig was located, but was prevented by Russia and Austria from gaining control over this port. Even though he now controlled four-fifths of the total foreign trade of Poland, Frederick blamed England for secretly preventing him from accomplishing his goal of total control.
33. Lowell, *The Hessians,* 54-55.
34. F.V. Melsheimer, *Journal of the Voyage of the Brunswick Auxiliaries from Wolfenbüttel to Quebec,* 137-142, republished in Quebec City by *Le Soleil,* 1927, translated by William Wood. Melsheimer was the chaplain of the Duke of Brunswick dragoon regiment. The first part of his journal was translated by William Wood, Council Secretary, and the second part by William L. Stone; it was published by *Transactions Literary and Historical Society of Quebec,* 1891, 45 pages.
35. Max von Eelking, *Memoirs and Letters and Journals,* vol, I, 1-17.
36. *Ibid.,* 30. Baroness von Riedesel was awaiting the birth of her daughter Carolyn, who was born at the beginning of March 1776. *Baroness von Riedesel and the American Revolution,* by Marvin L.Brown Jr., 1965, XXVIII.
37. For the figures and dates in this paragraph see:
    a)Max von Eelking, *The German Allied Troops in the North American War of Independence, 1783,* 87-90, translated by J.G. Rosengarten.
    b) Max von Eelking, *Memoirs and Letters and Journals,* 24.
    c) Archives of Canada, MG 13, War Office.
38. "Brunswickers" is the general name given to German Troops in Canada, since most of the soldiers stationed here were from the province of Brunswick. When the adjective "Brunswicker" is used, it refers specifically to the men of Brunswick only.
39. Georg Pausch, *Journals of Captain George Pausch, Chief of the Hanau Artillery during the Burgoyne Campaign.* Translated by William L. Stone, 33.
40. Edward Jackson Lowell, *The Hessians,* 56-57.

Chapter III

THE GERMANS AND THE WAR
FROM 1776 TO 1778

N orth America was finally sighted on the cold and rainy morning of May 16, 1776. A few days later, on May 20, the fleet reached the mouth of the St. Lawrence River and the German soldiers could admire the coast of Nova Scotia on their left. On May 23, two British soldiers lost their lives in a tragic accident when they disappeared into the cold waters of the St. Lawrence, right in front of their horrified comrades. After a series of starts and stops at the whim of the wind, the fleet finally dropped anchor at Quebec City on June 1, 1776, at 6 o'clock in the evening.[1] The first division of German auxiliaries comprised:[2]

Commander-in-chief of the German troops:
Major General Baron Friedrich Adolphus von Riedesel

Headquarters	22 men
Grenadier Battalion von Breymann, Lt. Col. Heinrich C. von Breymann	564 men
Dragoon Regiment. Prince Ludwig, Col. Friedrich Baum	336 men
Regiment Prince Friedrich, Lt. Col. Christian J. Praetorius	680 men
Musketeer Regiment von Riedesel, Lt. Col. Ernst Ludwig W. von Speth.	680 men
Total	2,282 men
The Hesse-Hanau Regiment, Col. Wilhelm R. von Gall	668 men
Hanoverian volunteers (wearing English uniforms), Lt. Col. Scheiter	250 men[3]
Wives of German soldiers	77 women[4]

General Carleton, Governor of Quebec, who had returned on May 30 from Trois-Rivières after successfully driving back the American revolutionaries, gladly welcomed the German major general and his troops. The very next day, Riedesel was invited to dinner by Wolfe's ex-quartermaster to review the 600 or so American soldiers imprisoned by the government in the last weeks.[5] On June 5, Riedesel was given command of a separate corps comprising his own regiment, the grenadier battalion, von Gall's infantry regiment from Hesse-Hanau, Col. Allan MacLean's Scottish battalion, the Royal Emigrants, plus 150 Canadians and about 300 Indians.[6] His orders were to proceed to the Sorel region and set up camp near the Americans, while a fleet and a land army commanded by Generals Carleton, Burgoyne, and Phillips would make their way to Trois-Rivières, Sorel and Montreal.

On June 6, Lt. Col. Baum was ordered to land in Quebec with the dragoons and the Regiment Prince Friedrich who were to remain in the garrison there to watch over military business in the capital. Two hundred men were thus assigned to the area surrounding Quebec City and Lévis, as "the loyalty of the inhabitants was still doubted."[7] The rest were sent to repair the fortifications. The troops bound for Trois-Rivières received their marching orders on June 7 and reached their destination on June 11. Meanwhile, on June 8 and 9, Lt. Col. von Speth and some men from the von Riedesel Regiment engaged in light skirmishes with the Americans. Some 2000 rebels had planned an attack against Fraser's 300 men. However, they were tricked by a royalist named Antoine Gauthier and quickly routed. Carleton arrived at this very moment, but to everyone's great surprise called off the pursuit of the American rebels, who were thus able to escape to their base near Sorel. On June 10, the governor called his officers together to announce that Fraser, Gordon, Powell, and Beckwith were promoted to the rank of Brigadier General, Burgoyne, Phillips, and Riedesel (who had arrived that same day) to the rank of General, and himself, despite his leniency towards the rebels, to the rank of Commander-in-chief.[8]

The English plan was to liberate Montreal and drive the Americans back beyond the Canadian border. Riedesel was in command of the

Modern Map of Northeastern North America

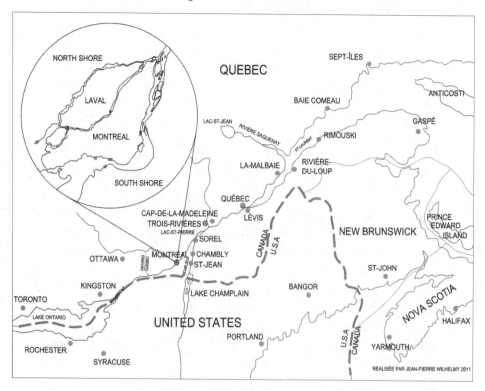

left flank, comprising all the regiments from Brunswick plus the one from Hesse-Hanau.[9] Fraser commanded the right flank, composed of the light infantry companies from all the English regiments in Canada, the British grenadiers and the MacLean regiment, plus a group of Canadians and Indians.[10] General Burgoyne was responsible for the entire operation. The fleet left for Montreal and anchored off Sorel on the evening of June 14. Some of Fraser's men went ashore to claim the town. The next day, Burgoyne, with the English brigade and a few pieces of artillery, set off in pursuit of the Americans who had just withdrawn to Fort St. Jean. The same day, the 29th English regiment set sail for Montreal, arrived on June 17, and took possession of Montreal, while the German troops, who had just landed on the south shore of the St. Lawrence, began a long and difficult march to La Prairie, south of Montreal. They spent their first night in Canada at

Verchères before continuing on their journey. An exhausted Riedesel wrote to Ferdinand of Brunswick from La Prairie on June 22, 1776:

> We have left the ships without taking any of our luggage, as the teams required for transporting it were needed for other purposes. We have marched about fourteen leagues in three days; during the whole of which journey myself an the other officers were obliged to go on foot. This is the seventh day that I have worn the same shirt and stockings. At first it was disagreeable, but we stood it. All the officers manifest the very best spirit, and our troops are the strongest and have the fewest sick. I am very happy to be under the command of General Carleton. He manifests such a contempt for the rebels, that I feel sure that we shall soon attack and get the best of them.[11]

In La Prairie, Carleton quickly organized the area's defences, then returned to Montreal with Burgoyne and Phillips to set up his headquarters. From there he proceeded to Quebec City where he reorganized the courts.

Meanwhile, in La Prairie, Riedesel was training his troops and working on discipline. He also taught them how to win the Canadians' confidence by paying cash and avoiding all forms of credit "in order," he said, "that the people of this province might be kept in good humour."[12] J.G. Rosengarten noted that money paid to officers increased their regular pay considerably. He added that General Riedesel, who had a keen business sense, admitted after returning to Bruswick that he had received 15,000 Thalers (US$11,000). It should be remembered that since the defeat of the French, the people of Canada had great difficulty exchanging their old currency and thus needed any cash the soldiers could provide. Since the soldiers were finding prices of provisions excessive in Canadian stores, Riedesel decided to set up his own business. Within a short time, however, the German soldiers were paying just as much as before.

For a few German soldiers, the Canadian climate posed no problem, but the majority suffered from it and had to spend time in hospital. Despite the language barrier, Germans and the French-speaking Canadians quickly established good relations, as we discover from the journal of Captain Pausch, chief of the Hanau artillery: "they find plenty of solace in the Canadian girls and women. For this reason, and in their companionship they are happy and contented."[13]

The second Brunswicker division reached land between September 14 and 17, 1776. They had embarked at Stade on May 30. The crossing had been difficult, like all ocean crossings at the time. Nineteen men had died and 131 contracted scurvy.[14] The second division comprised:[15]

COMMANDER: Col. J.F. von Specht
1 chief of staff
Musketeer Regiment von Specht, Col. J.F. von Specht
Light Infantry Battalion von Barner, Lt. Col. von Barner
A company of chasseurs, Capt. Ewald Richzet
An artillery company from Hanau, Capt. Georg Pausch

The artillery company, under Captain Pausch, according to his Journal, sailed past the others thanks to favourable winds, reaching Canada between August 19 and 26. Riedesel hastened to greet them before they were taken to La Prairie and from there to Fort Ile-aux-Noix, on the upper Richelieu River, which was still under construction. A few days later, the rest of the division arrived and joined their comrades at various tasks such as transporting provisions, building barracks and blockhouses, and strengthening the defences—occupations at which they would be employed throughout their stay in Canada.

In early September, Carleton learned from reliable sources that the American fleet had been spotted in Lake Champlain. An English scouting vessel and an American boat skirmished on September 6. On October 9, Captain Thomas Pringle's English fleet pursued Benedict Arnold and his fleet. During the night of October 10, while their scouts were combing the area to find the American hideout, Carleton and Pringle, on board the *Maria,* unwittingly dropped anchor a mere 24 kilometres from Arnold's fleet, which was moored "under the protection of Valcour Island. The water between the island and the mainland was deep enough for the purposes of navigation and yet sheltered enough to afford protection from stormy seas and from prying enemy eyes. (...) If the British ships did find him, they would have to beat up wind to get at him, thus giving him the advantage of manoeuvre. Arnold placed his vessels in line across the pass..."[16]

On the morning of October 11, with the wind in her sails, the English boat *Inflexible* spotted one of the rebels' scouting vessels and

Example of a sick list from the von Riedesel Regiment, dated
June 30, 1776.

gave chase "around the south end of Valcour Island," joined by a
Hanau gunboat and some English ships. Arnold and his ships were
waiting.

As soon as they were within striking distance, the British opened
fire. In the ensuing battle, the gunboat of the Hanau artillery was hit
and sank straight to the bottom. Fortunately for her crew, some
English ships were able to come to the rescue. The American ship,
Royal Savage, was also hit. "Owing to his losses in ships and manpower—sixty killed and wounded and two vessels sunk—Arnold's
officers questioned whether there was any point to further resistance."

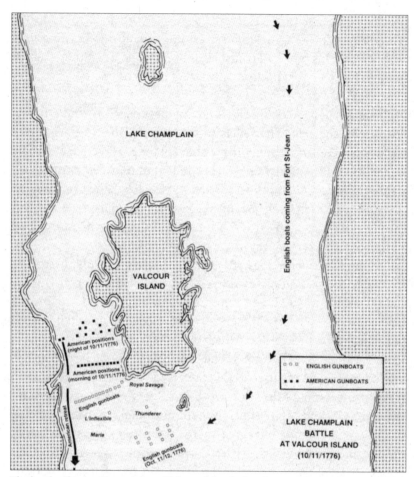

The battle of Lake Champlain at Valcour Island, October 11, 1776.
Drawn by Jean-Pierre Wilhelmy based on the original in *The Invasion of Canada*,
Stanley, Plate n° 8 by M.E.H. Ellwand.

Pringle had placed a cordon of gunboats across the exit from Valcour
Bay, and the Americans realized that in the morning light they would
be an easy target for British guns. But desperate times call for desperate measures. Unanimously, Arnold and his officers resolved to
attempt the impossible.

The night of October 11 witnessed an incredible *tour de force* as the
bold Arnold's battered little fleet sailed to safety right past the British

blockade. The British were waiting for daybreak to mop up the Americans. But to Pringle's utter astonishment, the morning light revealed that his prey had vanished as if by magic. He dithered about his next move, so that his fleet only set off in pursuit of the Americans the next day, October 13.

Pringle caught Arnold's slow-moving fleet near Crown Point and once more subjected the rebels to heavy fire. This time American losses were enormous; only three ships managed to escape. Arnold was on board the *Congress*. When the rest of his fleet surrendered, Arnold turned *Congress* towards the shore where... he grounded on the shale. After setting fire to his vessels, Arnold made his way through the woods towards Chimney Point, narrowly escaping an Indian ambush on the way.

For the Americans, this battle proved disastrous. Only three ships were able to reach Fort Ticonderoga where Major General Horatio Gates was waiting with 9000 militiamen and soldiers. Carleton and his men were only a few kilometres from Ticonderoga and in a good position to recapture the fort, which the Americans had taken eighteen months earlier. But Carleton hesitated; in all likelihood he had no real intention of attacking the fort. He preferred "collecting the prisoners taken from Arnold's fleet, giving them a lecture, praising them for their bravery and then releasing them and sending them home on condition that they would agree not to serve again against the British until regularly exchanged."[17] All the while, his men were cooling their heels in front of Ticonderoga's walls, and in the next few days, nothing of any importance occurred. Even when General Fraser daringly drew to within five kilometres of the fort, the rebels within stayed put and did not open fire, despite the English general's provocation.

A few days later, to everyone's astonishment, the governor declared that it was too late in the season to continue fighting and, on October 18, ordered his men to repair to their winter quarters.

Captain Pausch's journal details the winter placement of the troops. "The winter quarters of the Germans were in and around Three Rivers, as far down as Chambly, on the western side of Lake St. Pierre, and between the St. Lawrence and the Richelieu. The more special divisions were as follows: the regiment of Specht as far down as Champlain, near Three Rivers, and the place called Batiscamp (Batiscan); the regiment of Rhetz from the last named place to Fort St. Anna. These regiments sent off detachments to the parishes south of the St. Lawrence. The dragoons and regiments of Riedesel were quartered in Three Rivers. Two squadrons of the former, and three companies of the latter, had the town assigned to them. The two other squadrons were transferred to Cape-de-la-Madelain (Cap-de-la-Madeleine), the two other companies to Pointe-du-Lac. The regiments were also obliged to send detachments to the nearest parishes on the other side of the St. Lawrence. The regiment of Hesse-Hanau was removed to the parishes of Berthier and Masquinonge. It also sent out detachments to occupy St. François and Sorel. The regiment of Prince Frederick occupied the parishes of Rivière-du-Loup, and Machiche (Yamachiche). The grenadier battalion was quartered in St. Charles, St. Denis, and (St. Ours). Barner's light infantry was sent to Chambly, where it was joined by the company of sharp-shooters. The artillery of Hanau was quartered in Montreal."[18]

Both Germans and English were disappointed by Carleton's decision. One officer wrote in disgust, "this little army, I say, after having done as much as the Situation of the Country, and the Climate wo'd admit of, by driving the Enemy from Canada, destroying their Fleet, and then following closely to their Dens, was obliged to return to Canada to its great Regret, which it did the 2nd November in a very regular manner, without being in the least molested by the enemy, and the Whole got into their Winter Cantonnment abt. the 12th of the same Month."[19]

Since Carleton could not spend the winter at Crown Point, he returned to Canada with his men a few weeks later, which necessitated changes in the establishment of winter quarters. Breymann moved to Repentigny and St. Sulpice, Barner's battalion to St. François, St. Antoine, LaBaie, Yamaska, Becancour, and Nicolet, and the Hanau artillery to Lachine.[20]

Riedesel would also have liked to continue fighting. In a letter to Duke Ferdinand he wrote, "If we could have begun our last expedition four weeks earlier, I am satisfied that everything would have been ended this year;" and then added, "The rebels are losing courage.

They know that they are being led astray by some ambitious men, but do not yet see how to get out of the fix." Riedesel believed the Americans to be poor soldiers led by incompetent officers; he was convinced that an army of properly-disciplined regulars could easily crush them. He was not alone in thinking his side to be stronger: "We hold the key to Canada because we are now masters of Lake Champlain,"[21] wrote another officer. The Hanau artillery, which had helped destroy the fleet in Lake Champlain, was nevertheless satisfied with the outcome and was singled out by Governor Carleton in a letter he wrote to the Count of Hesse-Hanau praising the bravery of Captain Pausch and his men.[22]

In Canada, the soldiers were first billeted in public buildings; but the lack of space forced authorities to seek other solutions. The memory of the Canadians' indifference to the British cause was still fresh in Carleton's mind; harshly he told the people that they must not expect "to be treated with the same consideration as if they had exhibited the zeal and devotion owing to their king."[23] Thus, "billeting soldiers and fatigue-duty would be the cross they had to bear, and it was only fair that the majority of these drawbacks fall upon those cowards whose refusal to serve their country had made them necessary."[24] Then the governor instructed his officers to exempt those Canadians who had served during the campaign.

The journal of a certain Sanguinet provides an eye-witness account:

The army returned to Montreal at the end of October to set up winter quarters in the city and surrounding countryside, in the homes of all the inhabitants. Citizens of the city were mistreated and molested by the army without the possibility of legal redress. One Montreal citizen, who had certainly been a fine royalist, who was lodging two soldiers – an officer wanted to appropriate his bedchamber – despite the fact that he was ill and his wife – so that he refused. – Twenty-four soldiers with fifes and drums were sent to his house with orders to dance all night. – The incredible thing is that Governor Guy Carleton has refused to make any distinction between His Majesty's true and loyal citizens and the others. – On the contrary, he has confounded the two and the loyal subjects have been treated the worst, probably there are political reasons for this, but I believe, they are making a mistake – and those who have distinguished themselves the most and who have risked their lives and property in the service of the King – not only have they not been rewarded, but it seems as if they are being singled out for harsh treatment. Anyone who complained to Governor Guy Carleton rarely received a reply.[25]

At first the soldiers were billeted two or three to a house, but before long, four, six and even twelve were being assigned to the same lodging.[26] The English authorities were perfectly aware that this situation was potentially explosive, but they were determined to show the people what to expect if they failed to support the English king when he needed them. For the most part they used German mercenaries to carry out the vile task of repression.[27] While in no way exonerating the German soldiers, can we really blame them entirely for what happened?

As could be expected, a host of problems quickly arose and by 1777 pressure from the Canadians forced Carleton to set up a board of enquiry, composed of Saint-Georges Dupré, Edward William Gray, and Pierre Panet, to "investigate complaints about the exaction of fatigue-duty and billeting as well as the soldiers' conduct."[28] Of course, not all the soldiers were beyond reproach; but some Canadian writers like Ovide-M. H. Lapalice in his *Histoire de la Seigneurie Massue et de la paroisse de Saint-Aimé* (History of the Massue Seignory and of the Parish of Saint-Aimé)[29] —owing perhaps to a lack of exhaustive research—have badly misinterpreted certain facts. Here is a common example: "The Germans were repeatedly accused," wrote Lapalice, "of going into barns and stables, both night and day, and helping themselves to sheep, pigs and poultry."[30] All these claims are true; but the author seems to have omitted some important details which alter the picture he gives of these "thieves." A document entitled *Informations et procédés de la milice de Berthier (en haut) au sujet des troupes allemandes* (Information and Procedures of the Militia of Upper Berthier concerning the German Troops), dated Berthier, March 13, 1777, provides the following statement by the captain of the uppertown militia: "At the end of the month of last November, upon the arrival of the German troops in Berthier, the inhabitants with whom the soldiers were lodged went for nine consecutive days without receiving their rations, so that during this time, the said inhabitants were forced to receive said soldiers so that many of the said militia and others complained that said soldiers, lacking food as they did, killed several sheep and poultry."[31] This version of the story explains many things.

Other historians, lacking perhaps the research documents, have burdened the German soldiers with an undesirable reputation. In his *Histoire de la Seigneurie de Lauzon* (History of the Lauzon Seignory) Joseph-Edmond Roy wrote: "These soldiers possessed all the uncouthness of the Teutons and the insolence of badly taught German riders. More than one colonist thus had cause to complain about their extortions. Thanks to contemporary records, we can now read the complaints which were addressed to the governor or to his aides." Roy goes on to give an example: "On November 8, 1782, the inhabitants of St. Nicholas complained that they had been mistreated by Major Pausch of the Hesse-Hanau artillery:

> To Mr. François Babi Ecuier, lieutenant colonel of the militia of the Government of Quebec:
>
> Michel Bergeron an inhabitant of the parish of St. Nicholas, begs leave to ask your Intervention with His Excellency our peaceable commander general of this country, concerning the mistreatment he has suffered and which he fears (along with his fellow-citizens) will be repeated, at the hands of Major Pausch of the artillery which is winter-quartered in the said parish, who beat the plaintiff without cause so hard with a stick that he rendered him incapable of working he tried to avoid the blows but two soldiers and a sergeant with a sabre held him until the major had expended all his fury upon him etc... He immediately lodged a complaint with the Colonel who is in the parish of St. Antoine who listened calmly to his grievances and gave but a vague reply which is why he has thus along with the others named below dared to address the present petition to you.
>
> Michel Demers complains likewise that Major Pausch appropriated his stove by force for his own use which is contrary to regulations, etc., etc.
>
> The complaints lodged are correct,
> JEAN-BAPTISTE DEMERS
> Lieutenant of the parish of St. Nicholas.[32]

The following letter to Governor Haldimand from Colonel Leutz, Major Pausch's commanding officer, conserved in both the English and Canadian archives, answers these charges: [33]

Sir!

According to your Excellency's ordres which received by Capt Domerfeld, concerning Major Paeusch of the Hesse Hanau Artillery and the Capt of Militla Frichet, as well as the Inhabitants Michel Bergeron and Michel Demers from the parish of St-Nicolas, I do myself the Pleasure to send my Rapport about this matter to Your Excellency, I dit not think that one of those persons would have complained to you, and I dit flatter myself that wheen the Capt of Militia and Inhabitans complained to me about the behaviour of Major Pausch, that they would not trouble you with them too, as they have done in so much as I contented Michel Demers already with some Money, which I give him out of my poket, with promisses that he should for his stove be contented by Major Pausch.

The chief complaint of Michel Bergeron consisted of being flocked and having another soldier at his housse at the room of this who was allready quartered with his Family, which was done on the spot. The said Inhabitant when they were complaining to me, they went away quiet satisfied and contented, and I dit not thought otherweise, than that the whole affair was settled. - But for to execute Your Excellency's ordres as strictly, as it is in my power, I have satisfied and contented the said complaining persons and have the honor to send the inclosed reçeits of them to you. I shall put Major Pausch under arrest for ten days, if my proceeding in this affair finds Your Excellency's approbation...

Leutz Colonel

Even supposing Major Pausch were guilty of mistreating the inhabitants, should the blame for one officer's mistake or for one isolated example fall upon all the soldiers? Shouldn't the general behaviour of these men be considered in light of the way German authorities administered justice between civilians and soldiers when cases arose?

The soldiers were obviously not beyond reproach. Research leads nonetheless to the conclusion that severe discipline was maintained throughout German ranks and that whenever a misdemeanour occurred, the authorities ensured that if the perpetrator was a member of the German corps, he would be punished. In most cases, their punishment greatly exceeded what would have been meted out to a Canadian.

Within the army there was stern discipline. Guilty soldiers were brought before a military judge who sentenced them based on severe guidelines whose harshness would have surprised many a civilian. For instance, when 36-year-old Christoph Muller[34] of the Regiment von Speth from Brunswick was found guilty of stealing a silver spoon, he was given fifty strokes with a rod. Found guilty of desertion, he was sentenced to hang (42nd article of war). When some German soldiers were found guilty of theft and mistreatment of the inhabitants of the Rivière-du-Chêne region, their leader Col. Kreutzbourg wrote to Governor Haldimand instead of punishing them: "Their guilt is so clear that, according to Instructions from my master the Prince, I am not authorized to bring the trial to a close but must send the papers to court.[35] Nonetheless, I am confident that they will not be condemned to die, and that the prince will commute the death penalty to severe corporal punishment. Compensation was paid to the inhabitants in the presence of the captains of the parish militia."[36]

These historians' accounts continue to affect us today. For instance, *Les Beaucerons, ces insoumis* (Those Unruly People of the Beauce) Madeleine Ferron wrote: "Oral tradition gives no hint of serious trouble between occupier and occupied." She continues, "It would be naive to think that those eight years of occupation caused no disturbance and left no tangible reminders. Joseph Edmond Roy discloses several grievances addressed to the governor: acts of brutality and abuses of power by the German soldiers."[37]

Daily life for the Germans during the winter of 1776-77 can be summed up as follows: the soldiers received their provisions and paid the inhabitants for other services. Wood for heating was chopped in the bush nearby by soldiers who, according to the archives, were under constant supervision. Men billeted by Canadians were visited daily by an officer, frequently by a superior officer, and monthly by the colonel. Those housed in public buildings were also subject to severe discipline; they had to supply detailed reports on everything that occurred around their quarters.[38]

Weather permitting, Riedesel often had his men practice shooting. Like many others, he believed the Americans to be better shots than his soldiers.[39] He had good reason to think so. First, the English army was equipped with smooth-bore muskets which did not allow for accurate aiming; they were not designed to hit the bull's-eye but to fire into the brown. As a result, the strategy of the Anglo-German army consisted in resting the barrel on a fellow soldier's shoulder to take aim and spray the enemy with bullets.

The east-coast Americans used these smooth-bore muskets as well, but the English army also came up against the men of the west who used a different, lighter weapon that permitted more accurate shots, a necessity for men who used their guns daily and depended on them for survival. Ironically, these weapons had been perfected by German colonists who had settled in Pennsylvania. They replaced the smooth bore with a spirally grooved one that forced the bullet to spin through the air, thus keeping it straight on course. The barrel of the Pennsylvania rifle was also twice as long as the smooth-bore weapons. This was not a problem for the Americans, who wreaked such havoc on the English army that a loyalist wrote to a newspaper: "This province raised a corps of 1000 fusiliers. The poorest shot among them can shoot a man in the head from fifty or 200 metres. You had better warn your officers to make sure all their affairs are in order in England before they embark for America." This reputation for infallibility leads us straight to the myth of the American marksman who never misses a shot, like Buffalo Bill, Wild Bill Hickok, Annie Oakley, and Sergeant York.[40]

Despite early problems of adaptation to the Canadian mentality and Canada's harsh climate, and despite the language barrier, the German soldiers seem to have been fairly content in their first winter quarters on Canadian soil. This was especially true for the officers, most of whom spoke fairly good French. One officer from Lower Saxony wrote eight letters to his family between March 9 and April 20, 1777, while stationed in the parish of Ste. Anne. They offer a fascinating glimpse of eighteenth-century Quebec, quite different from the picture presented by the English and French and passed on by historians.[41] The following passages, despite their length, are particularly interesting.

Hessian Musket. Courtesy of West Point Museum Collections.

Letter no. 1:

(...) You had the kindness to express sympathy with our supposed lack of various necessities. To comfort our friends back home I must admit the truth that to date such want has been by no means significant and that we have more than enough beef, pork, and mutton, and since February 20th veal, also hens, capons, geese, duck, partridge, and hare. Nor have we lacked white cabbage, turnips, beets, turniprooted cabbage, or good dried peas and beans; to be sure, we have to forego red cabbage, cauliflower, lentils, and certain other vegetables, venison and wild pig; but your lady will tell you that with the above-named substantial things considerable variety can be secured in a well-equipped kitchen. Add the fact that now and then we have had many good fish, that from wheat flour and good butter many a pleasant pastry can be made, and that you can eat young bear, beaver-tails, caribou, and elk roast, and with such dishes at least give your table the appearance of luxuriousness; then you will be convinced that mouth and eyes can be satisfied in Canada. In praise of my dear Low Saxon countrymen be it said that their smoked and jellied meats, sausages, and various preserved meats will ever remain their own peculiar products, which the inhabitant of Swabia, Upper Saxony, the Rhineland, and the Canadian does not know. For good and natural reasons such things cannot be produced here.

Do not think that our privates are at any great disadvantage compared with the officers. Both must take their ration for which two and a half pence is deducted from their pay daily. In praise of our general-in-chief I must say that through his concern especially the German soldier gets for this deduction daily two and a half pounds of beef, and one and a half pounds of wheat flour, an allowance which even the healthiest stomach will hardly digest each day. If a soldier gets but one pound of meat and one pound of bread or flour, he gets excellent English peas and very good Irish butter and rice.(...)

Letter no. 4:

(...) How have we diverted ourselves this winter? Oh, at your service, very well! You see, we have some *seigneurs* and *curés* in our neighborhood, and with the help of our neighboring officers we have lived quite sociably, companionably, friendlily, happily, and at times also quite high. One *seigneur* in Ste. Anne, who is fairly rich, is *Grand Inspecteur des Forêts et des eaux royales* and holds a position *as aide-de- camp* to General Carleton, has often come from Quebec to visit us country folk, brought along company and city ladies, and given us many a little *fête* at his manorial estate here. The *curés,* too, are not to be despised. Nearly all are good royalists and holders of fat livings, by virtue of which they are in a position to give dinners of twenty covers and pass around very good— yes, often French wines. The *curé* in Batiscan, *Mr. le Fevre,* has several times given General von Riedesel very elaborate *fêtes,* without forgetting his neighbors at Ste. Anne. (...)

The 31st was the great festival, as on that day was celebrated the liberation of the City of Quebec on the 31st of last year, when the rebels also lost their great leader, General Montgomery. At 9 a.m. a thanksgiving service was held in the cathedral church and *Monseigneur* "the bishop" conducted the service in person; eight unhappy Canadians, who had assisted the rebels, had to do public penance in church with ropes around their necks, and to beg forgiveness of God, the Church, and the King. At 10 o'clock all the civil and military authorities and all foreign and native gentlemen, both Canadian and English, assembled at the Government House. All the gentlemen residing in Quebec wore, as *officiers de milice,* a green uniform with straw-colored facings, vest, and breeches, and silver epaulets...

Escorted by Major-General von Riedesel, Brigadier-General Specht, and all officers and English gentlemen present, he went at 11 o'clock to the great square in front of the *Recollets* monastery, where the French militia, or Canadian citizenry of Quebec, marched past in review in eight companies. and after the manner of the citizens of W—made a triple cannon salute and running fire and cried *Vive le Roi!!* From here the procession went to the upper city where we attended service in the English church. At the *Te Deum* the cannon in the citadel were fired, while the enthusiastic citizen fired rifles and shotguns at will out the windows. At three o'clock, sixty persons sat down to dinner at the General's; except for the two Ladies Carleton, no women were present.

At six in the evening the whole train betook itself to the great English *auberge,* where we found over ninety-four *dames* and two hundred *chapeaux*[42] already assembled in a great hall. The ladies sat on several rows of benches rising one above the other. A concert began at once, at which there was sung an English ode composed for this celebration in arias, ariettes, recitatives, and choruses. During this music tickets were distributed to those of both sexes who wished to dance. Each *chapeau* gets a ticket for his partner with whom he dances the whole evening. The ticket is numbered 1, 2, etc. In this some regard is paid to the rank both of the man and of the lady; strangers, however, were greatly preferred.

Of all the couples there, each danced its own minuet, and each time the lady names the minuet which is to be played. At great balls this gets tiresome. English dances are danced in two sections into which the long hall is divided in the middle by rows of benches. In taking places rank, or the familiar precedence, is abandoned, and the governor himself, who did not dance, took every conceivable pains to maintain equality. Ladies who do not desire to dance put on very tiny Bügelröcke[43] and the chapeaux who do not care to be asked to dance put on black cloth shoes with felt soles. All manner of refreshments were served, and although the place was rather crowded, one was not bothered by any spectators, since no one thinks of looking on. The streets in front of the house were as free from people as one can conceive. At midnight supper was served at several tables. Only cold dishes, to be sure, but a superabundance of delicacies and cakes. At 2 a.m. the dancing began again and lasted till broad daylight. All the English and French *officiers de milice* of Quebec gave this *fête* which easily cost several thousand reichsthaler.

January 1, 1777, the governor had a general reception for all persons of the church, the law, the sword, of commerce and navigation. The whole city teemed with sleighs as each one paid his New Year's calls on the others. We also had ourselves driven about, but also got rid of many a billet. At noon we dined at the home of Mr. de la Naudière, and in the evening there was a great assembly in the Government House, where there was play at some thirty tables. At ten o'clock every one went home to bed. The 2nd, we dined with Colonel St. Leger, commander of the 34th Regiment and present commandant in Quebec, with whom we got well acquainted in camp near Chambly. Since there were only *chapeaux* at table a tremendous number of toasts were drunk. In the evening we took leave of the General, despite the fact that we were invited to several other *fêtes* and especially to a sleigh-party of one hundred sleighs to the countryplace of Dr. --. This man is Doctor of Medicine, Counsellor at Law, and uncommonly rich; he is the Lucullus of Quebec and like him has no wife of his own.

January 20, Major-General von Riedesel celebrated the birthday of Her Majesty the Queen in Trois-Rivières. We covered the seven German miles thither by sleigh in four hours and dined at a table of forty covers, at which there were also several wearers of the Cross of St. Louis, who, nevertheless, seemed to be poor. Many healths were drunk in champagne to the firing of a small cannon in front of the house. Afternoon and evening there was a ball with thirty-seven ladies present who were also at supper. Miss *Tonnencour* enhanced her charm greatly by her jewels, to be sure, but poor Miss R--e in her wretched cotton gown won the preference of many by her natural gentle charm and her fine voice. You must know, Sir, that the Canadian beauties sing Italian and French *chansons* at table, and that several *chansons* in honor of General von Riedesel have been written and set to music and are often sung in Trois-Rivières.

I count the 5th of February as an unusual *fête* because seven couples were married in the church of Ste. Anne. The Brigadier escorted to the altar a niece of the *curé,* Major von Ehrenkrok, a savagess who was marrying a *sauvage de la nation des Têtes de Boule,* an Attikamek warrior, and I, a relative of the *Capitaine de milice.* One can only hold this honorary office in case of a bride whose father is dead; i.e., one represents the father. At noon we dined at the *curé's* and in the evening diverted ourselves in the various bridal houses, where polite attention alternated with little practical jokes, just as is the case at our own peasant-weddings. Since our musicians were in Quebec and they have no village musicians, the dancing was to the tralalara of a Canadian minuet. You had to stand the full-throated singing of *chansons.* However, by this we have, in a way, gained family rights in Ste. Anne, for all the women, from the aged dames of seventy to the little girls of sixteen, voluntarily offer us a kiss. This is the Canadian greeting among relatives and very good friends; men offer men, and women offer women only their hands. This custom is in vogue in the most distinguished families and is a right of friendship.

Letter no. 1:

(...) This year the winter has been such that all the inhabitants say they never had one like it. We ourselves have noticed no great difference between the cold of the winter here and at home, while we have marveled at the steady weather. Since November 24th of last year "1776", when it began to snow and freeze, we have had neither rain nor a real thaw; since then the first snow and ice have stayed. It has often snowed hard, but rarely over twelve hours, and all the snow has been fine and dry. You can easily imagine that in such a long even winter the earth rnust be covered with a compact coating of snow and ice four to five feet deep.

(Indeed, the winter of 1776-77, which seemed to have softened its usual severity out of kindness to the new arrivals, was so unusual in the Canadian experience that hence forth it was known as the "winter of the Germans.")

Letter no. 6:

Your pen seems to have frozen up; so hear something of the Canadian snow. It is a d--d bad business in Canada that the winds often—at least every three days—blow violently for about twelve hours, so that they shift the snow from place to place and gradually fill all ditches, holes, and chasms so full that they appear level with the heights. Though this looks very nice, it is dangerous to travel the without knowledge and foresight. One can, e.g., plunge into a gulch where you break a few bones or are buried alive in the snow for weeks, horse, sleigh, and all. The driver's lack of caution need not be great, for one foot to the side can cause such an ugly thing. But just as a good gunsmith can find a remedy for anything, so for this, too, there is help. Each *habitant* is obliged to mark off the road between his habitation and that of his two neighbors with young fir trees, so that it is broad enough for two sleighs, and the trees stand twenty feet apart on each side. In these artificial *allées* one rides safely. These roads are changed with incredible frequency according to the nature of the weather and circumstances, and are marked anew each time and the trees of the old road pulled up. On the rivers, too, the roads are marked, yes, even on the great St. Lawrence, and any one who notices a dangerous spot on it is obliged to mark it. Thus traveling in Canada is a curious matter, inasmuch as a road runs on the heights to-day and over a river to-morrow. (...)

People on foot can skip over all the snow like rabbits, just following their nose, if they wear snowshoes. These things are much like the *raquettes* with which we play shuttlecock, only twice as big, so you have to shuffle along with legs far apart and bandy-legged. The English regiments have had to do a lot of practicing with them this winter, but our regiments did not get any because they haven't been able to turn out enough. Every habitant has such machines, which are also absolutely indispensable for him, even to take a walk in his own neighborhood. (...)

Letter no. 2:

This time, dear Mama, I shall chat with you just about Canadian housekeeping matters, though I fear you will not be able to apply them...

In the middle of December comes the slaughter festival of the Canadians compared to which all European slaughter festivals are insignificant. All the fat four-footed beasts and all the plump feathered creatures in all Canada have to give up their lives in a period of eight or ten days, and everywhere you see signs of the general slaughter. All the fat oxen, swine, sheep, hens, geese, ducks, and turkeys must offer their throats without mercy and provide for the human race during the entire winter. But what a departure from our method! They cut all the four-footed creatures into roasting and baking pieces of any desired size, pluck the feathers from the domestic fowl without using warm water, but leave them on the tail, wings, and head, tie the wings and legs close to the body with bark fibers, and turn all the meat and poultry over to the care of Mother Nature, letting it freeze thoroughly in the open air and then laying it in an especially built *hangard* (storehouse) through which the winds sweep from all directions. All winter they take out one piece after the other at pleasure, cook and eat it in peace and with good appetite. What ails this way of doing things?... ... All frozen meat remains white, tender, fine-tasting...(...) The Canadians know nothing about preserving meat by salting, smoking, or other methods, and their houses are not built or equipped therefor. They lack good cellars because in most parishes there is no stone, and the best smoke rooms in wooden houses would hardly withstand the usual cold of Canada. So we must properly allow the Canadians their habit of keeping the meat fresh by freezing; all the more as they freeze everything that can stand frost. Hare, hazel-grouse, and other feathered things hang in their skins and feathers in the *hangards* all winter long; also very delicate fish, with which the parish St. François especially provides almost half Canada, await in these sheds the time when they will be taken out and cooked; thus one knows nothing of the fact that elsewhere fish vanish from the bill of fare. They even pour cows' milk into great vessels and let it freeze in any sized blocks desired, from which they break off one piece after another and cook it; rarely is the milk unkind enough to curdle.

Water, beer, wine, and other spirits, on the other hand, must be carefully guarded against freezing, and so one is not ashamed to take them into one's room or the adjoining closet, the door of which remains open. In the houses of the ordinary *habitans,* therefore, wooden water pails with covers stand in a corner of the living- room, and a japanned tin dipper hangs above with which any one may dip water and drink. More distinguished folk have vases of faïence in their rooms to which water can be brought by pipes, and so even in summer one finds a cool, refreshing drink in their rooms. The poorer people keep their strong drinks in little tuns, called *barils,* on a chair in their rooms right under their eyes and draw off grasses or bottles as wanted. Aristocratic and wealthy folk, on the other hand, have in their rooms great rectangular chests, made of beautiful wood and bound with brass, in which there are

cut-glass decanters holding three or more quarts. If the host is econom-
ical, he sets such an Apostle near himself and with a silver funnel fills
the small carafes on the table; after the meal he puts his big container
back in his cellar-box, locks this, and is sure his butler will not be able
to rob him.

All pregnant cattle are kept in the barn through the winter and are
fairly well cared for. The so-called *güste (not* pregnant) cattle, whether
beeves or sheep, run in the snow all day, straw and hay are shaken down
for them in the snow which they eat little by little with enough snow to
serve instead of water... Wretched and long- haired as the cattle look in
winter, in reality they are sound and sturdy, and a cure of fresh grass in
spring will in four weeks put them in such condition that the most
exacting German farmer would express his delight with them. Cattle
plague is totally unknown in Canada. (...)

Letter no. 3:

(...) You do not shoot anything of consequence near the parishes. The
habitans have killed off all the wild animals near the settlements. Hence...
he who desires a real hunt must go to one or the other Indian tribe, live
with them in their wild fashion, eat, sleep, march, swim, and roam four
hundred to five hundred leagues in the wilderness. It is incredible what
hunting trips the savages make through woods, over mountains, rivers,
lakes and marshes, and what means they know of overcoming all difficulties. They go fifty to sixty German miles into the wilderness, erect
huts, leave a few people there, and the rest go by twos and threes in every
possible direction, hunt and shoot whatever comes in their way, and after
four or five weeks return to the huts just as if regular roads led there.
Anyway, the savage can take a straight course for many hundred leagues
through wildernesses and all natural obstacles and end up in the place
he intended. On the trees, leaves, rivers, and other natural objects they
can find indications by which they can guide themselves just as accur-
ately and correctly as we do by our compasses. They make natural deduc-
tions in places where they have never been and predict two days in
advance: "at such and such a place comes a river from such and such a
region, but it must turn so and so"; and their statement proves correct.
This is a fine instinct which nature simply gave them and which is based
but little on reflection or ripe experience. If they are able -as they certainly are - to tell from a man's footprints by what nation they were made,
if they can follow these footprints in the dark and use their nose as their
only guide, if they can scent as well as our hunting-dogs and bird-dogs,

then the best-trained man's reason fails and cannot comprehend the fine animal senses with which God has endowed people whom we term savages. (...)

To help combat the chill of winter, Supply Officer Faucitt personally ensured that soldiers were dressed properly. Our officer friend from Saxony wrote home. "The whole army wears a special uniform in winter. This consists of cloth overtrousers reaching from the feet to the navel, a great pair of mittens, and a cloth cape which covers the face, neck, and shoulders. The English regiments wear in addition Canadian *capots* over their uniforms.

A more elaborate description of the winter uniform was given by Captain Pausch:

One pair of long blue cloth overalls such as are worn by sailors, which come high up above the hips and way down to the shoes. These are fastened under the feet with a leather strap, and have five buttons on the outside of each leg and extend about a quarter the way up from the ankle, also:
    One large blue woolen cap.
    One pair of blue mittens lined with corduroy material.
    One capacious under-jacket, the sleeves being made of strong white corduroy. One Canadian over-coat with a cape and facing of white sheep's wool, and bound with a light blue braid. The cape itself is made out of a whitish gray cloth a kind of melton. It is bound with light blue woolen ribbon, and in three places extending down in front to the waist it is fastened with rosettes - these latter being made out of this same blue ribbon. This garment is called throughout all Canada a *capot*.

Each soldier was charged 33 shillings 9 pence for this uniform.[44]

The summer of 1776 saw the failure of a plan to squeeze Washington's army between the forces of General Guy Carleton, coming south from Canada, and those of General William Howe, commander of the British army in America, pushing up from New York. Plans for a new campaign were laid in early March 1777. General John Burgoyne, who had been part of Carleton's disastrous expedition but who somehow managed to avoid taking any blame for it, returned to England in the fall of 1776 because of his wife's poor health. He was able to persuade Lord George Germain, the American secretary "whose responsibility it was to develop a strategy to crush the rebellion,"[45] that a second expedition was advisable—"this one under more aggressive leader-ship, which he himself would provide."[46] He proposed a three-pronged attack: Burgoyne and his men would proceed to Ticonderoga, while Lt. Col. Barry St. Leger would create a diversion by Lake Ontario before advancing towards the Mohawk River to capture the forts established there. Finally, General Howe would approach from the south, join them to encircle the Americans, and squeeze them within the powerful claw of the combined army.

John Burgoyne, known as "Gentleman Johnny," was a poet, writer, actor, and playwright (his most famous play was The Heiress, 1756). His military reputation was based on his actions in 1762 in Portugal, but during the American Revolution his military decisions were constantly questioned by higher authorities in the Anglo-German army.[47] However, his proposals for a new campaign were welcome in London. Burgoyne therefore returned to Canada in spring 1777 bearing a letter for Carleton[48] from Lord Germain ordering him to remain in Canada where "his unique concern was to maintain order and see that judicial system was set up."[49] Thus, in a few words, Carleton was relieved of his duties as commander-in-chief of military operations. His replacement was none other than Gentleman Johnny Burgoyne.

For Carleton and his supporters, this was the expected outcome of the festering antagonism between the general and Lord Germain, and the bitter-sweet tone of their recent correspondence had foreshadowed just such a reaction.[50] Lord Germain claimed his decision was the result of Carleton's laxity in pursuing the rebels. Most historians agree that despite his ambition, Burgoyne was in no way responsible for Carleton's disgrace. Carleton's subsequent behaviour supports this view. He made every effort to help the new commander-in-chief suc-ceed in this all-important British campaign. Riedesel wrote, nonethe-less, "A great mistake was undoubtedly here made by the British ministry." To the German general it seemed obvious that "Any one almost, in the absence of General Carleton, could have attended to the administration of Canada." On the other hand, Carleton's absence from the military campaign jeopardized its chances of success; Riedesel felt that only his vast experience could properly serve the

English crown. However, as a good soldier should, Riedesel obeyed his new commander without argument.[51]

On May 28, 1777 the German troops were ordered to prepare for immediate departure, except for 667 soldiers under Lt. Col. von Ehrenkrook. According to Carleton, these men were "the sick, infirm, and such as the regiments usually disburthen themselves of on like occasions."[52] They were in such poor condition that Carleton had to ask Howe for assistance in the event of another invasion.

Burgoyne's army consisted of English soldiers, 3016 Germans plus 250 Loyalists and Canadian volunteers, and about 400 Indians.[53] General Phillips was in charge of the right flank, Riedesel of the left. St. Leger's forces comprised 875 Loyalists and volunteers, plus 800 to 1000 Indians led by Joseph Brant. Colonel Kreutzbourg and his chasseurs were to have joined this group but were held up by a misunderstanding, with the result that they did not reach Quebec until July 11, 1777. By the time they reached Oswego on August 26, St. Leger had already begun his retreat from Fort Stanwix.[54]

The Hesse-Hanau chasseurs, sometimes called jaegers, had been recruited from the forests of Germany, like those from the other principalities who participated in this war. These Gameskeepers, foresters or simple huntsmen formed the elite of the Anglo-German army in North America. They were armed with short European rifles, each one unique because each man used his own personal weapon, purchased from or custom-made by his own gunsmith. These weapons generally measured about four feet and did not carry a bayonet. Instead, the soldiers wore short swords attached at their waists by a rope.[55]

The companies of Kreutzbourg, Francken, Wittgenstein, and Hildebrandt were highly skilled. They had left Hanau during May 1777, destined for service under General John Burgoyne.[56] However, the piece of cake they were promised in this campaign turned out to be cause for a bad case of indigestion once they reached Saratoga. The Americans certainly did not look like a traditional army, and rumour had it that they were exhausted and demoralized. The Anglo-German army, expecting to fight in the traditional way, completely forgot the lessons of history, particularly those famous battles between the Roman army and barbarians fighting on familiar ground unencum-

Organization of General Burgoyne's Army in 1777

Right flank under Phillips

Canadians　Canadians

Under Brig. General Fraser

24th English reg.　English grenadiers　English Lighte Infantry

Under Lt. Colonel Breymann

Under Brig. Gen. Hamilton

Under Brig. Gen. Powell

21st English　62nd English　20th English　47th Englishs　53rd English　9th English

Left flank under Riedesel

Indians　Indians

Under Lt. Colonel Breymann

Light Infantry von Barner　Grenadier batt. von Breymann

Under Lt. Colonel Breymann

Under Brig. Gen. Specht

Under Brig. Gen. Gall

H.-Hanau　Prince Ferdinande

Rhetz　Specht　Riedesel

Reserves

Brunswick Dragoons

bered by the heavy equipment which hindered the Roman advance through the marsh. Years had passed between these two wars, with no change in the scenario: the Anglo-German army made the same errors as the Romans. Moreover, the Americans in turn were to shut their eyes to history and suffer the same consequences during the Vietnam war. A baffled English officer wrote in disbelief, "They refuse to fight."[57]

At first it looked as if Burgoyne would have no trouble with the Americans. Major Arthur St. Clair surrendered Ticonderoga on July 5, 1777. But the rest of the campaign was a different story.

In the meantime, Baroness von Riedesel arrived at Quebec with her three daughters, Augusta (1771-1805), Frederika (1774-1854), and the baby, Caroline (1776-1861), who was born just after her father left Brunswick Wolfenbüttel. They were anxious to see their beloved husband and father after many months' separation. Accompanied by their faithful servant Rockel, they left Wolfenbüttel on May 14, 1776, reaching Calais on June 1 after a series of misadventures and frustrations which prevented them from continuing their journey towards America. On April 16, 1777 they were finally able to leave Portsmouth on board a merchant ship which landed at Quebec on June 11 at 10 a.m.[58]

After accepting a kind dinner invitation from Lady Maria, Governor Carleton's wife, they left at 6 p.m. on Captain Powell's ship and reached Pointe-aux-Trembles, near Quebec, around midnight. During the night of the June 12 they travelled by mail-coach, desperately trying to catch up with Riedesel who, they knew, was "constantly marching farther away."[59] Baroness von Riedesel later described the way the drivers spoke to their animals: "The Canadians always talk to their horses and give them all sorts of names. Whisking the whip they kept saying or singing, 'Allons, mon prince!' 'Pour mon général!' or sometimes, 'Fi, donc, madame!' I thought they meant me and said 'Plaît-il?' (excuse me?) 'Oh!' they replied, 'ce n'est que mon cheval, la petite coquine!' (It's only my horse, the little hussy.)"[60]

When they reached Batiscan they could not get a calash,[61] and were forced to continue their journey in a mere bark canoe. Despite a terrifying hailstorm, they reached Trois-Rivières in safety and were greeted joyfully by the German soldiers. They spent the night in a house the general had prepared for them and set out again at about 6 a.m. on the June 13 despite the continuing storm, this time in a covered calash belonging to Vicar-General Saint-Onge and determined to reach Berthier. After a brief rest, they set off at full speed for Montreal where they spent the night. At daybreak they once more resumed their journey and finally reached Chambly, where they learned with great disappointment that they had somehow missed General von Riedesel. He had set out to meet them by an alternate route to Berthier. Carleton and his officers hastened to reassure the baroness and her weary family that the general would be back in no time. The next day the joyful reunion at last took place: "My children and my faithful Rockel constantly stood in the road, watching so that they could bring me the news immediately when they saw my husband coming. At last a calèche, in which a Canadian sat, came into view. I saw the calèche halt, the Canadian step out, come nearer, and clasp the children in his arms. It was my husband! (...) With the infant Caroline in my arms I ran as fast as I could to join this darling group. My happiness was indescribable."[62]

After two all-too-brief days together, the family was forced to separate again on the June 18. The rest of the troops had arrived, and despite their ardent longing to accompany the general, the baroness and her daughters had to return to Trois-Rivières for safety's sake. A few days later they reached their destination, and Baroness von Riedesel wrote in her journal, "My sadness was intensified because the troops were marching toward the enemy, and my children and I were left to return alone and to live in a strange country among strangers. Sad and depressed I started on my journey. What a difference between this journey and the previous one! I was in no hurry this time, because my heart ached anew each time we reached another post station that increased the distance between my husband and me."[63] Despite the many distractions of life in Trois-Rivières, the baroness was so unhappy that her husband finally succumbed to her pleading and let his family join him. He arranged to have them escorted by boat to Fort Edward where he met them on August 15. This was the beginning of the great and perilous adventure of the Riedesel family during the American Revolution.

Nothing of any importance to the war occurred in Canada during the months following Burgoyne's departure with his army. However, the threat of a new invasion hung over the country. Carleton had his men repair the fortifications and maintained communication between the various posts scattered across the vast territory he administered. There were 667 German soldiers from Brunswick and Hanau in Canada at this time, under Lt. Col.—soon to be Brigadier—von Ehrenkrook, divided as follows:[64]

Names	Headq.	Capt.	Lt.	Offic.	Men
Grenadier regiment	0	1	1	1	72
Prinz Friedrich regiment	0	1	22	8	91
Von Rhetz regiment	1	1	2	7	91
Von Riedesel regiment	0	0	2	7	91
Von Specht regiment	0	1	2	7	91
Von Barner battalion	0	1	1	6	68
Hesse-Hanau regiment	0	1	2	7	96
Total	**1**	**6**	**12**	**48**	**600**

At the same time, further south, following the precipitous departure of the American Major Arthur St. Clair and his troops from Ticonderoga, Burgoyne decided to pursue the rebels. The Regiment Prinz Friedrich and the English 62nd were ordered to take over the garrison; Fraser and Riedesel were to capture one group of Americans who had taken the road to Hubbardton while Burgoyne himself chased St. Clair in the direction of Skenesborough (Whitehall, N.Y.).[65] On July 7 Fraser came under enemy fire. Riedesel and his men—von Breymann's Grenadier Battalion, the Prinz Ludwig's Brunswick Dragoon Regiment, and the von Barner Light Infantry Battalion— immediately came to his rescue. Meanwhile, Burgoyne had caught up with his prey and during the evening of July 6, St. Clair's entire fleet was destroyed. Three of its five ships were burned, the other two captured. When the Skenesborough insurgents learned of this disaster, they folded up camp and retreated to Fort Anne.

At the same time, Major General Philip Schuyler, commander of American operations in the northern sector, had assembled his troops at Fort Edward and began using guerrilla tactics to hinder the advance of the Anglo-German army. The king's troops found their route blocked by fallen trees, while their horses "escaped" into the wild, and the fields around them were burned. These obstacles proved so serious that before long Burgoyne began to consider a relief exped- ition to remedy this disastrous situation. Riedesel objected, arguing that it was too far to go and that the men would probably become targets for the enemy. But the English general was not the least inter- ested in the opinion of a mere German officer; ignoring Riedesel's recommendation, he chose Lt.-Col. Friedrich Baum to lead the exped- ition. Baum's detachment consisted of 551 men of whom 374 were Germans; the rest were Canadian volunteers, loyalists, and English soldiers with, in addition, 150 Indians.[66]

At the last minute, a report from Col. Skeene[67] reached Burgoyne, informing him that a huge store of provisions lay in Bennington, carelessly guarded by the enemy. Without bothering to check further, the English general immediately changed Baum's orders, sending him to Bennington instead. Unfortunately for the German officer and his men, Brig. General John Stark, an American leader from New Hampshire, was camped near Bennington with a force of 1500 to 1800 men. Baum and his detachment left on August 11, 1777,[68] unaware of impending disaster. Along the way, they managed to secure some provisions and even captured a few prisoners. On August 14, Baum learned of Stark's presence in the vicinity but proudly decided to pursue his route as planned. First, though, he prudently sent a mes- sage back to Burgoyne[69] in the hope of receiving some reinforcements. Burgoyne immediately sent 662 men under Lt. Col. Heinrich von Breymann, comprising 333 grenadiers from Brunswick, 288 men from Baum's light infantry regiment, and 21 artillerymen with two pieces of artillery, led by Lt.Spangenberg.[70] Hampered by the weight of their weapons,[71] as well as by the inclement weather, Breymann's relief troops could not advance very rapidly. On August 16, they learned that Stark's forces had crushed their comrades about eight kilometres from their present position. The next day they suffered the same fate when they met the Americans: only Captain Schlagenteuffel and 29 Brunswick dragoons escaped the enemy.[72] In less than two days, nearly 700 soldiers, including 400 Germans, had been taken prisoner by the rebels. Of Baum's men, 365 did not return to camp; and 231 of Breymann's men were either killed, wounded or missing.[73] For the Anglo-German army, this was the beginning of the end.

At the beginning of July 1777, Lt. Col. Barry St. Leger with nearly 900 soldiers and loyalists and about 1000 Indians led by Joseph Brant, left Montreal to proceed to Fort Stanwix[74] in accordance with the first part of Burgoyne's strategy; they were later to join the armies of Burgoyne and Howe at Albany. On August 4, St. Leger besieged the fort, thereby arousing the hostility of some 800 inhabitants of the Mohawk Valley. These people were primarily of German descent; they joined forces with General Nicholaus Herckeimer to aid the rebel soldiers in the fort. Although the Battle of Oriskany, as this confrontation was called, led to the loss of 500 American lives (out of 800 participants), it did not weaken their resolve. They fought on bravely, encouraged by the rumour that Benedict Arnold and 3000 men were on the way to save them.

A dramatic event suddenly changed British fortunes on August 22. The Indians deserted the cause. St. Leger panicked. Uncertain of his own strength without Kreutzbourg's chasseurs, and shaken by the news of Arnold's imminent arrival, he decided to retreat at once. This abandonment of Fort Stanwix constituted the second major English defeat in the North. Along with Bennington, it meant the failure of the triple rendez-vous at Albany and was the direct cause of the capture of thousands of German and English prisoners at Saratoga.

We know very little about the German soldiers who participated in the siege of Fort Stanwix, since they recorded practically nothing about this event. However, Captain Georg Pausch of the Hesse Hanau Artillery Company left a journal notation indicating that Lt. Hildebrandt's company of chasseurs from Hesse-Hanau,[75] along with 19 artillerymen and two pieces of artillery, formed part of the German contingent.[76]

Baroness von Riedesel and her daughters had accompanied the general to the battlefront where they endured many difficult moments. In her voluminous journal the baroness described these events in meticulous detail. Nowhere else do we find such a wealth of information about the German mercenaries. The days preceding the surrender at Saratoga were especially painful for the baroness, as these excerpts from her journal show: [77]

When the army marched again (September 11, 1777), it was at first decided that I was to stay behind, but upon my urgent entreaty, as some of the other ladies had followed the army, I was likewise finally allowed to do so. We traveled only a short distance each day and were very often sorely tried, but nevertheless we were happy to be allowed to follow at all. I had the joy of seeing my husband every day. I had sent back the greater part of my luggage and had kept only a few of my summer clothes. Everything went well at first. We had high hopes of victory and of reaching the "promised land," and when we had crossed the Hudson and General Burgoyne said "Britons never retreat," we were all in very high spirits. It displeased me, however, that the officers' wives were familiar with all of the army's plans and seemed all the more strange to me, as during the Seven Years' War I had noticed that in Duke Ferdinand's army every-thing was kept absolutely secret. Here, on the contrary, even the Americans were acquainted with all our plans in advance, with the result that wherever we came they were ready for us, which cost us dearly. On September 19, there was a battle, which, although it resulted in our favor, forced us to halt at a place called Freeman's Farm. I saw the whole battle myself, and, knowing that my husband was taking part in it, I was filled with fear and anguish and shivered whenever a shot was fired, as nothing escaped my ear. I saw a number of wounded men, and, what was even worse, three of them were brought to the house where I was.

(...) When we marched on, I had a large calash readied, with room for myself and the three children and my two maids; thus I followed the army right in the midst of the soldiers, who sang and were jolly, burning with the desire for victory. We passed through endless woods, and the country was magnificent, but completely deserted, as all the people had fled before and had gone to strengthen the American army under General Gates. (...)

... suddenly on October 7 my husband, with his whole staff, had to break camp. This moment was the beginning of our unhappiness! I was just taking breakfast with my husband when I noticed that something was going on. General Fraser and, I think, General Burgoyne and General Phillips also were to have had dinner that same day with me. I noticed a great deal of commotion among the soldiers. My husband told me that they were to go out on a reconnaissance, of which I thought nothing, as this often happened. On my way back to the house I met a number of

Northern New York Campaigns, 1777

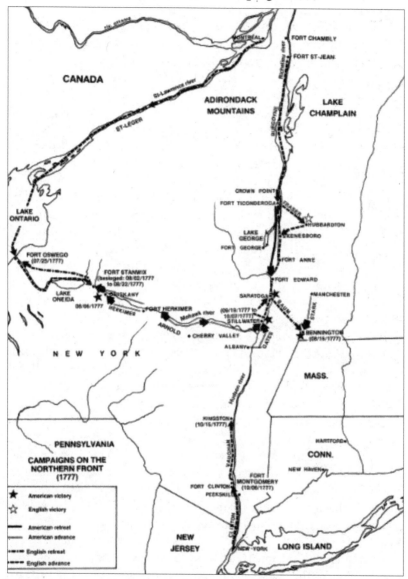

Map by Jean-Pierre Wilhelmy based on *The American Heritage Pictorial Atlas of U.S. History.*

savages in war dress, carrying guns. When I asked them whither they were bound, they replied,

"War! War!"—which meant that they were going into battle. I was completely overwhelmed and had hardly returned to the house, when I heard firing which grew heavier and heavier until the noise was frightful. It was a terrible bombardment, and I was more dead than alive!

Toward three o'clock in the afternoon, instead of my dinner guests arriving as expected, poor General Fraser, who was to have been one of them, was brought to me on a stretcher, mortally wounded. The table, which had already been set for dinner, was removed and a bed for the General was put in its place. I sat in a corner of the room, shivering and trembling. The noise of the firing grew constantly louder. The thought that perhaps my husband would also be brought home wounded was terrifying and worried me incessantly. The General said to the doctor, "Don't conceal anything from me! Must I die?" The bullet had gone through his abdomen precisely as in Major Harnage's case; unfortunately the General had eaten a heavy breakfast, so that the intestines were expanded, and, as the doctor explained, the bullet had gone through them, not between them, as in Major Harnage's case. I heard him often exclaim, between moans, "Oh, fatal ambition! Poor General Burgoyne! Poor Mrs. Fraser." Prayers were said, then he asked that General Burgoyne have him buried the next day at six o'clock in the evening, on a hill, which was a sort of redoubt. I no longer knew where to go; the whole hall and the other rooms were full of sick men, suffering from camp sickness. Finally toward evening I saw my husband coming; then I forgot all my sorrow and had no other thought but to thank God for sparing him! He ate in great haste with me and his aides behind the house. (...)

...wounded officers of our acquaintance kept arriving, and the bombardment was renewed again and again. There was talk of making a retreat, but no steps were taken in this direction. Toward four o'clock in the afternoon I saw flames rising from the new house which had been built for me, so I knew that the enemy was not far away.

We learned that General Burgoyne wanted to carry out General Fraser's last wish and intended having him buried in the place designated at six o'clock. This caused an unnecessary delay and served to increase the army's misfortune. At precisely six o'clock the body was actually carried away, and we saw all the generals and their staffs take part in the funeral services on the hilltop. The English chaplain, Mr. Brudenel, held the services. Cannon balls constantly flew around and over the heads of the mourners. The American General Gates said later on that, had he known that a funeral was being held, he would have allowed no firing in that direction. A number of cannon balls also flew about where I stood, but I had no thought for my own safety, my eyes being constantly directed toward the hill, where I could see my husband distinctly, standing in the midst of the enemy's fire.

The command had been given for the army to withdraw immediately after the funeral, and our calashes were ready and waiting. I did not want to leave before the troops did. Major Harnage, miserably ill as he was, crept out of bed so that he would not be left behind in the hospital, over which a flag of truce had been raised. When he saw me standing in the midst of danger, he ordered my children and the maidservants to be brought to the calashes and told me I would have to leave immediately. When I repeated my plea to be allowed to stay, he said, "All right, then your children must go without you, so that I can at least save them from danger." He knew the weakest spot in my armor and thus persuaded me to get into the calash, and we drove away on the evening of the 8th.

We had been warned to keep extremely quiet, fires were left burning everywhere, and many tents were left standing, so that the enemy would think the camp was still there. Thus we drove on all through the night. Little Frederika, was very much frightened, often starting to cry, and I had to hold my handkerchief over her mouth to prevent our being discovered.

At six o'clock in the morning we stopped, to the amazement of all. General Burgoyne ordered the cannons to be lined up and counted, which vexed everyone because only a few more good marches and we would have been in safety. My husband was completely exhausted and during this halt sat in my calash, where my maids had to make room for him and where he slept about three hours with his head on my shoulder. In the meantime Captain Willoe brought me his wallet with banknotes, and Captain Geismar brought me his beautiful watch, a ring, and a well-filled purse and asked me to take care of these things for them. I promised to do my utmost. Finally the order was given to march on, but we had hardly gone an hour when we stopped again, because we caught sight of the enemy. There were about two hundred men who had come out to reconnoiter and could easily have been taken prisoners by our troops, if General Burgoyne had not lost his head. (...)

Toward evening we finally reached Saratoga which is only half an hour on the way from the place where we had spent the whole day. I was wet to the skin from the rain and had to remain so throughout the night as there was no place to change into dry clothes. So I sat down before a good fire, took off the children's clothes, and then we lay down together on some straw. I asked General Phillips, who came up to me, why we did not continue our retreat while there was yet time, as my husband had promised to cover our retreat and bring the army through. "Poor woman," he said, "I admire you! Thoroughly drenched as you are, you still have the courage to go on in this weather. If only you were our commanding general! He thinks himself too tired and wants to spend the night here and give us a supper." In fact, Burgoyne liked having a jolly time and spending half the night singing and drinking and amusing himself in the company of the wife of a commissary, who was his mistress and, like him, loved champagne.

On the 10th at seven o'clock in the morning, I refreshed myself with a cup of tea, and we now hoped from one moment to the next that we would at last proceed. In order to cover the retreat, General Burgoyne ordered fire set to the beautiful houses and mills in Saratoga belonging to General Schuyler. An English officer brought a very good bouillon, which on his urgent entreaties I had to share with him, and after drinking it we continued our march; however, we got only to the next village, not far away. The greatest misery and extreme disorder prevailed in the army. The commissary had forgotten to distribute the food supplies among the troops; there were cattle enough, but not a single one had been slaughtered. More than thirty officers came to me because they could stand the hunger no longer. I had coffee and tea made for them and divided among them all the supplies with which my carriage was always filled; for we had a cook with us who, though an arch-rogue, nevertheless always knew how to get hold of something for us and, as we learned later, often crossed streams at night in order to steal from the farmers sheep, chickens, and pigs, which he sold to us at a good price.

Finally my own supplies were exhausted, and in my desperation at no longer being able to help the others I called to Adjutant-General Petersham, who was just passing by, and, as I was really very much worried, I said to him vehemently: "Come and look at these officers who have been wounded in the common cause and who lack everything they need because they are not getting their due. It is your duty to speak with the General about this." He was very much moved, and, as a result, about a quarter of an hour later General Burgoyne himself came to me and thanked me most pathetically for having reminded him of his duty. (...)

Toward two o'clock in the afternoon we heard cannon and musketry again, and alarm and confusion prevailed. My husband sent me word to get immediately to a house which was not far away. I got into the calash

with my children, and just as we came up to the house I saw five or six
men on the other side of the Hudson, who were aiming their guns at us.
Almost involuntarily I thrust my children onto the floor of the calash
and threw myself over them. The same instant the fellows fired and shat-
tered the arm of a poor English soldier behind me, who had already been
wounded and was retiring into the house. Immediately after our arrival
a terrifying cannonade began, which was directed principally at the
house where we sought shelter, presumably because the enemy, seeing
so many people fleeing thither, got the idea that the generals themselves
were there. But, alas, the house contained only the wounded and women!
We were finally forced to seek refuge in the cellar, where I found a place
for myself and the children in a corner near the door. My children lay
on the floor with their heads in my lap. And thus we spent the whole
night. The horrible smell in the cellar, the weeping of the children, and,
even worse, my own fear prevented me from closing my eyes.

Next morning the cannonade went on again, but from the other side.
I suggested that everyone leave the cellar for a while so that I could have
it cleaned, because otherwise we would all become sick. My suggestion
was carried out, and I got many to help, which was highly necessary for
this extensive task; the women and children, afraid to go outside, had
polluted the entire cellar. When everybody had gone out, I examined
our place of refuge; there were three fine cellars with well-vaulted ceil-
ings. I suggested that the most seriously wounded men be put into one
cellar, the women in another, and all the others in the third, which was
nearest to the door. I had everything swept thoroughly and fumigated
with vinegar, when, just as everyone was about to take his place, renewed,
terrific cannon fire created another alarm. Many who had no right to
enter threw themselves against the door. My children had already gone
down the cellar steps, and we would all have been crushed if God had
not given me the strength to keep the crowd back by standing in front
of the door with outspread arms; otherwise surely someone would have
been injured. Eleven cannon balls flew through the house, and we could
distinctly hear them rolling about over our heads. One of the poor soldiers who lay on a table, and was just about to have his leg amputated,
had the other leg shot off by one of these balls. His comrades had run
away from him, and when they returned they found him scarcely
breathing, lying in a corner of the room, where he had rolled himself in
his agony. I was more dead than alive, not so much on account of our
own danger as for the danger that hung over my husband, who kept
inquiring how we were and sending me word that he was all right.

Major Harnage's wife, Mrs. Reynell, who had already lost her husband, the wife of the good lieutenant who had been so kind as to share his bouillon with me the previous day, the wife of the commissary, and myself were the only ladies with the army. We were just sitting together and bewailing our fate when someone entered, whispered something to the others, and they all looked at each other sadly. I noticed this and that all eyes were upon me, although nobody said anything. This brought the horrible thought to my mind that my husband had been killed. I screamed; they assured me, however, that such was not the case but indicated with a nod that it was the poor lieutenant's wife to whom this misfortune had befallen. She was called outside a few moments later. Her husband was not yet dead, but a cannon ball had torn his arm away at the shoulder. We heard his moaning all through the night, doubly gruesome as the sound re-echoed through the cellar; the poor fellow died toward morning. However, we spent this night just as we had the previous one. In the meantime my husband visited me, which lightened my anxiety and gave me renewed courage.(...)

Our cook brought us food, but we had no water, and I was often obliged to quench my thirst with wine and even had to give the children some. Moreover, it was almost the only drink my husband would take. This finally began to worry our faithful Rockel, who said to me one day, "I fear that the General drinks all this wine because he is afraid of being taken prisoner, and that he is tired of living." (...)

Because we were badly in need of water, we finally found the wife of one of the soldiers who was brave enough to go to the river to fetch some. This was a thing nobody wanted to risk doing, because the enemy shot every man in the head who went near the river. However, they did not hurt the woman out of respect for her sex, as they told us themselves afterwards.

I tried to divert my mind by busying myself with our wounded. I made tea and coffee for them, for which I received a thousand blessings. Often I shared my dinner with them. One day a Canadian officer came into the cellar, so weak that he could hardly stand up. We finally got it out of him that he was almost starved to death. I was very happy to be able to give him my own dinner, which gave him renewed strength and won me his friendship. When we returned to Canada later on, I became acquainted with his family.

One of the worst things we had to bear was the odor which came from the wounds when they began to fester. At one time I was nursing a Major Bloomfield, aide to General Phillips, who had a bullet shot through both cheeks, smashing his teeth and grazing his tongue. He could not keep anything in his mouth; the pus almost choked him, and he could not take any nourishment at all except a little bouillon or other liquid. We had some Rhine wine. I gave him a bottle, hoping that the acid would cleanse his wounds. He took a little of it in his mouth, and this alone had such a fortunate effect that his wounds healed entirely, and I gained another friend. Thus even in these hours of suffering and sorrow I had moments of pleasure which made me very happy. (...)

Shortly afterwards General Burgoyne sent for all the other generals and staff officers to attend a council of war early in the morning, during which he suggested, on the basis of a false report, that the capitulation which had already been made to the enemy be broken. However, it was finally decided that this would be neither practicable nor advisable, and that was a lucky decision for us, because the Americans told us later that, had we broken the capitulation, we would all have been massacred, which would have been an easy matter, because there were only four to five thousand of us, and we had given them time to get more than twenty thousand of their men together. (...)

On October 17, the capitulation went into effect. The generals went to the American Commanding General, General Gates, and the troops laid down their arms and surrendered themselves as prisoners of war. The good woman who had fetched water for us at the risk of her life now got her reward. Everyone threw a handful of money into her apron, and she received altogether more than twenty guineas. In moments like this the heart seems to overflow in gratitude.

At last my husband sent a groom to me with the message that I should come to him with our children. I got into my beloved calash again, and while driving through the American camp, I was comforted to notice that nobody glanced at us insultingly, that they all bowed to me, and some of them even looked with pity to see a woman with small children there. I confess that I was afraid to go to the enemy, as it was an entirely new experience for me.

This campaign, of such crucial importance for the British, thus proved an unmitigated disaster from beginning to end. Altogether, counting the surrender at Saratoga and St. Leger's defeat, nearly 9,000 men were killed, wounded or taken prisoner. Howe and St. Leger were harshly criticized by the British authorities, but it was General John Burgoyne who, after returning to England, bore the brunt of the blame for the defeat. General von Riedesel, who was on very poor terms with Burgoyne, also blamed him for the disastrous results of the campaign.

The Germans did not take up their winter quarters in Canada that year until November 1777.[78] The men from Brunswick were assigned to Sorel, the chasseurs or light infantry, to the south shore of Montreal, and the Hesse-Hanau troops, to the region surrounding Berthier. Carleton was increasingly nervous after Burgoyne's defeat, and therefore sent Captain Zeilberg with a troop of 324 Brunswick soldiers and Hesse-Hanau chasseurs to Trois-Rivières in order to be prepared for anything. German patrols were increased south of the St. Lawrence and von Barner's light infantry, who were quartered between Montreal and the enemy, were much in demand in the days which followed.

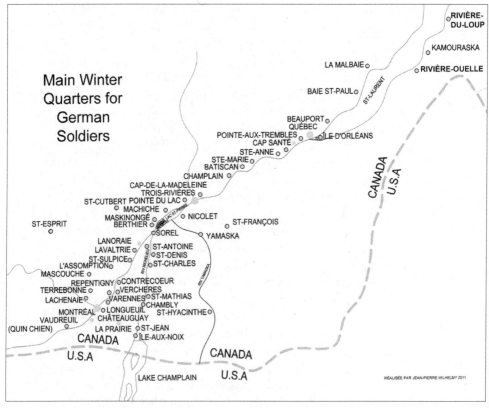

Map of Main Winter Quarters for German Soldiers, by Jean-Pierre Wilhelmy

LIST OF GERMAN SOLDIERS IN CANADA IN 1776

Units	jan.	feb.	mar.	apr.	may	june	july	aug.	sept.	oct.	nov.	dec.
Headquarters						22	24	24	24	25	27	29
Dragoon Reg.						325	330	324	319	316	313	311
Grenadier Reg.						559	558	559	555	553	548	544
Reg. von Rhetz						*	*	*	*	674	675	666
Reg. von Riedesel						671	682	669	665	682	658	656
Reg. von Specht						*	*	*	*	678	675	668
Reg. prince Friedrich						662	668	647	658	647	645	642
Brunswick Chasseurs						*	*	*	*	638	639	620
Bat. von Ehrenkrook						*	*	*	*	*	*	*
Reg. von Barner						*	*	*	*	*	*	*
Total Brunswick						2239	2262	2223	2221	4213	4180	4136
Hesse-Hanau Reg. von Schell Detachment						671	671	702	702	668	668	628
Hesse-Hanau Artillery						Inc. into. Hesse-Hanau Reg.						
Von Kreutzbourg Chasseurs						*	*	*	*	*	*	*
Total Hesse-Hanau						671	671	702	702	668	668	628
Headquarters						*	*	*	*	*	*	*
Reg. Alt. von Lossberg						*	*	*	*	*	*	*
Art. von Lossberg						*	*	*	*	*	*	*
Reg. von Knyphausen						*	*	*	*	*	*	*
Total Hesse-Cassel						*	*	*	*	*	*	*
Total of all the troops						2,910	2,933	2,925	2,923	48,81	4,848	4,764
Bat. maj. von Luke						*	*	*	*	*	*	*

* Not yet arrived

LIST OF GERMAN SOLDIERS IN CANADA IN 1777

Units	jan.	feb.	mar.	apr.	may	june	july	aug.	sept.	oct.	nov.	dec.
Headquarters	29	29	25	25	25	25	▲	▲	▲	▲	▲	11
Dragoon Reg.	311	311	311	304	308	305	▲	▲	▲	▲	▲	49
Grenadier Reg.	543	540	539	538	538	537	83	86	87	▲	▲	91
Reg. von Rhetz	658	659	657	651	653	652	104	111	151	▲	▲	173
Reg. von Riedesel	654	653	653	653	652	649	102	104	103	▲	▲	149
Reg. von Specht	668	665	663	662	661	659	106	108	111	▲	▲	141
Reg. prince Friedrich	641	638	637	636	636	635	105	108	108	▲	▲	617
Brunswick Chasseurs	596	579	573	572	570	568	80	80	146	▲	▲	169
Von Kreutzbourg Chasseurs	*	*	*	*	*	*	*	*	*	*	*	*
Reg. von Barner	*	*	*	*	*	*	*	*	*	*	▲	*
Total Brunswick	4,100	4,074	40,58	4,041	4,043	4,030	580	597	706	▲	▲	1,400
Hesse-Hanau Reg. von Scheell Detachment	627	622	620	612	611	610	111	113	112	▲	▲	157
Hesse-Hanau Artillery Incorporated into Hesse-Hanau												
Kreutzbourg Chasseurs	*	*	*	*	*	*	▲	■	■	■	■	424
Total Hesse-Hanau	627	622	620	612	611	610	111	113	112	▲	▲	581
Headquarters	*	*	*	*	*	*	*	*	*	*	*	*
Reg. de Alt. von Lossberg	*	*	*	*	*	*	*	*	*	*	*	*
Art. von Lossberg	*	*	*	*	*	*	*	*	*	*	*	*
Reg. von Knyphausen	*	*	*	*	*	*	*	*	*	*	*	*
Total Hesse-Cassel	*	*	*	*	*	*	*	*	*	*	*	*
Total of all the troops	4,727	4,696	46,78	4,653	4,654	4,640	691	710	818	▲	▲	1981
Bat. maj. von Luke	*	*	*	*	*	*	*	*	*	*	*	*

* Not yet arrived   ▲ No information available   ■ No longer in Canada

Notes

1. F.V. Melsheimer, chaplain of the Brunswick troops, *Journal of the Voyage of the Brunswick Auxiliaries from Wolfenbüttel to Quebec*, translated by William Wood (first part) and William L. Stone (second part). in *Transactions of the Literary, and Historical Society of Quebec*, no. 20, second part, 150 152. Henceforth, *Journal of the Voyage*.

2. Public Archives of Canada, *MG 13 War Office 17*, reel 1585, vol. 1570, monthly returns, 1776.

3. Max von Eelking, *The German Allied Troops in the North American War of Independence, 1776-1783*, translated and abridged by J.G. Rosengarten, 88. Henceforth, *The German Allied Troops*.

4. *Ibid.*

5. Baroness von Riedesel, *Letters and Memoirs relating to the War of American Independence and the Capture of the German Troops at Saratoga*, New York: Carvill, 1827, 46-47, letter no.XIV. Henceforth: *Letters and Memoirs*, Carvill, 1827.

6. Max von Eelking, *Memoirs and Letters and Journals of Major General von Riedesel*, translated by William L.Stone, vol.I, 242. Henceforth: *Memoirs and Letters*. Also in the German Archives: General von Riedesel to his wife, "Between Montreal and Quebec," June 8, 1776. Also in Marvin L. Brown Jr., p. 175.

7. F.V. Melsheimer, *Journal of the Voyage*, part. II, 157.

8. Part of the Regiment von Riedesel under Lt. Col. von Speth, which arrived on board the *Harmony* on May 27, was immediately dispatched to Trois-Rivières where it participated in the fighting of June 8-9, 1776. Max von Eelking, *Memoirs and Letters*, vol. I, 283-286. The Verreau Collection, carton 49, no. 6, mentions the name Nesbitt in place of Beckwith.

9. Max von Eelking, *The German Allied Troops*, 91. See the Verreau collection, carton 49, no.5.

10. Max von Eelking, *Memoirs and Letters*, vol. 1, 286. See the Verreau collection, carton 49, no.5.

11. *Ibid.*, 45-46.

12. Georg Pausch, *Journal of Captain George Pausch, Chief the Hanau Artillery during the Burgoyne Campaign*, translated by William L. Stone, 66. Henceforth, Journal of Georg Pausch.

13. *Ibid.*, 96.

14. Max von Eelking, *The German allied Troops*, 94.

15. Public Archives of Canada, *MG 13 War Office 17*, reel 1585, vol. 1570, monthly returns, 1776.

16. Stanley, *Canada Invaded*, 139-141. The rest of this account of the Battle of Valcour Island is taken from Stanley, pp. 137-143.

17. Stanley, *Canada Invaded*, p. 144.

18. *Journal of Capt.Pausch*, p. 93.

19. G.F.G. Stanley, *For Want of a Horse, being a Journal of the Campaigns against the Americans in 1776 and 1777 conducted from Canada, by an officer who served*

with *Lt. Gen. Burgoyne*, Sackville, 1961, p.71, quoted in Stanley, *Canada Invaded*, 144.

20. Max von Eelking, *Memoirs and Letters*, vol. 1, 80-82.

21. A.L. Schlozer, Letters of Brunswick and Hessian officers during the American Revolution, translated by William L. Stone, 54. Henceforth, *Letters of Brunswick*.

22. Public Archives of Canada, *MG 21, Transcriptions*, Haldimand Collection, letter dated May 28, 1777, from Carleton to Count Wilhelm of Hesse-Hanau.

23. Gustave Lanctot, *Le Canada et la Révolution américaine*, 175.

24. *Ibid., 176.*

25. Abbé Verreau, priest, *Invasion du Canada* (eye-witness accounts of the war, collected and annotated), *Journal de Sanguinet*, 135. The original style has been preserved.

26. A.L. Schlozer, *Letters of Brunswick*, 55.

27. Mascouche, in Abbé Verreau, *Le témoin oculaire de la guerre des Bastonnois en Canada*, 154-156.

28. Gustave Lanctot, *Le Canada et la Révolution américaine*, 176.

29. Ovide-M.H. Lapalice was a member of the Historical Society of Canada in Paris, the Historical Society of Montreal, Archeology and Numismatics Society of Montreal, and Historical Society of Canada. He was also the archivist at Notre-Dame Fabrique in Montreal.

30. Ovide-M.H. Lapalice, *Histoire de la Seigneurie de Massue et de la Paroisse St.Aimé, 122.*

31. Quebec City Seminary, *Verreau collection*, carton 17, no.28. Italics have been added.

32. Public Archives of Canada, Haldimand collection, series B, vol. 219, 153. Letter of March 8, 1782, in Roy, *op. cit.* The original style has been preserved.

33. Public Archives of Canada, *MG 21, Transcriptions*, Haldimand Collection, series B, vol. 152, 10. Letter dated 13, 1783. The style and spelling have been preserved. Haldimand succeeded Carleton as Governor in June 1778; see beginning of chapter 4.

34. *Ibid.*, series B, vol. 137, 77-81. Letter dated April 5, 1782: excerpt from the proceedings of the inquiry.

35. When soldiers from Hesse-Hanau were sentenced to death as a result of these investigations, the sentence was submitted to the Prince who had reserved the right to make life and death decisions about his men. For the treaty dealing with the men of Hesse-Hanau, see *Parliamentary Register*, Part I, vol. I

36. Public Archives of Canada, *MG 21, Transcriptions*, Haldimand collection, series B, vol. 151, 46-47.

37. *Op. cit.*, 96.

38. Max von Eelking, *Memoirs and Letters*, vol. I, 82.

39. *Ibid.*, 89.

40. Time-Life film on the American Revolution, produced by B.B.C. London and shown on Radio-Québec during the programme *America, America* on Jan. 31, 1981. Henceforth, *America, America.*

41. These letters appeared in a German periodical published by August Ludwig Schlözer and entitled *Briefwechsel*, 1776-1782, vol. IV, no.49, 288-323, letters I, IV, VI. The following observations were made by a high-ranking officer in the German army (Regiment von Specht), and it is highly unlikely that any of them wholly applied to the regular soldier particularly as regards the "fêtes".

42. Gentlemen.

43. A very short skirt, a mere ring over the hips, an antecedent of the crinoline.

44. *Journal of George Pausch*, 93-94.

45. Robert Middlekauff, *The Glorious Cause*, 366.

46. *Ibid.*, 366-367.

47. For the Burgoyne campaign of 1777, consult the following:

   a) William L. Stone, *The Campaign of Lieutenant General John Burgoyne and the Expedition of Lieutenant Colonel Barry St-Leger*, Albany, N.Y., 1877.

   b) Friederike Charlotte Luise von Massow von Riedesel, *Letters and Memoirs Relating to the War of American Independence and the Capture of the German Troops at Saratoga* translated at G. & C. Carvill, New York, N.Y., 1827.

   c) Friederike Charlotte Luise von Massow von Riedesel *Journal and Correspondence of a Tour of Duty*, 1776-1783, translated and revised by Marvin L. Brown Jr., *Baroness von Riedesel and the American Revolution*, North Carolina Press, 1965.

   d) Hoffman Nickerson, *The Turning Point of the Revolution*.

   e) Thomas Anburey, *With Burgoyne from Quebec*, Toronto, 1963.

48. Public Archives of Canada, *MG 11, Colonial Office*, series vol. 13, 73-79, letter dated March 26, 1777.

49. Pierre Benoit, *Lord Dorchester*, 105.

50. *Ibid.*, 105-112.

51. Max von Eelking, *Memoirs and Letters*, vol. I, 97-98.

52. Public Achives Canada.

53. See the table entitled "Organisation of Burgoyne's army for the campaign of 1777".

54. One company of chasseurs, under Lt. Hildebrandt, arrived several months before the rest of their fellows from Hesse-Hanau. Charles Rainsford, *Transactions as a Commissary for Embarquing Foreign Troops in the English Service from Germany with Copies of Letters Relative to it. For years 1776-1777*, in Collection of the New York Historical Society, vol. XIII, 1879, 421-423.

55. *Ibid.*

56. *Ibid.*, 421-423, 426.

57. *America, America ... .*

58. Friederike von Riedesel, *Journal and Correspondence*, 26-34.

59. *Ibid.*, 36.

60. *Ibid.*

61. A calash, or calèche, was a light small-wheeled carriage; it usually took four passengers; and the top folded down.

62. Friederike von Riedesel, 38. It is mind-boggling to imagine the physical conditions during the baroness's journey to her husband, barely pausing to eat or sleep,

and with three small children under the age of six. Modern readers who make elaborate preparations in order to pack a toddler into the car for a short afternoon visit (diapers, clothing, toys, stroller, perhaps a bed) will appreciate the baroness's courage in undertaking to bring her family to Canada!

63. *Ibid.*, 39.

64. Max von Eelking, Memoirs and Letters, I, 101. Note that in the Public Archives of Canada, MG13, War Office 17, vol. 1571, 385, the total is 711 men on November, 1, 1777, of whom 664 were ready to serve.

65. *Ibid.*, 252-254.

66. Lowell, *The Hessians,* 143.

67. Eelking, *Memoirs and Letters,* I, 262-264.

68. Eelking, *The German A llied Troops,* 131.

69. Eelking, *Memoirs and Letters,* I, 264.

70. Eelking, *The German Allied Troops,* 131-132.

71. To give an idea of the weight the German soldiers had to carry: their hats and sabres alone weighed as mush as all the equipment of their English counterparts. Lowell, *The Hessians, 145.*

72. Eelking, *The German Allied Troops,* 132.

73. Lowell, *The Hessians,* 147.

74. At this time the fort was defended by about 700 militiamen under Col. Gansevoort.

75. This company had arrived in Canada some time before the other chasseurs. Public Archives of Canada, *MG 21, Transcriptions,* Haldimand Collection, series B, vol. 39, 54: letter of June 26, 1777, Captain Edward Foy to Kreutzbourg.

76. *Journal of George Pausch,* 131.

77. Friederike von Riedesel, *Journal and Correspondence,* 47-67.

78. Public Archives of Canada, *MG 13, War Office 17,* vol. 1572, 257; and Max von Eelking, *The German Allied Troops,* 236.

Chapitre IV

THE GERMANS AND
THE WAR FROM 1778 TO 1783

France's entry into the war as allies of the American rebels in early 1778 sparked fears in Canada of a new invasion. As early as January there was talk of troops being mobilized in Albany. Governor Carleton, uneasy at the prospect of imminent attack, spread his troops out along the south shore of the St. Lawrence from Sorel to St. Jean on the Richelieu; then toward the end of the month Carleton placed the militia on full alert. In March rumours of an impending attack were strengthened by reports from prisoners returning to Canada. But just when the tension was at its height and the governor's troops were ready to march, the welcome news came that the invasion had been postponed. Throughout the fall, no major event occurred to disturb the Canadians' peace of mind.

On June 30, the capital welcomed the arrival of Canada's new governor and commander-in-chief of the armed forces, General Frederick Haldimand.[1] His double appointment was largely the result of Carleton's behaviour over the past few years and his thorny relationship with Lord Germain. Haldimand was actually appointed in August 1777, but because of unfavourable winds he was forced to postpone departure from England until the following spring.

The new governor received his instructions in a letter from Lord Germain dated April 16, 1778. First and foremost among his duties was to ensure the security and defence of Canada.[2] The British Secretary of State judged his 5000 men insufficient for this purpose and he was promised another 1200 soldiers, including the Princess of Anhalt's regiment,[3] as well as 600 recruits from Brunswick and Hanau. Moreover, Haldimand was authorized to raise a corps of 1000 Canadians to complete his forces if necessary.[4]

Thus at the end of May, as promised, 613 soldiers from the principality of Anhalt-Zerbst arrived at Quebec, along with 34 wives who were employed as nurses or as laundresses.[5] They had left Europe on April 26, but it was to be fully three months later before they would be allowed to set foot on dry land, for Governor Carleton, who had not been officially informed of their coming, insisted that their quarter-master return to London to obtain the necessary papers before allowing them to disembark.

At the head of this regiment were the two Rauschenplat brothers from Brunswick, who had been recruited through newspaper advertisements. The regiment was composed as follows:[6]

Regimental headquarters and its staff:

The first battalion under Major von Piquet:
1 company of chasseurs led by Capt. Nuppenau
1 company of grenadiers led by Major von Piquet
1 company of musketeers led by Col. von Rauschenpl
1 company of musketeers led by Prince Augustus Schwarzburg-
  Sondershausen

The second battalion under Major von Rauschenplatt:
1 company of chasseurs led by Lt. Jaritz
1 company of grenadiers led by Capt. von Wintersheim
1 company of musketeers led by Major von Rauschenplatt
1 company of musketeers led by Capt. Gogel
1 artillery company
3 chaplains of different religions
Of the 627 soldiers who left Europe, fourteen did not survive the
  arduous journey.[7]

When finally authorized by Governor Carleton, the troops from Anhalt-Zerbst left their ships, worn out from the long months on board, and stayed in Quebec to recuperate. On July 31, about sixty soldiers chosen from the different German regiments, along with the newly-arrived Hesse-Hanau artillery, joined the British army.[8] Despite these reinforcements, the new governor Haldimand noted the following summer that 600 of his 6700-man army were sick, had deserted or been captured, while 900 more were posted to various outposts and about 1000 were manning the garrisons,[9] which left relatively few men for defence purposes. Moreover, the governor entertained serious doubts as to the loyalty of many Canadians towards the British crown.

In September, the ranks of Haldimand's forces grew somewhat with the return of survivors of General Burgoyne's disastrous campaign. The troops from Brunswick had suffered severe losses in this defeat; their duke asked his prime minister, Feronce Rotencreutz, to reorganize them as soon as possible.[10] Until such time as Lt. Col. von Speth should return, therefore, the three new regiments of the Brunswick army in Canada were commanded by Lt. Col. von Ehrenkrook, who was promoted to Brigadier General. The Prinz Friedrich Regiment was led by Lt. Col. C.J. Praetorius; Major von Barner led his own regiment, as did Lt. Col. von Ehrenkrook.[11]

The governor raised no major objection to these changes, merely pointing out that the treaty with the Duke of Brunswick had specified five regiments, not three. However, given the circumstances,[12] he went along with the changes and capitalized upon the situation by requesting more officers from the duke.

As Germain had suggested, the governor used the army to rebuild some of the more dilapidated fortifications at such strategic locations as Sorel, St. Jean, and Ile-aux-Noix; stores and barracks were also slated for these locations.

In mid-January, winter quarters were finally assigned as follows:[13] from the von Ehrenkrook Regiment, Brigadier von Ehrenkrook's company would proceed to Trois-Rivières along with Captain von Zielberg's company, while Captain von Plessen's went to the parish of Champlain and Captain von Schlagenteuffel's, to Pointe-du-Lac. From the von Barner Regiment, Captain Hambach's company was assigned to Vaudreuil, Captain Thomae's to Maskinongé, Captain Rosenberg's to St.Cuthbert, and Lt. Col. von Barner's to Rivière-du-

Loup. The Prinz Friedrich Regiment was quartered in the St. Hyacinthe region.

Under Haldimand, familiar problems arose regarding lodging, provisions, borrowed vehicles, and unpaid bills, but the new governor was in a better position than his predecessor to deal with them. On January 7 and 9, 1779 he wrote to Ehrenkrook and his men and to the captains of militia defining once and for all the duties and obligations of both soldiers and civilians.[14] Henceforth, offenders could quickly be identified and the proper punishment meted out. In his civilian role as governor, Haldimand had to protect the interests of the inhabitants and of the captains of militia, but he did not allow any of them to shirk their duties at the expense of the German visitors among them. The Trois-Rivières merchant Malcolm Fraser provides a case in point. Fraser wrote to the governor[15] asking, because of his name, to be exempted from lodging Lt. Col. von Barner, whom he accused of forceful entry into his house and the destruction of his personal belongings, etc. Barner was informed of the merchant's complaints and was given the opportunity to defend himself.[16] After considering the evidence, Haldimand requested that his secretary Conrad Gugy inform Fraser that he would have to lodge Lt. Col. von Barner as scheduled. But he also credited Fraser for the billeting he had done to date and for whatever he might be expected to provide in the future.[17]

When a conflict arose between Haldimand's civilian and military roles, he assigned another judge to hear the case and pronounce judgment. For example, Militia member Carnivaux was accused of assaulting an officer, Lt.Kress. Knowing an impartial hearing would be held, Lt. Col. von Loos, Kress's superior, asked him to take his case to Judge Dunn, appointed by Haldimand for this purpose, rather than arresting the captain.[18] Haldimand later wrote to Loos[19] commending him for his handling of the problem so as to maintain harmony between civilians and army personnel.

These hearings were generally serious affairs in which every attempt was made to shed light on thorny and often delicate issues. In the case of Julien Leblanc vs Captain School, for instance, the search for truth led to a verdict in favour of the accused. On February 8, 1779 Julien Leblanc, Militia Captain in the parish of St. Martin on Jesus Island,

wrote to Haldimand that on February 4, two German soldiers commanded by Captain von Schoel "tried to abduct and rape the young
daughter of a certain Joseph Lorrain."[20] Fortunately for Schoel and his
men, during a rigorous examination of the evidence, the complainant
finally admitted that he had made up the whole story, hoping to get out
of billeting soldiers. Captain Leblanc was accused of recording the
complaint too hastily and was punished accordingly.[21]

Not only soldiers received justice at these trials. Civilians and captains of militia also often benefited. For example, Hesse-Hanau chasseurs who chopped down some trees without permission from Militia
Captain François Maupassan were ordered to pay damages of forty
pounds.[22]

The way officers constantly "borrowed" the civilians' carriages—
ordinary soldiers had no access to them—was another major source
of friction between civilians and the military. Before the new regulations were established by Governor Haldimand, German officers often
requisitioned vehicles on the slightest pretext, claiming loftily that it
was their right. A document entitled "Information and Procedures
of the Militia of Upper Berthier concerning the German Troops" records several complaints about this practice, among them that of Pierre
Pénélan, captain of a militia company in Berthier, who confirmed
"that continually, he was requested to furnish all the officers of troops
lodging in his company with a considerable quantity of carriages,
which he furnished at their demand, said officers threatening to ill-
treat him, should he refuse, that said inhabitants were not paid for
these journeys, which was causing them much complaining and waste
of time."[23] A similar complaint was lodged on March 15, 1777 in
Lavaltrie by Louis Roy Desjardins, captain of the Lanoraie militia,
who declared "that apart from the regimental carriage which he provided for the commander ever day, he was continually obliged to
arrange provision of considerable quantity of vehicles for various
German officers for which the inhabitants were not paid, that these
vehicles were retained for several days in Montreal at their expense.
(...) Forty-one vehicles were provided, which he stressed represented
less than one quarter of the requests."[24] Another militia captain,
André Moudon from Lavaltrie, told of having procured 127 vehicles

for German officers, but when he refused to provide them without written orders he was placed under guard by Captain Schell.[25]

Fortunately for the inhabitants Haldimand's new directives ordered officers to pay before hiring a vehicle.[26] But for some officers, this posed a real problem: one of their duties was to pay regular visits to their men, who were often billeted a considerable distance from the officers' own quarters, and their salaries were too low, or so they claimed, to cover the cost of these trips. A number of them decided to submit alternative proposals to the governor. One idea was to set up their own system of transportation. But Haldimand's treasury could not cover the costs involved and the proposals were all rejected one after another. The former procedure had to be reinstated. The governor would provide adequate funding but the inhabitants' vehicles were to be borrowed only when strictly necessary.[27]

Unpaid bills also caused tension between soldiers and civilians. Haldimand's regulations merely restated a rule established by Carleton that no debts were to be incurred between the two groups; but here again, both sides broke the rules occasionally. The case of the tailor John Diehle,[28] a Quebec merchant, is a good example. In an insolent letter addressed to Governor Haldimand, Diehle complained that officers of the Hesse-Hanau Corps of Chasseurs had, under orders from Lt. Col. Kreutzbourg, bought uniforms from him on credit, but now that these gentlemen had changed quarters, he was afraid he would not be paid. Kreutzbourg, surprised by the tailor's demands, informed the governor: "When I was at Point Levy, I myself told Mr. Diehle not to extend credit to anyone in my Corps, and that I would not answer for the consequences if he did. But he went ahead anyway and offered to make uniforms for the officers and chasseurs, telling them they could pay when it was convenient."[29] Nonetheless, Kreutzbourg quickly found the men in question and forced them to settle part of their debt immediately; the rest was paid in monthly instalments until Diehle was fully reimbursed.[30]

Despite these incidents, relations between soldiers and civilians were not always tense or hostile. While it is impossible to know what the Canadian *habitant* or the ordinary German soldier thought about their relationship, the journals of many of the higher ranking German officers and militia captains, fortunately better educated than their men, indicate that the Canadians and Germans got on fairly well. To begin with, many German officers greatly appreciated Canadian hospitality. As General von Riedesel once remarked in a letter to his wife, "The inhabitants are remarkably civil and obliging, and I hardly think that under similar circumstances our peasants would behave as well."[31] His wife likewise devoted many pages of her journal to descriptions of Canadians, written with a warmth that reveals her unmistakable admiration for these people—an admiration which was fully reciprocated as well. She often related little chats she had with the farmers she met while walking in the country. In her descriptions of daily life one senses her great sympathy for Canadians and theirs for her, and the mutual wish to know each other better. The Riedesels paid a fine compliment to Canadians when they named one of their daughters "Canada."[32]

The correspondence of some German officers reflects the same good will and respect for Canadians. Think of the officers who gave away three brides at St. Anne—the role of "substitute fathers" was an honour conferred upon them as friends. Another officer from headquarters at Batiscan said of Canadians that, "they are very good people, serious, pleasing and very honest. (...) Their friendship, once gained, knows no bounds. (...) Of an excellent turn of mind, many of them have a very fine wit. (...) No other nation could endure the efforts, the work, and fatigue with as much patience and without ever complaining."[33]

Other officers' reports add to this picture of good relations between the two groups. Lt. Col. von Loos reported on a visit "to Kamouraska, where I found the regiment of Anhalt Zerbst in the best order and discipline upon diligent inquiry of the militia captain about the conduct of the troops in the different parishes, they declared their satisfaction and made no complaints whatever."[34] On another occasion he wrote, "The Militia Captains in the different parishes are fully satisfied with Colonel Leutz's arrangements and did not hear any complaints against either officers or men."[35]

Reports by the militia captains confirm these German statements of reciprocal good will. For instance, a report dated February 25,

1781, signed by Militia Captain Pierre Mancan and Ensign Pierre Janelle of Baie de Saint-Antoine, declares: "we are quite satisfied with the behaviour of troops billeted in this parish, and Major von Rauschenblatt and his officers have always maintained proper discipline."[36]

The winter of 1779 was typically Canadian—long and difficult. The German soldiers were still not used to the cold, nor were they properly dressed for it. Captain Thomae's company from the von Barner Regiment unfortunately paid dearly for this carelessness. During an expedition to Lac St. Pierre in January 1779, fourteen soldiers and two women perished from the cold because they were inadequately dressed, while thirty of their comrades suffered varying degrees of exposure. Thomae was court-martialled and exonerated on the plea that proper clothing had never been issued; but he had been warned of the danger of exposing his men at such a season.[37] Indeed, it may well be that this misfortune was due in part to the all too frequent delays in providing the German army with clothing and ammunition. Such poor planning—one might almost say indifference—on the part of the London bureaucrats was common. Lowell suggests that evidence of this negligence can be found from the start, as early as when the Germans were first hired as part of the British army: "The Brunswickers were reviewed and mustered into the English service by Colonel Faucitt, who was not pleased with the appearance of the soldiers. (...) The uniforms of the first division were so bad that the English government was obliged to advance, 5000 to Riedesel to get his men a new outfit in Portsmouth. He was cheated by the English contractors, and when the cases of shoes were opened at sea, they were found to contain ladies' slippers. For a Canadian campaign no overcoats had been provided. New uniforms for the first division were after them in the course of the summer."[38] These problems obviously caused great discontent among the troops.[39]

In February, a Montreal bookseller began distributing American propaganda posters dated October 1778 and signed by the Count d'Estaing, urging all French Canadians to renew their pledge of allegiance to the king of France. However, the hoped-for results did not materialize.[40]

During the year, several incidents involving the Hesse-Hanau chasseurs were serious enough to exasperate the governor. In August, for instance, Kreutzbourg, the commander of the elite corps, refused to lend his chasseurs to Haldimand to help rebuild the barracks on Carleton Island.[41] He was not trying to disobey, Kreutzbourg assured the governor in a letter, but was merely going by the treaty signed by his prince in 1776, which stipulated that the British governor could call upon troops from Hesse-Hanau for duties of a strictly military nature only. Moreover, the work of reconstruction was rather risky, since at any time one of his men might be injured, thereby becoming an expensive burden on his prince. The Seven Years' War had shown that, in similar circumstances, the British government had refused to pay disability pensions to German soldiers; the burden of paying for these accidents had been borne by his prince alone; and now, he concluded, he was worried that a similar situation might arise.[42]

The governor admitted the soundness of these arguments but replied that unusual circumstances forced him to seek help from the Hanau chasseurs, since without them there would be no one to replace the Canadians at the onerous task of rebuilding the fortifications.[43] Nonetheless, he assured Kreutzbourg that if he really felt he could speak for his prince on this matter, he would respect their views: the chasseurs would be exempted from extra duty as requested, even though they were being paid just as much as the English soldiers who were doing similar chores. The matter was debated for several years until the Count of Hanau finally gave overt support to Kreutzbourg, requesting that his men be exempted from all paramilitary fatigue duty.[44]

The men from Brunswick caused the governor no such headaches, since they were willing to perform any task he set them. The same was true of the troops from Anhalt Zerbst, while those from Hesse-Cassel were so cooperative that they were cited by Lord Germain for being "full of good will" towards the governor. The Secretary of State for American Affairs rewarded them by periodically sending them special little presents of clothing, shoes, tobacco etc.[45]

In July 1779, Lt. Col. von Speth, Ensign Haeberlin, and 25 Brunswick soldiers returned to Canada as part of an exchange of prisoners with the Americans.[46]

Authorized by the governor to take over as head of the German troops, Speth relieved Ehrenkrook of his temporary command and was promoted to Brigadier General.[47] Speth reviewed his troops at the end of August and sent all those soldiers too old for combat duty back to Germany.[48] The Germans were gearing up for the coming winter, determined to avoid the mistakes of the previous year. In October, 174 new recruits from Anhalt-Zerbst arrived to join the German army.[49]

A little later, winter quarters were assigned. Headquarters and the von Ehrenkrook Regiment would be at Berthier, the von Barner Regiment in Montreal, and the Prinz Friedrich Regiment would remain where they were, with one company at Fort St. Jean and an officer with fifty chasseurs at Ile-aux-Noix. Kreutzbourg and his chasseurs were assigned to La Prairie and the surrounding area, Captain von Schoel's detachment to Quebec, while a company from Wittgenstein would remain on Carleton Island.[50]

The German soldiers were just as occupied the following year. They worked at building the temporary fortifications, while also serving as policemen and counterespionage agents. On June 26, 1780, the adjutant general assigned the eight companies of Brigadier General von Rauschenplatt of Anhalt-Zerbst to the task of rebuilding the temporary citadel at Quebec;[51] and on August 22, it was the turn of Loos' men.[52] The soldiers performed a wide range of skilled tasks, for each regiment was composed of men from all walks of life, such as carpenters, masons, blacksmiths, carters, engineers, etc. [53] Their work as policemen and counterespionage agents led to the arrest of many American sympathizers. In May 1780,[54] for instance, Lt. Col. Praetorius organized a series of patrols up and down the Richelieu River to keep an eye on likely looking suspects. To this end, Lt. Wiesener devised a map showing the major hotbeds of American espionage activity, many of which were homes of Canadian sympathizers, sometimes even militia captains.[55]

Towards the end of June 1780, reinforcements from Hesse-Cassel finally arrived via the U.S.A. They were supposed to have reached Canada in September 1779, but damage to their ships during a bad storm forced them to turn back. These reinforcements consisted of the Alt von Lossberg Fusilier Regiment under the command of Col. Johann August von Loos, soon Brigadier General, as well as a detachment of the von Knyphausen Fusilier Regiment under Col. von Borck.[56] In August news reached Canada that Duke Karl of Brunswick was dead and that his son, Karl Wilhelm Ferdinand, had already succeeded him.[57] At the end of August, English ships reached port at Quebec after a very difficult crossing. On board were a few recruits from Brunswick as well as stores for the next two years.[58]

When an army is composed of very distinctive groups, as with the Anglo-German army from 1776 to 1783, the situation is ripe for misunderstandings and friction. When men are weary of fighting, or depressed because of recent defeats or homesick, or simply when groups with different languages and customs are thrown together, the tensions that result can quickly escalate into serious hostility. Archives for 1781 indicate that the authorities kept a watchful eye on the situation, to forestall any trouble. The Barner-MacLean affair is an example of how they dealt with potential problems. In March of that year, the German Major von Barner complained that an English lieutenant, Archibald MacLean of the 84th, had had "the audacity to attack" his reputation on several occasions, "publicly in Montreal." [59] Because the two men belonged to different armies, Barner realized it would be unwise to reprimand MacLean directly; so, instead, he took his case to the English soldier's superior, Brigadier General Francis MacLean, who recognized the accuracy of the charge. Wishing to make an example of the dispute, he asked Barner to address Governor Haldimand directly.[60] The governor did not want to penalize one group because of another; he therefore ordered the English officer to write a personal letter of apology—not as an Englishman writing to a German, but as one man to another.[61] Thanks to such diplomacy and careful vigilance by the leaders of each group, the English and Germans were able to maintain a relatively civilized front with one another—most of the time.

In September 1781, Major General von Riedesel announced he would soon return to Canada. After surrendering at Saratoga in October 1777, he was held prisoner until 1780, when he was released during an exchange of prisoners. He was immediately promoted to

Lt. General by General Clinton[62] and was given command of Long Island.[63] He settled in Brooklyn, where he was joined by his wife in the spring of 1781. Their decision to return to Canada was made in the hope that the move to a northern climate would prove beneficial to Riedesel's health. In fact, he never fully recovered from the sunstroke that had weakened him.[64]

On July 22, therefore, Riedesel and his family, along with some English soldiers, several German officers, and 900 soldiers from Brunswick and Hanau who had also been freed by the rebels,[65] began their journey to Canada.[66] Captain von Schlagenteuffel and seventy Brunswick soldiers had recently returned as well, after an earlier exchange of prisoners with the Americans.[67]

Since Sorel was one of the key military positions in the war, its fort second in importance only to those of Montreal and Quebec, Lt. General von Riedesel, leader of all the German forces in Canada, was given command of this vital area in recognition of his skill and judgment as a military leader.[68]

Following the defeat at Saratoga, the Brunswick army was reorganized into three regiments. But with the return of Riedesel and his men, in addition to new recruits from Europe, a second restructuring was necessary. On October 20, 1781, Captain Schlagenteuffel became leader of the dragoon regiment, while Lt. Col. Praetorius retained his position as commander of the Prinz Friedrich Regiment and Lt. Col. von Ehrenkrook remained at the head of the von Rhetz Regiment. Lt. Col. von Hille was in charge of the von Riedesel Regiment, Major de Lucke led the von Specht Regiment, and Lt. Col. von Barner retained command of the von Barner Light Infantry Battalion (chasseurs). In addition to these six regiments, General von Riedesel could count on half the Hesse-Hanau Regiment, one regiment and a detachment from Hesse-Cassel, and the Princess of Anhalt's regiment. The grenadier battalion was divided into companies which joined the various infantry regiments. Finally, a company from the Prinz Friedrich Regiment joined the depleted von Rhetz Regiment which had suffered the most losses.[69]

Some time later, at Clinton's request, Riedesel suggested to Governor Haldimand that an army be sent to harass the American rear guard in Virginia. Haldimand would only authorize two small expeditions, one to Vermont and the other to Oswego, which proved utterly useless, since the Americans easily repelled them.[70]

On October 8, winter quarters were designated as follows: Major General von Riedesel's men to the north shore of Lake Champlain from La Prairie to Sorel and from Bécancour to Pointe-au-Fer, Brigadier General von Speth's troops to Montreal and Yamachiche on the north shore of the St. Lawrence, and from Côteau-du-Lac to La Prairie on the south shore. The Hesse-Hanau chasseurs were assigned to St. Thomas (Lt. Col. Kreutzbourg's men), St. Vallier (Major von Francken's), Berthier (Lt. Young's), St. Pierre (Capt the Count of Wittgenstein's), St. François (Capt. von Leth's) Quebec (Capt. Castendyck's), Carleton Island (Lt. von den Velden's), and Île-aux-Noix (Lt. Krass or Krafft). The troop from Anhalt-Zerbst were quartered at Bécancour, Pointe-du-Lac, St. Pierre, Gentilly, Nicolet, St. Antoine, St. François and Quebec.[71]

During her return journey to Quebec, Baroness von Riedesel, whose interest in the lifestyle of Canadians was as keen as ever, recorded the following in her journal:

> Every inhabitant has a good house, which he takes the pains to clean every year. This gives them a very immaculate look and makes them glisten in the distance. When sons marry they build their houses close to their parents, as do also sons-in-law, with the result that handsome settlements spring up, for which reason these people are called habitans (settlers), and not peasants. The dwellings, to each of which adjoins a stable, an orchard, and a pasture, are situated along the St. Lawrence, and make a very picturesque sight, especially to those who sail up and down the river. Each house has an ice cellar, which is made with little difficulty. A hole is dug in the ground and lined around with boards, and it is filled with ice. Then water is poured in, which in freezing fills the crevices and makes all smooth as glass. Over this the inhabitants place a very clean board on which to put the items to be preserved, observing the greatest cleanliness and taking special pains to keep out of the ice cellar any straw or hay, which, they say, causes the ice to melt more quickly. These ice cellars are all the more indispensable, since everyone slaughters his own cattle, which otherwise would not keep in the heat of summer there. Ordinarily these ice cellars are dug under the barns.

These people keep a lot of livestock in the summer, which at the start of winter they slaughter and bring to the city for sale. The smaller stock— beefs, sheep, and swine—which they keep for themselves, they drive into the forest in the morning to graze, and only in the evening do they give them fodder in the stable. In this part of the country they also have a small fish, called small cod, which is caught under the ice. This is done by cutting large holes in the ice, three or four hundred paces apart. Into these are placed nets of stout cord fastened on strong beams. In this manner they sometimes catch five or six sledges full. They throw the fish onto the ice where they are frozen in a moment and where they remain until they are needed. Then they are gotten, thawed out, thrown directly into the kettle, and eaten. These fish taste particularly good when fried in butter.

The dwellings are very comfortable, and one finds the beds remarkably good and clean. All people of property have curtained beds, and as their living rooms are very large, they have their beds in them. They have large stoves, in which they also cook. Their soups are very substantial, and for the most part consist of bacon, fresh meat, and vegetables, which are cooked together in a pot and served as a side-dish. The Canadians make their sugar themselves from maple trees, which for this reason are called sugar maples. Early in the year they go into the woods with kettles and pots, in which they catch the sap from cuts made in the trees. This they boil, and the part that comes to the top, which is the best, they particularly use. The only thing wrong with maple sugar is that it is brown: otherwise it is very good, especially for (troubles in) the chest. The natives are hospitable and jovial, singing and smoking all the time. Frequently the women have goiter. Otherwise the people are healthy and live to an old age. Not infrequently one sees people, old as the hills, living with their great- grandchildren, who take the best of care of them.[72]

In December 1781, the Riedesel family was finally able to take up residence in the fine new home in Sorel which Governor Haldimand had had built for them.[73] This house was to shelter a host of important personalities, like the Baroness of Fortisson, Prince Edward, Duke of Richmond, Captain Charles Peel, and the Count and Countess of Dalhousie, and it was also the site of the first illuminated Christmas tree in Canada.[74] Although the house has been somewhat altered in the past 200 years, it still stands in the town of Sorel, where it is known as "the governor's house" (see photo on page 210). On December 10, 1966 representatives from the Trans-Canada Alliance of German Canadians commemorated that Christmas of 1781 by unveiling a bronze plaque bearing the following inscription in French, English, and German:

"Dans cette maison, le 25 décembre 1781, fut illuminé un arbre de Noël à la tradition allemande par le général von Riedesel. Cet arbre de Noël est le premier du genre enregistré au Canada."

"In this house, a Christmas tree was lit by General von Riedesel on the 25th December 1781 in German tradition, which is recorded as the first Christmas tree in Canada"

"In diesem Hause entzündete am 25 Dezember 1781 General von Riedesel den ersten Weihnachtsbaum deutscher Art in Kanada."

The winter of 1781-82 was another very difficult one, with endless piles of snow and bitter winds which vanquished even the hardiest souls. In April, Carleton was named commander-in-chief of New York to succeed General Clinton, who had asked to be replaced after five weary years as commander which had given him nothing but headaches.[75] Carleton immediately asked Haldimand to strengthen the defences. Throughout the summer months, Riedesel and his men worked on the fortifications at Île-aux-Noix, which was so crucial to the defence of Lake Champlain that an additional fifty chasseurs from Hanau were posted to the Lacolle River.[76]

Haldimand was concerned about the fate of the Vermont Loyalists and wanted to offer them the protection of the British crown. He therefore sent a large detachment of soldiers to the Vermont border in early 1782. At the end of the summer, an invading army composed of English and German soldiers was secretly built up, using the refortification of Île-aux-Noix as a screen. But it never received its marching orders—news of Cornwall's defeat at Yorktown quickly ended thoughts of another invasion.

In November 1782, Baroness von Riedesel announced to her husband the birth of a new daughter, whom they named "Canada" in honour of their adopted home. But alas, their mutual joy turned to grief when the infant died five months later. The baroness was worried about the child's tomb: "My little girl, whom we had named Canada, having been buried in Sorel, the officers promised to have an inscription engraved upon her tomb, to save it from any profanation, which it might suffer, on the score of our religious principles, from some zealous Canadian Catholic."[77]

Winter quarters for 1782-83 were assigned as follows: [78] the dragoons of the Prinz Ludwig Regiment to St. Antoine in the western section of St. Charles and Beloeil; the grenadier battalion to Berthier, La
Noraie and Lavaltrie, and one officer with 25 men to Pointe-du-Lac;
the von Rhetz Regiment, with the exception of the Guard Corps and
Captain Olers' company, was sent to Sorel, St. Denis in the eastern
section of the parish of St. Charles, and Beloeil as well as to Pointe
d'Olivier; the von Riedesel Regiment to Sorel; the von Specht Regiment
to Yamaska, St. François, La Baie and Nicolet (this regiment provided
an officer with 25 men under General Clark for the barracks at Trois-
Rivières); the von Barner Light Infantry Battalion to St. Sulpice,
Repentigny, and l'Assomption; and Riedesel distributed the recently
arrived recruits among the different regiments.

On December 29, 1782 Riedesel ordered his men to change their
footwear: "The frequent snows in this province render it necessary
that those who go on expeditions, perform advance duty, etc., should
wear snow shoes. This cannot be done unless each man is supplied
with moccasins; the wearing of which in the winter, in place of shoes,
on or off duty shall be allowed, except in case that a regiment in
Quebec or in garrison is forbidden to parade in them."[79] Henceforth
these new articles formed a regular part of the German soldiers'
equipment, to the vast amusement of the local population for whom
they had long been a necessity in the winter.

LIST OF GERMAN SOLDIERS IN CANADA IN 1778

Units	jan.	feb.	mar.	apr.	may	june	july	aug.	sept.	oct.	nov.	dec.
Headquarters	-	-	-	-	-	-	-	-	-	-	-	-
Dragoon Reg.	50	50	50	50	50	50	50	50	50	inc. into. v. Barner Reg.	inc. into. v. Barner Reg.	inc. into. v. Barner Reg.
Grenadier Reg.	104	113	113	113	113	113	113	113	113	inc. into. v. Barner Reg.	inc. into. v. Barner Reg.	inc. into. v. Barner Reg.
Reg. von Rhetz	171	171	171	171	171	171	171	171	171	inc. into. v. Barner Reg.	inc. into. v. Barner Reg.	inc. into. v. Barner Reg.
Reg. von Riedesel	150	150	150	150	150	150	150	150	150	inc. into. v. Barner Reg.	inc. into. v. Barner Reg.	inc. into. v. Barner Reg.
Reg. von Specht	153	153	151	149	148	148	148	148	148	inc. into. v. Barner Reg.	inc. into. v. Barner Reg.	inc. into. v. Barner Reg.
Reg. prince Friedrich	605	604	601	600	600	599	598	597	597	592	621	620
Brunswick Chasseurs	170	171	169	167	167	167	167	167	167	inc. into. v. Barner Reg.	inc. into. v. Barner Reg.	inc. into. v. Barner Reg.
Bat. von Ehrenkrook	*	*	*	*	*	*	*	*	*	609	602	604
Reg. von Barner	*	*	*	*	*	*	*	*	*	587	588	584
Total Brunswick	1,403	1,412	1,405	1,400	1,399	1,398	13,97	1,396	1,396	1,7,8	1,811	1,808
Hesse-Hanau Reg. von Scheell Detachment	102	149	148	152	152	152	152	260	262	282	259	259
Hesse-Hanau Artillery			Inc. into. Hesse-Hanau Reg.					31	31	32	32	32
Von Kreutzbourg Chasseurs	424	407	409	413	413	409	409	466	466	464	487	464
Total Hesse-Hanau	526	556	557	565	565	561	561	757	759	778	778	755
Headquarters	*	*	*	*	*	*	*	*	*	*	*	*
Reg. Alt. von Lossberg	*	*	*	*	*	*	*	*	*	*	*	*
Art. von Lossberg	*	*	*	*	*	*	*	*	*	*	*	*
Reg. von Knyphausen	*	*	*	*	*	*	*	*	*	*	*	*
Total Hesse-Cassel	*	*	*	*	*	*	*	*	*	*	*	*
Prince Anhalt-Zerbst Reg.	*	*	*	*	613	613	613	613	608	604	585	574
Total of all the troops	1,929	1,968	1,962	1,965	2,577	2,572	2,571	2,766	2,763	3,170	3,174	3137
Bataillon du major von Luke	*	*	*	*	*	*	*	*	*	*	*	*

* Not yet arrived   - No info. avaible

LIST OF GERMAN SOLDIERS IN CANADA IN 1779

Units	jan.	feb.	mar.	apr.	may	june	july	aug.	sept.	oct.	nov.	dec.
Headquarters	-	-	-	-	-	-	-	-	°	°	°	°
Dragoon Reg.				inc. into v. Barner Reg. + Bat. v.E hrenkrook								
Grenadier Reg				inc. into v. Barner Reg. + Bat. v.E hrenkrook								
Reg. von Rhetz				inc. into v. Barner Reg. + Bat. v.E hrenkrook								
Reg. von Riedesel				inc. into v. Barner Reg. + Bat. v.E hrenkrook								
Reg. von Specht				inc. into v. Barner Reg. + Bat. v.E hrenkrook								
Reg. prince Friedrich	614	614	614	612	613	613	612	613	613	612	678	677
Brunswick Chasseurs				nc. into v. Barner Reg. + Bat. v.E hrenkrook								
Bat. von Ehrenkrook	604	603	601	600	600	600	600	600	633	640	699	698
Reg. von Barner	581	586	583	581	559	557	555	555	582	584	695	701
Total Brunswick	1,799	1,803	1,798	1,793	1,772	1,770	1,767	1,768	1,830	1,838	2,074	2,078
Hesse-Hanau Reg. von Schell Detachment	280	260	259	259	259	259	259	259	263	225	226	227
Hesse-Hanau Artillery	32	32	32	32	32	32	32	32	34	73	72	72
Von Kreutzbourg Chasseurs	461	459	461	460	458	459	457	458	481	581	586	582
Total Hesse-Hanau	773	751	752	751	749	748	746	747	778	879	884	881
Headquarters	*	*	*	*	*	*	*	*	*	*	*	*
Reg. Alt. von Lossberg	*	*	*	*	*	*	*	*	*	*	*	*
Art. von Lossberg	*	*	*	*	*	*	*	*	*	*	*	*
Reg. von Knyphausen	*	*	*	*	*	*	*	*	*	*	*	*
Total Hesse-Cassel	*	*	*	*	*	*	*	*	*	*	*	*
Prince Anhalt-Zerbst Reg.	558	556	555	549	544	543	542	538	536	539	698	698
Total of all the troops	3,130	3,110	3,105	3,093	3,065	3,061	3,055	3,053	3,144	3,256	3656	3,657
Bataillon du major von Luke	*	*	*	*	*	*	*	*	*	*	*	*

* No info. avaible   - No info. avaible

LIST OF GERMAN SOLDIERS IN CANADA IN 1780

Units	jan.	feb.	mar.	apr.	may	june	july	aug.	sept.	oct.	nov.	dec.
Headquarters	9	9			9	9	9	10	10	10	10	-
Dragoon Reg.			inc. into. v. Barner Reg. + Bat. v.E hrenkrook									
Grenadier Reg.			inc. into. v. Barner Reg. + Bat. v.E hrenkrook									
Reg. von Rhetz			inc. into. v. Barner Reg. + Bat. v.E hrenkrook									
Reg. von Riedesel			inc. into. v. Barner Reg. + Bat. v. Ehrenkrook									
Reg. von Specht			inc. into. v. Barner Reg. + Bat. v. Ehrenkrook									
Reg. prince Friedrich	683	681	679	679	678	678	678	676	674	675	675	-
Brunswick Chasseurs			inc. into. v. Barner Reg. + Bat. v.Ehrenkrook									
Bat. von Ehrenkrook	700	700	700	699	700	696	695	732	719	719	720	-
Reg. von Barner	699	697	696	696	696	697	693	725	719	719	720	-
Total Brunswick	2,091	2,087	2,084	2,083	2,083	2,080	2,075	2,143	2,122	2,123	2,125	-
Hesse-Hanau Reg. von Schoell Detachment	227	263	263	263	263	263	280	282	282	282	281	-
Hesse-Hanau Artillery	72	34	34	34	34	34	41	41	41	41	41	-
Von Kreutzbourg Chasseurs	584	587	587	587	587	586	586	582	581	579	568	-
Total Hesse-Hanau	883	884	884	884	884	883	907	905	904	902	890	-
Headquarters	*	*	*	*	*	-	-	5	5	5	5	-
Reg. Alt. von Lossberg	*	*	*	*	*	-	-	350	349	350	350	*
Art. von Lossberg	*	*	*	*	*	*	*	*	*	*	*	*
Reg. von Knyphausen	*	*	*	*	*	-	-	199	198	198	197	-
Total Hesse-Cassel	*	*	*	*	*	-	-	199	198	198	197	-
Prince Anhalt-Zerbst Reg.	698	698	698	698	698	697	697	698	698	698	698	-
Total of all the troops	3,672	3,669	3,666	3,665	3,665	3,660	3,679	4,300	4,276	4,265	4,272	-
Bataillon du major von Luke	*	*	*	*	*	*	*	*	*	*	*	*

* Not yet arrived   - No info. avaible   * No longer in Canada

LIST OF GERMAN SOLDIERS IN CANADA IN 1781

Units	jan.	feb.	mar.	apr.	may	june	july	aug.	sept.	oct.	nov.	dec.
Headquarters	10	10	10	10	10	10	10	10	10	10	-	-
Dragoon Reg.		inc. into. v. Barner Reg. + Bat. v.E hrenkrook							130	255	255	
Grenadier Reg.		inc. into. v. Barner Reg. + Bat. v.E hrenkrook								149	149	149
Reg. von Rhetz		inc. into. v. Barner Reg. + Bat. v.E hrenkrook								312	312	312
Reg. von Riedesel		inc. into. v. Barner Reg. + Bat. v.E hrenkrook								373	373	373
Reg. von Specht		inc. into. v. Barner Reg. + Bat. v.E hrenkrook								349	349	349
Reg. prince Friedrich	672	670	669	668	668	668	667	667	666	662	644	644
Brunswick Chasseurs	inc. into. v. Barner Reg. + Bat. v.E hrenkrook										•	•
Bat. von Ehrenkrook	726	726	725	724	723	722	721	721	721	722		
Reg. von Barner	722	721	720	719	718	718	716	715	714	711	413	413
Total Brunswick	2,130	2,127	2,124	2,121	2,119	2,118	2,114	2,113	2,111	-	-	-
Hesse-Hanau Reg. von Schoell Detachment	278	278	278	278	278	278	278	278	278	305	295	295
Hesse-Hanau Artillery	41	41	41	40	40	40	40	40	40	52	57	57
Von Kreutzbourg Chasseurs	563	562	563	560	560	558	557	555	553	545	613	613
Total Hesse-Hanau	882	881	882	878	878	876	875	873	871	902	965	965
Headquarters	5	5	3	5	5	5	5	5	-	-	-	
Reg. Alt. von Lossberg	349	349	347	347	346	346	346	345	346	396	400	400
Art. von Lossberg	*	*	*	*	*	*	*	*	*	24°	24°	24°
Reg. von Knyphausen	197	196	196	196	195	195	195	195	193			
Total Hesse-Cassel	551	550	546	548	546	546	546	545	539	420	424	424
Prince Anhalt-Zerbst Reg.	677	677	675	675	674	673	672	670	673	678	702	702
Total of all the troops	4,240	4,235	4,227	4,222	4,217	4,213	4,207	4,201	4,194	-	-	-
Bataillon du major von Luke	*	*	*	*	*	*	*	*	*	231	•	•

LIST OF GERMAN SOLDIERS IN CANADA IN 1782

Units	jan.	feb.	mar.	apr.	may	june	july	aug.	sept.	oct.	nov.	dec.
Headquarters	22	22	22	21	21	21	21	21	21	21	21	24
Dragoon Reg.	256	255	254	254	254	254	254	255	255	256	254	274
Grenadier Reg.	150	150	150	150	150	149	150	149	150	148	146	253
Reg. von Rhetz	314	313	312	313	313	313	314	311	311	311	314	404
Reg. von Riedesel	375	375	375	375	370	372	369	369	367	367	363	397
Reg. von Specht	349	349	349	349	349	347	347	346	344	343	339	403
Reg. prince Friedrich	642	642	640	639	637	638	636	637	635	636	637	615
Brunswick Chasseurs					inc. into. v. Barner Reg. + Bat. v. Ehrenkrook							
Bat. von Ehrenkrook	•	•	•	•					•	•	•	•
Reg. von Barner	413	413	413	413	413	411	409	406	402	398	394	426
Total Brunswick	2,521	2,519	2,515	2,514	2,507	2,505	2,500	2,494	2,485	2,480	2,468	2796
Hesse-Hanau Reg. von Schoell Detachment	295	293	290	290	289	289	289	289	290	292	329	326
Hesse-Hanau Artillery	57	58	58	58	58	58	60	60	60	60	67	67
Von Kreutzbourg Chasseurs	609	608	608	608	607	607	607	604	603	600	599	640
Total Hesse-Hanau	961	959	956	956	954	954	956	953	953	952	995	1033
Headquarters	-	-	-	-	-	-	-	-	-	-	-	-
Reg. Alt. von Lossberg	400	400	400	400	397	396	395	392	391	392	415	415
Art. von Lossberg	24	24	24	24	24	24	24	24	24	24	24	24
Reg. von Knyphausen	°	°	°	°	°	°	°	°	°	°	°	°
Total Hesse-Cassel	424	424	424	424	421	420	419	416	415	416	439	438
Prince Anhalt-Zerbst Reg.	701	701	701	700	700	700	700	698	699	693	693	693
Total of all the troops	4,607	4,603	4,596	4,594	4,582	4,579	4,575	4,561	4,552	4,541	4,595	4960
Bataillon du major von Luke	•	•	•	•	•	•	•	•	•	•	•	•

* Not yet arrived - No info. avaible * No longer in Canada • Disbanded

LIST OF GERMAN SOLDIERS IN CANADA IN 1783

Units	jan.	feb.	mar.	apr.	may	june	july	aug.	sept.	oct.	nov.	dec.
Headquarters	24	23	23	23	23	23	23	14				
Dragoon Reg.	274	270	269	269	268	269	262	204				
Grenadier Reg.	253	253	253	252	252	250	250	200				
Reg. von Rhetz	400	401	400	399	399	398	391	318				
Reg. von Riedesel	397	397	397	396	395	394	394	312				
Reg. von Specht	402	403	402	402	402	402	398	306				
Reg. prince Friedrich	615	614	614	613	613	611	608	487				
Brunswick Chasseurs	inc. into. v. Barner Reg. + Bat. v. Ehrenkrook											
Bat. von Ehrenkrook	•	•	•	•	•	•	•	•				
Reg. von Barner	423	423	421	419	417	416	414	212				
Total Brunswick	2,788	2,784	2,779	2,773	2,769	2,763	2,740	2,053				
Hesse-Hanau Reg. von Schoell Detachment	325	325	322	322	321	321	371	377				
Hesse-Hanau Artillery	67	68	66	66	66	66	68	57				
Von Kreutzbourg Chasseurs	640	636	636	634	632	595	578	378				
Total Hesse-Hanau	1,032	1,029	1,024	1,022	1,019	982	1017	812				
Headquarters	-	-	-	-	-	-	-	-				
Reg. Alt. von Lossberg	405	404	404	406	406	406	407	388				
Art. von Lossberg	24	24	24	23	23	23	23	23				
Reg. von Knyphausen	•	•	•	•	•	•	•	•				
Total Hesse-Cassel	429	428	428	429	429	429	430	411				
Prince Anhalt-Zerbst Reg.	688	687	687	690	690	690	690	674				
Total of all the troops	4,937	4,928	4,918	4,914	4,907	4,864	4,877	3,950				
Bataillon du major von Luke	•	•	•	•	•	•	•	•				

Notes

1. Haldimand, Swiss by birth, spoke much better French and German than English, which he mangled. He was one of the better governors of Canada and a good friend to Canadians (Francis-J. Audet, *"Mes Fiches,"* in Histoire du Canada), although some considered him harsh (H. Manners Chichester, *"Haldimand, Sire Frederick"* in the Dictionary of National Biography). "Riedesel who was fond of him noted himself that Haldimand was of a morose character and kept to himself." General Riedesel, II, 108, trans. Stone; Marvin L. Brown Jr., *Baroness von Riedesel and the American Revolution, A Revised Translation and Introduction and Notes.*

2. Public Archives of Canada, *MG 21, Transcriptions,* Haldimand Collection, series B, vol. 43, 28-29.

3. The regiment was named for the Princess of Anhalt, although it had been raised by Prince Frederick of Anhalt-Zerbst.

4. Public Archives of Canada, *MG 21, Transcriptions,* Haldimand Collection, series B, vol. 43, 29.

5. *Ibid,* vol. 151, 4F-4G, letter dated September 12, 1778.

6. Max von Eelking, *The German Allied Troops,* 236-238.

7. Public Archives of Canada, *MG 13, War Office 17,* vol. 1572, 343, 344, monthly returns. Quebec, September 5, 1778.

8. Max von Eelking, *The German Allied Troops,* 239.

9. Public Archives of Canada, *MG 11, Colonial Office,* series Q, vol. 15, 177, monthly returns, July 1778.

10. Public Archives of Canada, *MG 11, Colonial Office,* series C.o.5, vol. 141, 114-115. Letter dated Feb. 23, 1778. Note from Rotencreutz.

11. Public Archives of Canada, *MG 21, Transcriptions,* Haldimand Collection, series B, vol. 83, 88. General order dated Nov. 20, 1779.

12. A great many officers were missing just then, following the surrender at Saratoga. Riedesel himself was a prisoner of the Americans. The reorganization of the troops into fewer regiments meant that far fewer officers were needed.

13. Max von Eelking, *The German Allied Troops,* 240.

14. Public Archives of Canada, *MG 21, Transcriptions,* Haldimand Collection, series B, vol. 153, 53-59. Instructions of Jan.7, 1779.

15. *Ibid.,* vol. 217, 534-535. Letter dated March 3, 1779.

16. *Ibid.,* vol. 151, 80-85. Letter dated March 16, 1779.

17. *Ibid.,* vol. 164, 50. Letter dated March 23, 1779.

18. *Ibid.,* vol.164, 50. Letter dated September 5, 1782. Loos to Haldimand.

19. *Ibid.,* vol. 153, 53-99. Letter dated September 6, 1782.

20. *Ibid.,* vol. 218, 125-126.

21. *Ibid.,* vol. III, 65. Letter dated March 27, 1779, Campbell to Haldimand.

22. *Ibid.,* vol. 189, 99-100. Letter dated Feb. 9, 1789, Carleton to Haldimand.

23. Quebec Seminary, Viger-Verreau Collection, carton 17, no. 28, Berthier, March 13, 1777. The style of the original has been preserved.

24. *Ibid.*, Lavaltrie, March 15, 1777. Ditto.
25. *Ibid.*
26. Public Archives of Canada, *MG 21, Transcriptions*, Haldimand Collection, series B, vol. 171, 18-24. Letter dated Jan. 9, 1779, instructions of the militia captains.
27. *Ibid.*, vol. 83, 4. Carleton's order, June 5, 1776.
28. *Ibid.*, vol. 151, 307. Letter dated Aug. 19, 1782.
29. *Ibid.*, vol. 151, 310-311. Letter dated Aug. 25, 1782.
30. *Ibid.*
31. Friederike von Riedesel, *Letters and Memoirs*, 50.
32. *Ibid.*, 256-275.
33. August Ludwig Schlozer, *Briefwechsel*, 1776-1782, vol. III, no.42, 320-341, Batiscan, Nov. 2, 1776.
34. Public Archives of Canada, *MG 21, Transcriptions*, Haldimand Collection, series B. vol. 152, 13. Report dated Feb. 28, 1783, Loos to Haldimand. Style and spelling of the original have been preserved.
35. *Ibid.*, vol. 152, 22. Report dated March 28, 1783, ditto.
36. *Ibid.*, vol. 151, 231. Letter dated Feb. 25, 1781, certificates of the officers of militia.
37. Max von Eelking, *The German Allied Troops*, 241.
38. Edward Jackson Lowell, *The Hessians*, 119.
39. Public Archives of Canada, *MG 11, Colonial Office, series Q*, vol. 20, 410. Letter dated August 13, 1782, Riedesel to Carleton.
40. Max von Eelking, *op. cit.*, 241.
41. Public Archives of Canada, *MG 21, Transcriptions*, Haldimand Collection, series B, vol. 151, 113-114. Letter dated Aug. 29, 1779, Kreutzbourg to Haldimand.
42. *Ibid.*, vol. 151, 120. Letter dated Oct. 3, 1779, ditto.
43. *Ibid.*, vol. 153, 66. Letter dated April 20, 1780, Haldimand to Kreutzbourg.
44. *Ibid.*, vol. 151, 293. Letter dated July 5, 1782, Kreutzbourg to Haldimand.
45. *Ibid.*, vol. 44, 25. Letter dated March 24, 1780, Germain to Haldimand.
46. Eelking, *op. cit.*, 241.
47. *Ibid.*, 242-243.
48. *Ibid.*, 243.
49. Public Archives of Canada, *MG 13, War Office 17*, vol. 1573, 272, monthly returns, Quebec, Nov.1, 1779.
50. Eelking, *op. cit.*, 244.
51. Public Archives of Canada, *MG 21, Transcriptions*, Haldimand Collection, series B, vol. 81, part 1, 32. Letter dated June 26, 1780, from the adjutant general to Rauschenblatt.
52. *Ibid.*, vol. 83, 138. Letter dated Aug. 22, 1780 from the adjutant general to Loos.
53. *Ibid.*, vol. 155, 68. Reports of May 23 to May 31, 1782. Also vol.151, 12, letter dated Sept. 12, 1778.
54. *Ibid.*, vol. 151, 177. Letter dated May 26, 1780, Praetorius to Haldimand.55. Stephen Francis Gradish, 1969 "The German Mercenaries in North America During the American Revolution: A Case Study", Canadian Journal of History, vol. 4 (mars), p. 23-46. The German Mercenaries in Canada, 1776-1783, 80.

56. Public Archives of Canada, *MG 11, Colonial Office, series Q*, vol. 17, part 11, 120. Letter dated July 12, 1780.

57. Max von Eelking, *Memoirs and Letters*, vol. II, 88.

58. Max von Eelking, *The German Allied Troops*, 247.

59. Public Archives of Canada, *MG 21, Transcriptions*, Haldimand Collection, series B, vol. 151, 243-267. Letter dated March 27, 1781, Barner to MacLean.

60. *Ibid.*, vol. 151, 244-276. Letter dated March 28, 1781, MacLean to Barner.

61. *Ibid.*, vol. 139, 45. Letter dated April 1781, Haldimand to MacLean.

62. Sir Henry Clinton was commander-in-chief of the British forces in North America after 1778, succeeding Sir William Howe.

63. Max von Eelking, *Memoirs and Letters*, vol. II, 89.

64. *Ibid.*, 209.

65. Riedesel brought with him: five officers from headquarters, 16 captains, 24 subalterns and 400 Brunswickers, the rest being troops from Hanau and Anhalt-Zerbst. Among the Brunsickers was Major de Lucke's battalion, made up of German survivors found in the New York region. Max von Eelking, *The German Allied Troops*, 247.

66. Max von Eelking, *Memoirs and Letters*, vol. II, 105-108.

67. Max von Eelking, *The German Allied Troops*, 247.

68. Max von Eelking, *Memoirs and Letters*, vol. II, 109.

69. *Ibid.*

70. Max von Eelking, *The German Allied Troops*, 248.

71. Max von Eelking, *The German Allied Troops*, 248. 7 1. Max von Eelking, *Memoirs and Letters*, vol. II, 110. For the troops from Hesse-Hanau and Anhalt-Zerbst, see Public Archives of Canada, *MG 13, War Office*, 240 and 251, monthly returns, 1781.

72. Marvin L. Brown Jr., *Baroness von Riedesel and the American Revolution*, 115-117.

73. *Ibid.*, 117-118.

74. A. Couillard Després, *Cité de Sorel*, a small brochure on the subject of "the governor's house" published during the bicentennial of the first illuminated Christmas tree in Canada.

75. Pierre Benoit, *Lord Dorchester*, 119.

76. Max von Eelking, *The German Allied Troops*, 250-251.

77. Friederike von Riedesel, *Letters and Memoirs*, 275.

78. Max von Eelking, *Memoirs and Letters*, vol. II, 137-138.

79. *Ibid.*, 149-150.

Chapter V

THE GERMANS AFTER THE WAR:
RETURN OR SETTLEMENT AND THEIR
LASTING CONTRIBUTION IN CANADA

D isillusioned by the repeated defeats, the British authorities began
secret negotiations with the Americans that led to the signing of
a provisional peace treaty on November 30, 1782.[1] But the Americans
continued to launch little offensives, collecting a string of further vic-
tories. Canada buzzed with conflicting rumours of war and peace. At
the end of March 1783, the war officially came to an end. For Major
General von Riedesel and his troops this meant a quick return to
Europe, because every day that the Germans spent on American soil
added to the costs which the British government could ill afford.[2] The
expected orders came in mid-June, in a letter to Riedesel from Lord
North, George III's Prime Minister, praising "the merits and services
of yourself, and the brave conduct of your officers and men." In it, the
Germans' imminent departure was announced: "Preliminary negotiations for peace between his majesty and the United States of America
having begun, and it being the intention to refrain from all operations
against Canada, I have received orders from the king to inform you
that instructions have been given to Governor Haldimand to make the
necessary preparations for the return of yourself and the troops of his
highness, the duke of Brunswick."[3]

With the governor's cooperation, swift preparations were made,
and on the evening of August 2, 1783, the Riedesel family and part of
the German army boarded the ships that would take them back to
their native land. The fleet comprised sixteen ships in the first division
and eight in the second:[4]

I.   *Troops from Brunswick*
     Commander: Major General von Riedesel
     A-Dragoon Regiment Prinz Ludwig, led by Major Baum
     B-Regiment Prinz Friedrich, led by Lt. Col. Praetorius
     C-Musketeer Regiment von Riedesel, led by Col. Hille
         D-Regiment von Rhetz, led by Major de Lucke
     E-Musketeer Regiment von Specht, led by Major von
         Ehrenkrook

II. *Troops from Hesse-Cassel*
     Commander: Major General von Loos
     A- Fusilier Regiment Alt von Lossberg, led by Major General
         von Loos

III. *Troops From Hesse-Hanau*
     Commander: Col. Lentz
     A- Hesse-Hanau Artillery Company, led by Captain Pausch
     B- Corps of Chasseurs, led by Col. Kreutzbourg
     C- The first battalion of the Hesse-Hanau Regiment, led by
         Col. Lentz

IV. *Troops From Anhalt-Zerbst*
     Commander: Col. von Rauschenplatt
     A- The Anhalt-Zerbst Regiment (Frie Corps), led by
         Col. Rauschenplatt

After a record crossing of only nineteen days, Riedesel wrote a glad letter to Duke Ferdinand on September 26, from Stade: "Gracious Sovereign, I have the honor of announcing to your highness the safe arrival of myself and the rest of the Brunswick troops on the coast of Germany."[5] On the way to Wolfenbhttel, he took the opportunity of thanking the commanders of his regiments: "I cannot let the opportunity pass of expressing to your honors my thanks for the great zeal and fidelity you have manifested in the service."[6]

On October 8, the troops finally reached the city of Brunswick, after an absence of several years; they were greeted by the duke himself and by a huge crowd of enthusiastic fellow citizens.[7]

In the United States, the recruits from Hesse-Hanau, Waldeck, and

Anhalt-Zerbst left New York in July 1783, followed a month later by the troops from Anspach-Bayreuth and the first division from Hesse-Cassel, while the second division came on a short while later. The first division, under the command of Major General von Kospoth, consisted of the following regiments: Fusilier Regiment von Knyphausen, Fusilier Regiment von Dittfürth, Musketeer Regiment Prinz Friederich, Musketeer Regiment von Bose, Garrison Regiment von Porbeck, Garrison Regiment von Bünau, Garrison Regiment von Benning, Garrison Regiment von Knöblauch, and the Grenadier Regiment d'Angelleli. They put to sea on August 15, 1783, reaching Europe in October and November. The second division, under the command of Major von Wurmb, set sail in November and reached England at the end of December. Forced to winter at Plymouth, Deal, Portsmouth, Dover, and Chatham, this division finally left England in April 1784 and reached Germany at the end of the month.[8] Upon their arrival they were greeted by the crown prince and inspected by the landgrave.

The Chasseurs from Hesse-Cassel, stranded in America with no means of transportation, weighed anchor only in November 1783; after a long stay in England they finally reached home in May 1784.[9]

Many German soldiers were also held prisoner in the United States. The rebels released them in May 1783 at Frederick, Maryland. According to the journal of Johann Conrad Döhla, they then marched 236 miles in thirteen days to their former quarters, where they received new uniforms and blankets. They finally reached the ports of embarkation in August-September 1783. These 1500 men from Brunswick, Hesse, Anhalt-Zerbst, and Waldeck set sail in fourteen ships and two frigates for home, where they were given the same red-carpet treatment their comrades had received.[10] Major Baurmeister's journal records the jubilant welcome given to the troops from Waldeck: "they were received amid demonstrations of joy, like heroes returning from a victorious campaign."[11]

The military experience gained by the German army in America proved particularly useful for German Princes during the French Revolution of 1789. General Valentini, a military historian, wrote of the troops from Hesse-Cassel: "Of all the troops sent against France in the later wars, the soldiers from Hesse Cassel showed the highest military skill, endurance, good spirit, and a true love of war."[12]

For other German mercenaries—Herbert Wilhelm Debor speaks of 4549 men[13]—1783 marked the official beginning of their new life in North America, "official" because some mercenaries had already been discharged by German military authorities and settled here. Debor, who did exhaustive research into this subject, claims that 2300-2400 soldiers immigrated to Canada. Of this number, 1300-1400 settled in Quebec (Lower Canada) and founded families, while 950-1000 others went to Ontario (Upper Canada), and the Maritimes. Debor suggests that many of the soldiers who settled in Quebec would already have developed close ties with the local population during the seven mainly peaceful years they had spent there. Moreover, the young Germans were always very respectful of authority, in this case the British crown, which proved to be far more generous in giving land and other rewards at the end of the war than the American Continental Congress. An American study by Dr. Virginia Easley DeMarce, lends weight to Debor's arguments. DeMarce's genealogical research is of particular interest, as it provides a good many details on each of the soldiers who immigrated to Canada.[14]

Some soldiers had no choice but to stay in North America. Because the Duke of Brunswick wanted to reduce his military strength by nearly half at the end of the fighting, he decreed that any soldier convicted of a crime or bad conduct, or deemed unfit for future combat, must remain in Canada.[15] "Foreigners," or in other words, men who wore the Brunswick uniform but who were not natives of that duchy, were strongly encouraged to remain as well. Other soldiers were pressured in a similar fashion. For instance, on December 23, 1777, Feronce Rotencreutz, the Duke of Brunswick's Prime Minister, wrote to Faucitt: "We must at all costs prevent these capitulating cowards (of Saratoga) from returning to Germany, they will be discontented and their exaggerations will disgust everyone with your American war; send these leftovers to one of your islands in America..."[16] The same fate was reserved for the Hessians of Trenton.[17] Nonetheless, not all the German soldiers were forced to stay in America; on the contrary, some had to return to Europe, like the Anhalt-Zerbst Regiment whose services had already been promised to the Austrian emperor.[18] But when the actual moment of departure came, many deserters from all the regiments, as well as those soldiers whose princes had discharged them, chose to remain in Canada where many had already married local women. Their numbers might strike us as insignificant when compared with later waves of immigrants, but for those days the figures are considerable. In 1783 the population of Canada was approximately 110,000; the German soldiers who stayed after the war represented, therefore, three to four percent of the entire male population. Their assimilation into Canadian society was so rapid and complete that the vast majority of their descendants are unaware, even today, of their German ancestry. In both English and French-speaking Canada the German names were altered, so that only the most determined genealogists can hope to trace them.

The corps of chasseurs provided the most immigrants of all the German regiments serving in Canada. Nearly half the Hesse-Hanau chasseurs stayed behind. One Hessian officer quoted by Max von Eelking suggested that a possible reason for this phenomenon was the similarity between the lifestyle here and what they had known at home. Recruited from European forests, these men delighted in the outdoors way of life epitomized by the Indians. Unlike their compatriots further to the south who were involved in heavier fighting and the repercussions of war, the chasseurs saw comparatively little action and were much more able to appreciate what America could offer them.[19]

Although several of the German mercenaries stayed in urban centres like Montreal, Quebec, Trois-Rivières, Sorel, and Chambly, many others chose to settle in the small communities where they had wintered, or else on lands given to them at the end of the war. Alexander Fraser, seignior of St. Gilles, granted them plots of land in the northern section of his domain on condition that they "clear an acre of land the first year and pay an annual rent of three Tours pounds per arpent of frontage and three sols[20] of quit-rent."[21]

Unfortunately, not everyone received land like Alexander Fraser's. Even though the soldiers were given government land grants in the same way the Loyalists were, their early elation yielded to despair in the face of interminable delays and appalling living conditions. On June 26, 1784 Baron von Reitzenstein and a group of German soldiers with their families landed at Cataraqui (now Kingston, Ontario) after overcoming a veritable "sea of troubles" which were merely the beginning of their woes. Upon arrival, they were astounded to discover that none of their land grants had been surveyed. By July, this work was still barely begun. With the dread prospect of winter arriving before homes could be erected on these unsurveyed lands, Baron von Reltzenstein decided to appeal directly to the governor. On August 1, he wrote: "Your Excellency will be gracious enough to permit your humble servant to tell you of the desperate situation of the discharged soldiers, whose plight is infinitely worse in every respect than that of the Loyalists and certainly worthy of Your Excellency's Compassion. The Loyalists having received from the government Blankets and Clothing, although they already had more of these items than the poor soldiers since they were established in one place for a considerable length of time and had therefore the advantage of organizing their households, are in a position to deal with the vagaries of the weather while others are forced to sleep on the ground, half naked and without blankets; exposed to all the elements and to the evil vapours which the earth after it rains, and the fog which is so common here, give off; with the result that sickness is spreading rapidly, and within a short time these poor soldiers will no longer have the strength to continue their work and will begin dropping like flies. And if the men are in such a way, Your Excellency can imagine the sorry plight of the women and their poor children!"[22]

Two weeks later, with the government still dragging its feet, Reitzenstein wrote another letter, this time to Major Mathew whom he hoped would intercede on behalf of the Germans. He described the pitiful state of his men: "You were kind enough, Sir, to promise me that you would do all in your power to provide the poor Discharged Soldiers with Blankets; please allow me then, Sir, to entreat you to consider the pitiable situation of these unfortunate people, who are left to sleep on the ground without blankets of any sort, exposed to the force of frequent seasonal rains and to the evil vapours given off by the ground after the fog which is almost a daily occurrence, and during nights which are as cold as in autumn; with their wives and poor children. When you consider this sorry situation, Sir, I am certain that Your Generous Heart will take pity on these poor abandoned creatures."[23]

Not everyone underwent such suffering. In Nova Scotia, for example, the Germans as well as the Loyalists were given free transportation, 300 acres of land with no taxes to pay for twelve years, and other perks of a similar nature.[24] The generosity of the Nova Scotian offer attracted, as we have mentioned, many Germans; Debor estimates that 950-1000 men settled in Ontario and Nova Scotia, most of them going to the latter.

Many of these soldiers were already quite familiar with the Halifax region, having spent time there after prisoner exchanges or upon arrival in Canada as new recruits. Halifax was then the port where the soldiers waited before proceeding to their next destination, be it in Canada, the U.S., or Europe. In fact, the city continued to fulfil this function through the two World Wars in our own time. Troop trains from across the country carried soldiers to the waiting ships in Halifax harbour, and at the end of the war returning soldiers—and their European war brides—were carried home by trains that met them there.

Soldiers from the Regiment von Stein/von Seitz/von Porbeck, of the Hesse-Cassel army, occupied the garrison at Halifax from 1778 to 1783.[25] Another 500 recruits from various Hessian regiments who were supposed to be sent to the colonies in the south, wound up spending the last two years of the war in Halifax when their orders were changed.[26] Others, like some soldiers from Ansbach-Bayreuth and Waldeck, were granted crown lands in Nova Scotia at the end of the hostilities. Maxwell Sutherland mentions them in his "Case History of a Settlement,"[27] He asserts, erroneously in this author's opinion, that the German soldiers who settled there left their lands a short while later. Their "disappearance" can be better explained by a rapid assimilation into the English-speaking milieu so that it is practically impossible to trace them.

When hostilities ended, many German soldiers chose to settle in the United States close to their well established compatriots, as many observers have attested. On the other hand, as Debor points out, many of those who served in the U.S. during the war preferred to leave a country where they had known much hardship in favour of Canada. So the numbers balanced out in the end.

During the American Revolution, many German soldiers fought in uniforms other than their own. Some, mostly Hanoverians, wore British uniforms; but others fought for the rebels or their allies. This makes the genealogists' task of tracing these men all the harder. While exact numbers are difficult to determine, a letter from Barrington to Carleton on May 28, 1776 informs us that 449 German soldiers were distributed throughout the English army as follows: 81 recruits to the 9th regiment, 53 to the 20th, 14 to the 21st, 35 to the 24th, 5 to the 31st, 102 to the 33rd, 42 to the 34th, 74 to the 53rd and 43 to the 62nd.[28]

One of the biggest mysteries for genealogists is the case of Germans who immigrated to Canada and served the rebel cause, an enigma explored by Clifford Neal Smith in the Encyclopedia of German-American Genealogical Research in an article entitled "German mercenaries serving with the French in the American Revolution". According to Smith, "At least one German-speaking military unit, the Régiment royal allemand de deux ponts (Royal German Zweibrücken Regiment) from the principality of Zweibrüken, served with the French during the American Revolution. (...) It seems probable that some members of this unit remained in the United States after the Revolution, and it remains an unfinished task of genealogical researchers to discover who these men were."

Smith goes on to mention an article entitled "Die deutschen Truppen im französischen Hülfsheere des amerikanischen Unabhängigkeitskrieg" (German troops in the French auxiliary army during the American Revolution)[29] which gives what little information is available about this regiment. According to this article, a battalion of (Kurtrier) grenadiers served with the Saar regiment—known as a detachment of the "La Sarre" regiment—which later joined the Saintonge regiment under Col. Adam Philipp, Count von Custine. Several soldiers recruited in Alsace and Lorraine were regrouped into chasseur companies in the Bourbon and Soissons regiments. In addition, a large proportion of the French cavalry under the Duke of Lauzon was German, and 600 men from a regiment of Anhalt-Zerbst

Extract of a petition to obtain Crown lands at Barford and Hinchinbrook

GERMAN ARMIES IN AMERICA
1776-1783   29,867 SOLDIERS

GENERAL STAFF

HESSE-CASSEL STAFF

- REGIMENT VON LINSINGEN grenadiers
- *REGIMENT VON KNYPHAUSEN fusiliers
- BATTALION VON BLOCK grenadiers
- REGIMENT VON MIRBACH musketeers
- BATTALION VON MINIGERODE grenadiers
- REGIMENT VON TRÜMBACH musketeers
- REGIMENT DE CORPS musketeers
- REGIMENT VON RALL grenadiers
- REGIMENT VON WUTGENAU musketeers
- REGIMENT VON WISSENBACH musketeers
- REGIMENT PR. HEREDITARY Fusiliers
- REGIMENT VON HUYNE musketeers
- REGIMENT PRINCE CARL musketeers
- REGIMENT VON STEIN musketeers
- REGIMENT VON DITFURTH fusiliers
- REGIMENT VON BUNAU musketeers
- REGIMENT VON DONOP musketeers
- ARTILLERY CORPS artillery
- *REGIMENT VON LOSSBERG musketeers
- CHASSEURS-YAGERS chasseurs
- COMBINED REGIMENT (temporary)

BRUNSWICK STAFF

- *REGIMENT PRINCE LUDWIG grenadiers
- *REGIMENT PRINCE FRIEDRICH musketeers
- *REGIMENT VON RIEDESEL musketeers
- *REGIMENT VON SPECHT musketeers
- *REGIMENT VON RETHZ musketeers
- *REGIMENT VON BREYMANN grenadiers
- *REGIMENT VON BARNER musketeers, chasseurs
- ESTABLISHED WITH THE SURVIVORS FROM SARATOGA
- *REGIMENT VON EHRENKROOK musketeers
- *REGIMENT VON BARNER garrison

HESSE-HANAU STAFF

- *REGIMENT PRINCE HEREDITARY grenadiers, musketeers
- *FREE CORPS Light infantry (chasseurs)
- YAGERS CORPS yagers

ANSBACH-BAYREUTH STAFF

- REGIMENT ANSBACH
- REGIMENT BAYREUTH
- CHASSEURS

WALDECK STAFF

- 3RD REGIMENT WALDECK musketeers, grenadiers

ANHALT-ZERBST STAFF

- *REGIMENT PRINCESS OF ANHALT

HANOVER

BEARING ENGLISH COLOR WITH ENGLISH UNIFORMS

A regiment or battalion had 5 or 6 companies

A regiment was made of:

1-Infantry
- 21 officers with commission
- 60 officers without commission
- 22 musicians
- 5 non-fighting officers
- 525 soldiers

2-Grenadiers
- 16 officers with commission
- 44 officers without commission
- 20 musicians
- 1 non-fighting officers
- 420 soldiers

A regiment was made of:

1-Chasseurs
- 4 officers with commission
- 12 officers without commission
- 3 musicians
- 1 non-fighting officers
- 105 soldiers

2-Artillery
- 5 officers with commission
- 14 officers without commission
- 3 musicians

*CANADA-BASED REGIMENTS

formed part of the army of the Count d'Estaing. The latter, according to the article, might be the Viscount of Noailles' men; the Viscount, of the West Indies Corps, was responsible for the capitulation of the British Islands of St. Vincent and Grenada in 1778. The article suggests that the French may well have hired a battalion but no documentary evidence exists indicating whether or not it was sent to America.

In Quebec, marriages between German soldiers and local women can be easily traced. A glance at the old registers from parishes where these men were billeted turns up several records of marriages, births, and deaths. However, in just as many cases of marriage between a soldier and a French Canadian Catholic girl, no records remain to aid the hapless genealogical researcher. About half the soldiers were Protestants, and it would appear that many lovesick maidens temporarily forgot their duty to the church which held sway over their lives, and married without permission in the rite of their future husbands.

In is *History of the Catholic Church in Quebec 1608-1975*, Nive Voisine writes, "From the time of the conquest, the Catholic French Canadians lived in close proximity with a Protestant population which could contaminate their faith. These foreigners, moreover, were a very real presence, since many soldiers were billeted in the habitants' home. This promiscuity created a serious problem for religious authorities, namely mixed marriages. (...) This new situation posed both a theological and a moral problem..."[30] The bishops gradually adopted a uniform policy for dealing with it: priests were to try as far as possible to discourage their parishioners from entering into mixed marriages. If they failed to either prevent such a union or convert the non-Catholic spouse, they must insist that the marriage be celebrated by a Catholic priest, and the couple must promise to raise the children as Catholics.

As for the women who married in the Protestant faith in defiance of their priest, it is remarkable how many of them later returned to Catholic Church, bringing their husbands and families with them. This return to the Catholicism can be determined from birth records of children born to Catholic mothers and Protestant fathers. One possible reason was the lack of Protestant places of worship at the time. But there is an exception to every rule. Joseph-Edmond Roy's *Histoire de la Seigneurie de Lauzon* (History of the Lauzon Seigniory) recounts the way in which one avant-garde priest performed his duties as he understood them from his readings of ancient texts: "From the time that St. Gilles was first settled, the priest of St. Nicholas served the spiritual needs of the colonists. But as the parish was part Protestant and part Catholic, he performed his duties with truly evangelical charity without worrying about beliefs. He baptized, married and buried his parishioners as if they all belonged to the same flock."[31]

One reason for the large number of marriages between German soldiers and French-speaking Canadian women was that many of the mercenaries were from the Rhine region or Alsace and spoke French, while many others came from French-speaking countries—France, Switzerland or Belgium. But the major cause of these matches was the billeting of the German soldiers in the homes of the *habitants*. At first, as could be expected, a few problems arose as both sides tried to adapt to the new circumstances; such issues as a lack of food or too many soldiers billeted in one home created tension on both sides. But as time passed, the forced intimacy led to mutual tolerance, then to understanding, and often without their being aware of it, to deep and abiding friendship. In many cases, so much was shared between a soldier and his host's daughter that they decided to unite their destinies. A few men returned to Europe with their new wives, but the vast majority adopted Canada as their homeland.

Recruited from all across Germany and Europe, and even beyond when it became harder and harder to find new recruits, these men bequeathed us names as different as their countries of origin. Difficult to pronounce, many were changed, so that Koch became Caux, Maher—Maheu, Loeder—Laître/Letter, Beyer—Payeur, Pfeiffer—Fiffre, Schumpff—Jomphe, Stein—Schetagne. In other cases, German names were simply translated, so that Zimmerman became Carpenter, Stein—Stone, Schwartz—Black, Jaeger—Hunter, Vogel—L'Oiseau, and so forth. But in cases where the name did not lend itself to adaptation, little or no change occurred in the spelling, for instance,

Bartholomae, Baumann, Braun, Carl, Duff, Eschenbach, Fischer, Franck, Glackemeyer, Grimm, Grothe, Heinemann, Henckel, Hoffman, John, König, Krafft, Kühn, Lange, Loedell, Löw, Ludwig, Lutz, Mauck, Mayne, McDonald, Metzger, Mines, Minoni, Moro, Moses, Nieding, Peterson, Phillips, Reich, Reinhard, Reitz, Richter, Rosenthal, Sander, Sauer, Schaffalisky, Schell, Scherrer, Schiller, Schmidt, Schneider, Singer, Smith, Spahn, Steiger, Troestler, Verner, Vicario, Vogeler, Voges, Voss, Wagner, Wilhelmi, Wolf, Ziegler and so on.[32]

As a further way of integrating into Quebec society, many German soldiers changed their first names as well as their family names. Thus, Wilhelm became Guillaume, Jacob—Jacques, Andreas—André, Ernst—Ernest, Gottlieb—Théophile, Johann—Jean, Friedrich— Frédéric, Stephan—Étienne, Heinrich—Henri, Kaspar—Gaspar, Ludwig—Louis, etc. Phonetic confusion changed the "Sch" in some family names to "G" or "J", so that Schenck became Juinque, Schumpff —Jomphe, Schaeffer—Geffre, Stein—Schetagne. Confusion between the sounds of "B" and "P," as in certain German dialects, led to Pohle for Bohle, for instance, while the substitution of "J" for "Y" turned Yurgens into Jurgens.[33]

As for the many Brunswicker family names which were Gallicized but which came from French-speaking countries in the first place or which were the result of French infiltration in areas like the Upper and Lower Rhine in the Moselle region or the Saar, it is hard to imagine that they were once names of German mercenaries. It is also quite impossible to distinguish them from French Canadian family names. In this category we find: Albert, Allé, Bartholomé, Beauclair, Berger, Bésette, Biennommé, Boland, Bossé, Caux, Claude, Chenaille, Coache, Conrad, Dallaire, David, De Pincier, De(s) Coudres, Durdy, Duvinet, Hébert, Faille, Fausse, Ferdinand, Fiffre, Frédéric, Gabriel, Gallant(d), Gagné, George, Gervais, Gille, Godiché, Grothé, Guérard, Hamel, Hinse, Hotte, Hubert, Jacques, Jenot, Jomphe, Jordan, Laitre, Lamarre, Lambert, Laparé, Lemaire, Léonard, Lessard, Lettre, Loiseau, Maher, Maheu, Maillé, Major, Martin, Mayer, Miller, Millon, Molle, Mouché, Noé, Olivier, Pagé, Pambrun, Pape, Paul, Payeur, Piquette, Plasse, Platte, Pousse, Presser, Raymond, Rinier, Robin,

Roussel, Rose, Saint-Pierre, Telle, Thomas, Tornier, Tyssère, Viger, etc.

The same is true for many English names, such as Arnold, Baker, Bowman(n), Brown, Busch, Carl, Duff, Fischer, Franck, Fraser, Hill, Holland, Hoppe, Hunter, John, Krafft, Kuhne, Lake, Lange, Lowe, Ludwig, MacGraw, Mack, Martin, Mauck, Mayne, McDonald, Moro, Page, Peters, Reltz, Russel, Rose, Sander, Sauer, Schiller, Schmidt, Schmit, Schutt, Singer, Smith, Sommer, Steiger, Stone,

Stengel, Sweet, Thomas, Ulrich, Will, Wolf, Young, Ziegler and many others.[34]

Integration into the French-speaking Canadian population of so many Germans casts doubt upon the popular notion of homogeneity. As far back as June 1945, Gabriel Nadeau wrote in his memoirs of the French Canadian Genealogical Society:

> It is said, and perhaps rightly so, that we are the only people on earth who truly know our roots. But, while the origins of the French Canadian race have been carefully examined, we remain ignorant of the many other peoples, foreign and otherwise, whose blood has enriched ours for the past two centuries. For this reason, a myth has been perpetuated of a pure and homogeneous Canadian race which has remained so throughout its history. But this notion was only true during most of the French regime. There were many foreign elements added to the French in the past, and they have not ceased. (...) This commingling really began at the end of the French regime. Canadians had been a cloistered people up until then. Suddenly, a considerable number of men who were not from France were plunked down into their midst, and they had to deal with them. (...) Fortunately, most of these newcomers were men, so that the Canadians only had to give them spouses. For their own wives they could continue to choose women of their own blood, thus maintaining their racial purity for a while longer. But the idea of a pure French Canadian race as it is conceived today must be recognized as false when the various heteroethnic strains which compose it are known..." Then he adds, "There are almost no general studies on the Germans and the role they have played among us.[35]

Sadly enough, sixty years after Nadeau wrote that, practically no exhaustive studies have been conducted on the importance of the Germans, particularly the Brunswickers, to Quebec's heritage. Their importance does not stem merely from their numbers but from the class of immigrants that they were. In 1783 the Canadian population was largely uneducated; most of the intellectuals and merchants had departed after the French defeat of 1760. About eighty percent of the population was rural. One can well imagine, then, how the influx of qualified soldiers, with their wealth of experience gleaned through service in a highly disciplined army, affected the social and economic picture of the time. Army doctors, merchants of every kind, men from every craft and profession[36] musicians and heaven knows what else, all of with a vast military experience, held a variety of important posts and contributed to the development of Canada. Although so many of them settled in Quebec, their role is almost entirely unknown.

Several Brunswickers stood out in science andparticularly in medicin.[37] One of these was Friedrich Wilhelm Oliva. Born around 1749, he married Catherine Couillard des Islets on June 14, 1782; the couple had eight children. To quote Murray Greenwood, "During the American War of Independence, Friedrich Wilhelm Oliva served as surgeon major with the Fusilier Regiment Alt von Lossberg, lent to Great Britain. His army experience must have been highly beneficial to him professionally, for the German army suffered their fair share of wounds and injuries, as well as such diseases as scurvy, smallpox and dysentery. When the war ended, Oliva took up practice in St-Thomas-de-Montmagny but in 1792 he moved his family to Quebec where he practiced for the rest of his life."[38]

Like many of his fellow countrymen who also settled in Quebec, Oliva was a Catholic. He integrated the French-speaking society, not English, by marrying the daughter of the co-seignior of Rivière-du-Sud, Louis Couillard des Islets. Along with several of his fellow citizens, he signed the Loyalist Manifesto in 1794, drawn up in opposition to the French Revolution and to "wicked persons of evil intent" who might follow the same course. The manifesto exalted the British constitution and condemned the French leaders of the time.

Oliva seems to have been quite concerned about his patients' well-being, whatever their social class; he is known to have asked the authorities to delay sending an *habitant* to prison until the man was fully recovered from a serious case of dysentery. His medical theories, popularized largely through the memoirs of Philippe Aubert de Gaspé, seem to have been based on a healthy dose of skepticism concerning the orthodoxy of the day. Aubert de Gaspé, for instance, was himself vaccinated against smallpox at the age of five by Dr. Oliva. He wrote that the doctor pioneered in prescribing fresh air and daily exercise for those who suffered from smallpox or who had been vaccinated against it, as opposed to the traditional treatment consisting of heat and alcoholic beverages. According to Gaspé, Oliva said during a smallpox epidemic: "How fortunate people would be if they caught this disease in a forest, near a stream under the shade of a pine tree: 90 percent of them would probably recover." Although many people thought he was crazy, he prescribed ice-cold baths for the treatment of typhus fever, and apparently cured his son, Frédéric-Godlip, in this manner.

In 1788, Oliva was appointed to the first Medical Examiners Board for the Quebec region. This organization was created by law that year both in Quebec and Montreal, to oversee the practice of medicine and surgery. In his role as examiner, Oliva seems to have made a thorough study of the fundamental questions in medical therapy. We know, for instance, that when testing a certain Pierre Fabre dit Laterrière, he asked him neither to identify surgical instruments nor to describe the circulation of the blood, but to explain the differences between a patient as described in a medical textbook and a real bedridden one. In 1795, Oliva, along with James Fisher, John Mervin Nooth and George Longmore, was questioned by the Assembly about contagious diseases which ocean-going ships brought into the colony. That year, the Assembly voted a law authorizing the governor to quarantine any ships suspected of spreading contagion. Despite his many successes, Oliva was apparently a modest man. Unlike his colleagues, whose boastful advertising spoke grandly of their European training, Oliva opened his office in Quebec by means of an unpretentious announcement. For a doctor he displayed charming humility regarding nature's own curative powers. His death, wrote Aubert de Gaspé, "was an irreparable loss for the city of Quebec, where good doctors were few and far between."

Another Brunswicker also had a brilliant medical career. Dr Henry Nicholas Christopher Loedel began as a surgeon in Captain Lohneissen's company of Brunswick grenadiers. After the defeat at Saratoga, he was surgeon for Captain Hambach's company in the von Barner Light

Infantry Battalion. On July 21, 1783 he was released from duty by the German authorities and, despite his youth, quickly gained a reputation as a doctor and surgeon. An excellent article by Louis Richard in 1950 described the Loedel family's contribution to Canada.[39] On January 1 he joined the practice of the eminent Dr. Charles Blake, an Irish Protestant military surgeon who arrived in Canada during the war with the 34th Infantry Regiment of Ireland.[40] Upon leaving the army, Dr. Blake quickly earned an enviable reputation with his wealthy patients.

Both doctors' talents were soon recognized. Working together very actively, Blake and Loedel laid the foundations of their respective fortunes. The terms and conditions of their partnership were established in a contract dated April 30, 1787 and drawn up by Montreal notary J.-G. Beek, and stipulated that the doctors would share all assets, debts and profits with a two-thirds share going to Dr. Blake, who was doubtless the elder, more experienced partner, and one third to Dr. Loedel. In addition to practicing medicine, the two doctors were apothecaries, a sideline which proved most profitable.

Once his future seemed secure as Blake's partner, Dr. Loedel decided to settle down. On January 30, 1794, at Christ Church in Montreal, in an Anglican service performed by David Chabrand Delisle, Loedel wed Marguerite Gamelin. The bride was born in Montreal on October 22, 1762, the daughter of Pierre-Joseph Gamelin and Marie-Louise de Lorimier. Through his marriage, Loedel entered one of the most powerful merchant families in Montreal, with connections to the English establishment where three of the daughters were to find their husbands.

In 1771, Loedel's father-in-law was at the centre of considerable controversy when it was discovered that he was a member of a Masonic lodge, deemed incompatible with his position as church warden of Notre-Dame parish. The resulting brouhaha led Archbishop Briand to intervene and apparently persuade Gamelin to leave the Freemasons, since he continued to occupy the wardens' pew.[41]

Towards the end of the eighteenth century, the members of the medical profession began lobbying the government for some sort of protection from the growing number of quacks and unlicensed practitioners who were posing an increasing threat to public health.

On April 30, 1788, the Legislative Council passed Law George III, chap. 8, forbidding the practice of medicine and surgery in the province of Quebec, and of midwifery in Quebec and Montreal, to anyone not licensed by a competent examining board.

Dr. Loedel's partner, Dr. Charles Blake, along with Drs. Selby, Syrn, Bender and Jobert, was one of the first examiners and received one of the first licences. The very first licence issued by the commission was to Dr. Henry Loedel.

> We, whose names are hereunto subscribed, examining Commissioners appointed under an Act or Ordinance His Excellency the Governor and Council of the Province of Quebec, made and passed the thirtieth day of April in the twenty eighth year of His Majesty's Reign, intituled, 'A Act or Ordinance to prevent persons practicing Physic an Surgery within the Province of Quebec, and Midwifery in the Towns of Quebec and Montreal without license' do certify to His Excellency The Right Honorable Lord Dorchester, that we have examined Henry Loedel of the parish of St. Mary[42] in the District of Montreal, and find that he has been regularly bred to the profession of Surgery and Pharmacy or as an Apothecary, and Man-Midwife. (Signed) Chas.Blake
>
> Geo.Selby R.Sym X.Bender
> Jean-Bte Jobert
>
> We do certify that we were present at the examination for the said Henry Loedel. (Signed) Picotté de Belestre
>
> J.E. de Longueil
> J.Fraser
> Hertel de Rouville.[43]

A few years later, Loedel was himself an examiner on the commission. His name appears in this capacity in 1795, 1797, and 1798.[44]

In addition to the revenue from treating their wealthy patients, both Drs. Blake and Loedel received military pensions. At the time of his marriage, Loedel was "surgeon at the garrison hospital headquarters in Montreal."

About thirty years later, on July 22, 1813, he filed a complaint with the governor, claiming several months of back pay as a "hospital mate," at the rate of 7s. 6d. per day, and stating that he had been receiving this remuneration for several years from the "Agent for Army Hospitals" in England.[45]

Dr. Daniel Arnoldi, a contemporary of Loedel's in Montreal, paid tribute to his colleague's courage, recounting how, during a typhus epidemic at the end of 1799, when other doctors refused to help, Loedel did not hesitate to treat the soldiers and officers of the 41st Regiment who had contracted the disease, until he caught it himself. Dr. Arnoldi went on to say that Loedel was so ill with the fever that he nearly died. He convalesced very slowly, never fully recovering.[46]

On May 16, 1794, Drs. Blake and Loedel appeared again before Notary J.-G. Beek in Montreal to renew the terms of their contract. This time, they had equal shares in the partnership; everything was to be divided equally, apart from the half-pay that Blake received as army surgeon upon his retirement.

Their properties consisted of "a house at the water's edge" where Blake lived, "a house in the rue Notre-Dame" which was probably where Loedel lived with his wife and their five young children, and "a farm outside of Quebec." The new contract also listed money owing to the partners from 433 debtors, totally £2,681 55s. 11d., a princely sum in those days.

The list of debtors is very interesting. It reveals the quality of persons whom the two doctors treated or to whom they sold medication, and it also shows how their reputation had spread beyond the confines of Quebec. The list include patients from Johnstown in the U.S., from Michilimakinac, as well as from Kingston, Osmegatchy, Varennes, and other faraway places.

The man who owed them the most money—£126—was Sir John Johnson. Other names on the list included Alexander Henry, Miles McDonnell, the captain of Lord Selkirk from the Red River, Captain Fortune, Major Murray, William England, who owned the land where Montreal's General Hospital would later be built. Twenty-three doctors' names are also listed, along with clients from other walks of life: "William Smith, gardener," "Fynn, king's carpenter", "Simon, barrel-maker," "Abraham, the Jew, tailor," "Pickard, butcher," "Mr. Chewatt, surveyor," "Shiller, balliff," "John Jones, shoemaker," "John Long, publisher."[47]

In 1785, Dr. Blake had purchased four Negro slaves who, documents show, remained in his possession for many years. Given that, as we have seen, the two doctors divided all their goods equally, apart from

Blake's half-pay from the army, we may suppose that these slaves belonged half to Loedel too.[48] Did he use them? Their professional and business interests were so closely linked, and their personalities so similar, that the two partners forged ever closer ties of friendship and esteem. As time passed, their families preserved and extended these ties and the social relationships they engendered.

Loedel's fortune enabled him to educate his two eldest sons, Henry-Pierre and Pierre-Charles, in England. They both followed in their father's footsteps, studying medicine and surgery. They received their licences at the time of the continental wars. Soon both young men found themselves fighting against Napoleon in the English army.

Henry-Pierre, the elder brother, treated wounded artillerymen from the Duke of Wellington's forces at Waterloo on June 18, 1815.[49] Pierre-Charles graduated from the Royal College in London. In later years, he liked to tell his friends back home in Joliette how he was with Napoleon on board the "Northumberland," the ship that transported the French emperor to his final exile on St. Helena, and how he saw the emperor in the attitude in which history generally depicts him.

Upon returning to Canada, Henry-Pierre settled in Montreal, and Pierre-Charles in L'Assomption. Henry-Pierre, in addition to his practice, taught medicine and, along with Drs. Coldwell and Robertson, was among the founders of the English General Hospital in Montreal in 1819. These three doctors later co-founded the Faculty of Medicine at McGill University in Montreal, around 1823. Dr. Henry-Pierre Loedel died prematurely in 1825 after catching typhus fever, like his father, from patients he was treating at the general hospital.

Dr. A.-A. Foucher of Montreal, in a speech to the Second Congress of the Association of French-speaking Doctors of North America of which he was president, made the following remarks: [50]

> The regulations of the English General Hospital, founded in Montreal in 1819, contained the following decree in article 3, chapter 3: "Positions as doctors or surgeons are reserved for those who have obtained their diploma from a college or university within the British Empire." This stipulation effectively meant that locally-trained doctors would have no access to the hospital.

If on the one hand this meant that all doctors at the hospital would have received proper training, it also ensured that the fortunate few who were able to study abroad would be guaranteed places which their personal merit would not necessarily have obtained.

These remarks seem to be directed against doctors like the two Loedels, both of whom studied in England; but Dr. Foucher hastened to add:

> Nonetheless, the doctors at this institution have played such an important role in the history of medicine in this country that we must point out that these remarks do not apply to them.
>
> For we know that Drs.Coldwell, Robertson and Loedel taught medicine privately; they were the first doctors at the English General Hospital and later (in 1829) founded McGill University.[51]

Pierre-Charles Loedel settled in l'Assomption. On the eve of March 5, 1821, at the seigneurial manor in Lavaltrie, he married Marie-Antoinette Tarieu Taillant de Lanaudière, youngest daughter of the late Charles Gaspard de Lanaudière, seignior of Lavaltrie, and Suzanne-Antoinette Margane de Lavaltrie. He thus became the brother-in-law of Mr. Joliette, who married Marie-Charlotte Tarieu Taillant de Lanaudière, another daughter of the seignior of Lavaltrie.

Dr. Loedel's marriage was performed by the Anglican priest John Jackson, the minister of Christ Church in William-Henry, as Sorel was known then. The marriage was recorded by Father Jackson in the church register there.

Pierre-Charles Loedel and Marie-Antoinette de Lanaudière had a daughter who married Dr. Bernard-Henri Leprohon. Their son was Charles-Bernard-Henri Leprohon, former sheriff of Joliette.

John Justus Diehl[52] brother-in-law of Dr. Arnoldi, was a close friend of Drs. Blake and Loedel; he made them executors of his will. After his death, his young son, Pierre, served as apprentice to the two doctors, who then undertook to pay for his medical studies in Europe. They sent him to the University and Royal Infirmary in Edinburgh, Scotland. There he met Jacques Labrie of St. Eustache, who was then a student.

Diehl returned to Canada after graduation; in 1811, he became an examiner for the Montreal district. He joined the practice of his uncle,

Dr. Arnoldi, and the brilliant career which followed fully justified the encouragement he had received from Drs. Blake and Loedel, who had treated him like a son and to whom he was always grateful.[53]

Dr. Charles Blake died on April 22, 1810. His widow, Harriet Antill, remarried in 1814; her second husband was Bernard-Antoine Panet. The Blakes' daughter married Judge Thomas Cushing Aylwin.

On April 15, 1818, in recognition of his former militia service, Dr. Loedel received letters of patent from the government, granting him lot 11 of the fourth line and lot 11 of the fifth line of the township of Godmanchester in the county of Huntingdon, just north of the United States border. Situated to the north-west of the Châteauguay River, about half way between Dewitt and Huntingdon, these lots are crossed by a little stream which is still called the Loedel River on modern survey maps of the Ministry of Colonization of the Government of Quebec, although to the best of our knowledge no member of the Loedel family ever lived there.

Dr. Loedel's health remained shaky following his attack of typhus fever in 1799. On January 14, 1830, at about 7 in the morning, he suffered a stroke at his home on St. Urbain St. in Montreal. Despite the best medical attention, he died at about 2 p.m. the same day.[54] His funeral was held on January 20 and he was buried in Dr. Blake's vault in the Anglican cemetery of Montreal. He was said to be 75 years old. His death certificate was countersigned by his son Pierre-Charles and by his son-in-law, William Hall.[55]

His widow, Marguerite Gamelin, survived her husband by nine years, and spent her last years in Joliette, where she lived with her son, Pierre-Charles. She died on February 11, 1839, and was buried in the Church of St. Paulin de Lavaltrie on the south side in the nave, on the 15th. An inscription which still exists in this church recalls her memory.

As we have seen from the careers of Drs. Oliva and Loedel, the Brunswickers left us some excellent doctors. Auguste-France Globensky (Glaubenskindt) was another of them. Born in Berlin on January 1, 1754, he was the son of Joseph Globensky vel Glaubenskindt, whose origin was Polish, and of Marie Richter. He served as lieutenant surgeon in the Free Corps of Light Infantry of Hesse-Hanau. Soon after the war ended, he married Marie-Françoise Brousseau dit Lafleur de Verchères on February 23, 1784. The couple had sixteen children, ten sons and six daughters.[56] Jacques Prévost and Yvon Globensky provide some details on the life of their ancestor: "He was 30 at the time of his marriage at Verchères in 1784," writes Mr. Prévost. "He practiced medicine there for about ten years. During this period, he received a pressing invitation from his father to return to Germany. Globensky Sr., who was both wealthy and influential in Berlin, hired a ship's captain to go to Canada to bring back his son and daughter-in-law; but the latter refused to leave Canada."[57] A few years later, Auguste-France Globensky yielded to the entreaties of Father Mailloux and of the seignior Eustache Lambert-Dumont and settled in St. Eustache, where he was noted as an excellent doctor, according to one of his descendants, Yvon Globensky. Although few factual details about his career remain, the number of years he was in practice (36) shows the extent of his devotion to the people of St. Eustache until his death on April 19, 1830. His last words are said to have been, "I am not a Globensky, my real name is..." He died before completing the sentence. His confessor hastened to reassure those present that he was in reality much more than a simple Globensky, but that it was not within his power to disclose any more. If we consider that his father was secretary to the King of Prussia, says Yvon Globensky, that the Polish Prince of Locowitz attended his baptism and that in addition the family silver brought over from Germany shows the remains of a half-obliterated family crest, we arrive at the same conclusion as his confessor: Auguste-France was of noble, possibly even royal, birth.[58]

Like their Brunswick brothers Oliva, Loedel, and Globensky, other company surgeons helped advance their new country. Dr. Xavier Bender, surgeon-major with the Hesse-Hanau troops, became a member of the first Commission of Medical Examiners in the Montreal district in 1788;[59] Theodore Besserer, surgeon's mate of the Prinz Friedrich Regiment of Brunswick, practiced medicine at Château-Richer near Quebec and Sainte-Famille on the Île d'Orléans,[60] while another surgeon's mate named Conrad Just was a doctor and apothecary at Sainte-Famille.[61] As for Edmond von König, the ancestor of all the Konig/Koenigs in the Quebec region,[62] he was the second son of a baron, a

member of an influential Prussian family. He was discharged by the
German authorities in 1783; but in 1782, even before the fighting ended,
he married a French-Canadian girl, Marie-Louise Jean, with whom he
had eight children, five daughters and three sons. He settled in the
parish of Notre-Dame de Bonsecours de l'Islet, on the Lower St.
Lawrence, where no doubt he practiced medicine. The former lieu-
tenant-surgeon of the Prinz Friedrich Regiment died in this parish at
the ripe old age of 83.[63] Lastly, Dr. Charles Schiller of the Regiment von
Riedesel chose to exercise his skills as a doctor in the region of Sorel.[64]

There is very little documentation on the company surgeons who
remained in Canada after the war. But there is one very interesting
document which deserves mention. Entitled *List of Surgeons of the
Brunswick troops who are staying in Canada*,[65] it is of particular interest
because it gives an evaluation of each man and of his performance.

Regiments	Names	Remarks
Grenadiers	Loedel	A very skilled man of exemplary conduct, who speaks several languages and who works in the hospital in Montreal under Dr. Blake.
Prince Friedrich	Just and Besseres	We can praise their knowledge and skill, having had on numerous occasions proof of both.
Prince Friedrich	Dœren and Diller	They hold fine principles and have never been unwilling so that if they continue to apply themselves as they have done to date they would be very useful subjects.
Riedesel	Henckel	A very good subject with an irreproachable conduct and always tireless with his patients.
Grenadiers	Stein	A young man without much experience but whose assiduity augurs well for the future.

In science, Anthony von Iffland (1799-1876), son of a Brunswicker,
also founded Canada's first school of anatomy in Quebec City in
1822.[66]

Theodore de Pincier made another contribution to the field of civil engineering. Pincier was the natural son of the Duke of Brunswick and was nicknamed the "hermit of Sorel" because of the many disappointments he suffered. His background is related by Father Couillard Després in a history of Sorel.[67] "He was born in Saxony," recounts the abbey, "on July 8, 1750. His mother's husband, Captain de Martigny, committed suicide in a fit of jealousy; two years later she married a Frenchman, Georges-Henri de Pincier, who was a captain of the grenadiers with the German army. Pincier adopted the duke's son, gave him his name and brought him into his family. The future surveyor of Sorel owed his education and his advancement to this protector. He studied history, geography, mathematics, philosophy, civil engineering, the Talmud, Sanskrit, English, and French. When his studies were finished, he joined the army as a cadet in the first battalion of the Prinz Friedrich Regiment. He was made ensign on March 26, 1767. One day, in a rash moment, his mother decided to unburden her soul and revealed the secret of his birth. The young Pincier was so upset by the news that he resolved to leave his mother. He joined the troops bound for America. Not only was he determined never to see his mother again, according to his memoirs, but he never wrote to her either. He served in the English army during the American War of Independence." In a muster roll drawn up at Trois-Rivières on August 29, 1779, Théodore de Pincier's name appears as second lieutenant in Captain von Plessen's company from Lt. Col. Von Ehrenkrook's infantry battalion.[68] "When peace was concluded," continues Després, "he began to practice his profession. Colonel McDonnell recommended him to Sir John Johnson, 'the only rich American,' he said, 'who sided wholeheartedly with the king in the Revolutionary War.'

"With such a patron, he went to work for the government and surveyed several townships along the shores of Lake Ontario. In 1796 he was in Sorel. Robert Jones gave him the enormous task of surveying the seigniory. One by one he visited the wooded lands of Bellevue, Hunterville, Prescott, and Pot-au-Beurre. On June 12, 1772 he verified an earlier survey performed by Marcouillé, and on September 4, 1798 he checked the work of another surveyor named Daly. In his

memoirs, he gave many details which explain the difficulties encoun-
tered by surveyors in the performance of their duties. All his assist-
ants are named, with descriptions of their work methods..." These
men used to leave early in the morning, carrying their meals of bacon,
bread and biscuits. On November 5, they were only able to survey five
acres because they had to cut down some big trees which blocked the
road. The next morning, at dawn, they ate their frugal breakfast and
set to work. "There are only three axes," wrote Pincier; "we have to
cross some swampy ground covered with underbrush, tamaracks difficult to chop down because of their size. Our messenger arrived this
afternoon with five loaves of bread..." He described how he discovered
a lake about two arpents by six. "The water flows clear and trans-
parent, with no reeds. On our side the shore is low; alders grow all
about and there is a small beach overgrown with wild hay. On the far
side there's a hill that would be the perfect site for a house. Lots 38
and 39, which we have just marked out, will be the nicest concessions
in this seigniory." Després continues, "He went on to describe the
difficulties of getting to and from the camp, and of the rain and snow
which constantly forced them to interrupt their work...

"Later on Pincier was commissioned by Robert Jones to open a
road between the Cibouette River and Acton Township. Pincier had
received a fine education," says Després, "and he carried his observ-
ance of the rules of proper etiquette to an extreme. He felt, justifiably,
that notaries were in general too careless when drawing up contracts."
In a letter of December 24, 1806, "Pincier advised Robert Jones to
engage Mr. Henry Crebassa, a provincial notary who had just settled
in William-Henry" (the former name of Sorel). In the same letter, "he
outlined a proposal for colonizing the area. He suggested asking
the priests of Sorel and Berthier to spread some propaganda among
the Canadians, to draw them to lands which had not yet been
granted..."

According to Després, "Pincier recognized that Canadians were
excellent settlers and colonists" because of their "virtues of patience,
courage, and perseverance." Robert Jones' successor, John Kent Welles,
became his patron and employer. One day, Pincier recommended
"giving the name of St. George to the line situated behind the one called

Hunterville, in honour of the king. The governor, he added, is also named George, and Canadians always prefer to live under the patronage of a saint. I will offer the 80th line to His Excellency Governor Prescott, and I'll name it Prescottville..."

Towards the end of his life, Pincier ceased to admire the English. Since the government remained deaf to his pleadings, he turned to Seigneur Cuthbert of Berthier, begging him to intercede for him because of the many services he had performed. But help did not arrive soon enough, and in another letter he announced his intention of putting an end to his misery. This letter was in effect the last will and testament of the "hermit of Sorel." His last thought was for his mother. "This man," says Després, "had no faith, otherwise he would have endured his trials right until the end. He was a man of noble feelings, and proud enough to blush at having to ask for bread. At the end, burdened with illness, and despite the good advice of his friends, he killed himself in a moment of despair. He was 74."

A few of his friends recognized his good qualities nonetheless. Upon his death, Major Thomas Huxley gave the following order: "I humbly beg the commander of the garrison of William-Henry to allow his detachment to escort to the cemetery, with full military honours, the casket of a former lieutenant who served England for seven years with the troops from Brunswick, during the Revolutionary War of 1783. While granting this request, if the youngest officer should pick up the naked sword laid across the tomb, it will be a lasting reminder for him of the catastrophe which ended the sad life of Theodore de Pincier, the 'hermit of Sorel'." Pincier was buried in the Anglican cemetery on April 19, 1824.

Few Brunswickers or their descendants distinguished themselves in politics. Among those who did we find: Jean-Joseph Troestler, who was an M.P. for the county of York from June 1808 to October 1809,[69] and the son of Jean Georges Pozer,[70] Christian Henry Pozer, who represented the Beauce region in the House of Commons from 1867 to 1876 before becoming a senator.[71]

As for the arts, Friedrich Heinrich Glackemeyer, drum major of the "colonel" company of the Brunswick Regiment von Ehrenkrook, made a name for himself in Canada as a teacher, organist and music director. Later generations acknowledge him as the first professional musician in Canada. According to the biographical dictionary of Canadian musicians, "he was only five years old the first time his father placed a viola in his hands. He had a remarkably fine ear and a marvellous memory for sounds. It did not take long before he was able to play on his viola all the rnelodies he heard or read. His family was well placed in Hanoverian society. Young Glackemeyer quickly gained a reputation as a child prodigy and was in constant demand as a performer by the many people who wished to hear him play. His childhood was spent this way, right up until adolescence." He joined Riedesel's troops and subsequently taught music to the general's daughters. At the war's end, Riedesel granted him a discharge and a handsome sum of money, he also gave him an excellent recommendation and the possibility of returning to Germany as organist of Lauterbach. But Glackemeyer declined this generous offer, preferring to remain in the new world. He settled in Quebec City.

> He was welcomed by the cream of Quebec society. He immediately set himself up as a music teacher, and the students flocked to him. In addition to the viola and bass viol, he taught piano, though he seldom played that instrument.
>
> As a way of helping his students, and also out of professional interest, he began importing orchestral works and musical instruments. During 1872, the year following its creation (August 21, 1871), the Haydn Septet managed to locate and buy all this music. Since the lithography stones used for the impression of this music in Germany had been destroyed, these works can be found almost nowhere else in the world today, except for the collection deposited at Laval University in Quebec by the Haydn Septet. The collection is about 140 years old.
>
> In 1820 Glackemeyer was organist at the cathedral in Quebec and music director; he founded a musical society called the Harmonic Society of Quebec, and was its director and first president.
>
> He composed a number of unpublished works: March in Honour of the Battle of Châteauguay, dedicated to Colonel de Salaberry, etc.
>
> Lutheran by birth, Glackemeyer converted to Catholicism in order to marry Marie-Anne O'Neil in September 1784.[72]

Following a similar path, Francis Vogeler, fifer in the Prinz Friedrich Regiment, settled in Quebec where he taught music and sold instruments. In 1789, he imported three pianos for his customers.

Brunswickers also shone in other activities. Louis Chrétien Heer, George Rush, and Lt. Reineking made their mark as painters.[73] Another well known painter was Henry Ritter, son of a discharged German soldier, who was born in Montreal and later pursued his artistic studies in Dusseldorf and Hamburg. His magnificent seascapes were very popular in Germany.[74]

After the seventeenth century, geographical maps of Canada and North America were printed in Germany.[75] The art of modern printing—invented by the German Johann Gutenberg (1398-1468)—fascinated William-Edmond Blumhart, grandson of a Brunswicker. "Self-taught, enterprising and incredibly resourceful, at the age of forty W.-E. Blumhart became the secretary—and the son-in-law—of a very important man in Montreal: Louis Adelard Senecal."[76] In 1883, Blumhart became a correspondent for the Paris paper *L'Univers*, and his "letters on Canadian affairs" were highly appreciated. On October 15, 1884, he founded *La Presse*, which appeared for the first time on October 20. Over the years the paper grew highly successful, until it became the best selling French-language daily in North America.

German soldiers were also successful in business. Jean-Joseph Troestler,[77] a soldier in the corps of chasseurs of Hesse-Hanau is a good example. After the death of his first wife, Marguerite Noël, he acquired two concessions in Quinchien from Charles Vallé and his wife Magdeleine Bourcier, the property measuring three arpents wide by forty arpents deep. This transaction occurred on July 18, 1792. In 1794, the young German businessman married Marie-Anne-Joseph Curtius, who was eleven years his junior. "Troestler's establishment," according to Robert Lionel Séguin, "soon became one of the most popular west of the island of Montreal. He also ran a very profitable fur trade. On December 26, 1800, he purchased two building sites from Paul Petit dit Lamarche, in Vaudreuil, near the mill. Around the same time he built himself a spacious stone house which is quite rightly considered the finest in the entire region. The house is still in perfect condition today"[78] thanks to Louis and Judith Dubuc who restored it. This magnificent house, situated in the town of Dorion, was classified as a historical monument by the Canadian government in 1969 and by the Quebec government in 1976. It is 139 feet wide and 40 feet deep, and consists of three parts built respectively in 1798, 1805, and 1806. The year the house was completed, tragedy struck the Troestler famlly. Nine-year-old Michel-Joseph drowned accidentally near the family property; he was buried in Vaudreuil on August 8, 1806.

Not satisfied merely to reap the benefits of his business successes, Jean-Joseph Troestler began to take an interest in politics. On June 18, 1808, he was elected member for York, and held this post until October 2, 1809. At the height of his powers, he died at Vaudreuil on December 7, 1813, at the age of 56.

Another successful Brunswicker businessman was Christian Friedrich Heinemann, whose story is told by his descendant Pierre Heynemand in volume II of Father Floriant Aubin's history of the parish of St. Cuthbert.[79] Heinemann was sergeant major in Captain Schlagenteuffel's company of the von Rhetz Regiment from Brunswick. After the war, he played an important role in the parish of St. Cuthbert (Berthier county), where he might have spent a winter. At the age of 25, he and Ernst Harborth, a corporal from the same regiment, set up a general store known as Harborth and Heinemann. An article by another Brunswicker, John Justus Diehle[80] in the *Gazette de Québec,* of February 17, 1785, informs us that wheat, oats, and tobacco were used as legal tender. Despite the early break-up of the partnership (did Harborth die?), Heinemann carried on the business under his own name. By 1787, business was booming. Papers found by Pierre Heynemand give an excellent idea of the volume of sales: a mere supplementary order to finish the season consisted of a tun of rum, a butt of red wine, half a case of pipes, and fifty minots of salt,[81] as noted by Notary Faribault. According to Mr. Heynemand, the size of these orders, quite substantial for those times, suggests a German business network of which Heinemann was undoubtedly a member. Such a network would have been the peace-time equivalent of the well-organized system for distributing stores, arms, and clothing which was set up and run by the adjutants, quartermasters, company clerks and others who were responsible for the logistics of the German army during the seven years of the war. "The rapid development of our region, of the seigniory of Berthier and St. Cuthbert," writes Father Aubin, "is largely due to the expertise of talented men like Christian Friedrich Heinemann. The seigneur of Berthier and his heirs gave him the lifelong task of administering, developing and peopling their territory, which in those days encompassed all the lands between Lanoraie and Maskinongé, and from the St. Lawrence River to the Laurentians. It is not surprising that one line in St-Félix-de-Valois still bears his name: the Frederick line."

Other Brunswickers contributed to the growth of Canada in other ways. Albert Cleing/Kleing, Christian Cretschmann, Christophe Hartman, Adam Hoffman, John Iffland, Henry Riemenschneider and Conrad Weyand became tavern keepers,[82] while their comrade-at-arms, Charles Schneider, an innkeeper from Lachine, moved to Upper Vaudreuil and turned his large stone home into a hotel.[83]

Caspar Discher, Christian Gundlach and Jean Spath became bakers[84] Jacob Henckel/Inkel was a farmer in St-Philippede-la-Prairie, as was Peter Pfeiffer, but in addition he worked as a bailiff.[85] Carl Johann Ackermann, Jean Kielburg, Friedrich Lentze, Johann Christophe Müller and Michael Schloczmacher were shoemakers,[86] while André Heinllen, Georges Rath and Christian Schumpff/Jomphe made their contribution to their adopted land as tailors.[87] Conrad Christophe Beyer (Payeur), who was held in high esteem by his fellow citizens, was made Militia Captain of the St. Gilles company of the parish of St. Nicholas.[88] Anthony Wolmand became a tanner;[89] Augustus Welling, a customs officer;[90] William Vondenvelden, a printer and surveyor;[91] Henri Saillie, a blacksmith;[92] Jean Rullmann, a butcher;[93] Friedrich Gründler and Christophe Kreger, cabinet makers;[94] François Everhard, a schoolmaster;[95] Christophe Brandt, a wig-maker;[96] Henri Kremer/Cramer, a carter;[97] (Georg Conrad, Christopher Schaeffer and Georg Teffner, masons.')[98] And a letter dated October 1813 informs us that Friedrich, Baron Schaffalisky, A. Mucadelle, seigneur of Freudenthal, and lieutenant in the Corps of Chasseurs of Hesse-Hanau, fulfilled the duties of assistant barrack master in the year of our Lord, 1812.[99]

These examples give us an idea of the contribution of the Brunswickers to the people of Quebec and of all of Canada. Much

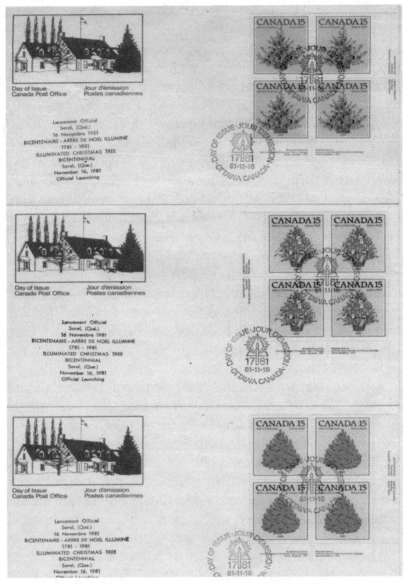

Stamps celebrating the bicentennial of the first Christmas tree illuminated in
Canada. Courtesy of Canada Post, Sorel, November 16, 1981.

work remains to be done, and it is to be hoped that future researchers will be able to shed more light on the important role the mercenaries and their descendants have played in Canada.

A very cherished tradition is the lighting of Christmas trees. But as we string lights around our Scotch pines or spruce trees each December, bringing joy to the hearts of young and old and uniting the generations in the annual ritual, how many of us stop to wonder where this tradition came from? Baron von Riedesel and his family had but recently moved into their new house in Sorel when the governor appointed him military chief of the entire region. That Christmas eve in 1781, the Riedesels decided to give a party for some of the English officers and other friends, to celebrate both their reunion and the holiday together. Out of consideration for the English officers, they served the traditional plum pudding; but in every other respect the atmosphere was distinctly German, with a marvellously illuminated pine tree dominating the room, to the great astonishment of the admiring guests. Baroness von Riedesel explained the meaning of the candle-lit tree with its decoration of various fruits, and then cookies and candies were handed around to the guests, in accordance with German tradition.[100]

This tradition took root thanks to the Riedesels and their guests. In 1981, to honour the bicentennial of the first illuminated Christmas tree in Canada, the minister of the Canadian Government responsible for the Post Office, unveiled three new stamps at the site of the Riedesels' tree; their home is known now as the "governors' house" in Sorel. Present at the unveiling were the German Consul, Madame Hélène Schoettle, the German-Canadian president of the Canada Council, Mr. Aksel Rink, the artist who designed the stamps, and many other guests. These stamps will broaden public awareness of the German—and particularly the Brunswicker—contribution to our country.

Notes

1. Samuel Eliot Morrison and Henry Steele Commager, *The Growth of the American Republic*, vol. 1, 229.
2. Max von Eelking, *Memoirs and Letters*, vol. Il, 174.
3. *Ibid.*, 175.
4. *La Gazette de Québec*, Aug. 1, 1782 - Dec. 31, 1787.
5. Max von Eelking, *Memoirs and Letters*, vol. 11, 181.
6. *Ibid.*, 182.
7. Major Baurmeister, *Confidential Letters and Journals*, 23.
8. Max von Eelking, *The German Allied Troops*, 259-260.
9. *Ibid.*, 260
10. *Ibid.*
11. Major Baurmeister, *op. cit.*, 22-23.
12. Max von Eelking, *op.cit.*, 255.
13. Herbert Wilhelm Debor, *German Soldiers of the American War of Independence as Settlers in Canada*, translated by Dr. Udo Sautter, 2.
14. *The Settlement of Former German Auxiliary Troops in Canada After the American Revolution*, Arlington, 1982, 223 pp.
15. Lowell, *The Hessians*, 291. Journal of the Grenadier Battalion von Platte. Eelking's "Hülfstruppen," vol.II, 253-255. Appendix D.
16. Friedrich Kapp, *Der Soldatenhandel*, 254. XIX, letter from Rotencreutz to Faucitt, State Papers Office, German State, vol. 109. 17. *Ibid.*, XIX, 254, letter from the Landgrave of Hesse-Cassel to the commander of the Hessian troops in America, library of the Historical Society of New York.
18. Virginia Easley DeMarce, *The Anhalt-Zerbst Regiment in the American Revolution*, VI.
19. Max von Eelking, *The German Allied Troops*, 253.
20. An *arpent* was an old French Canadian measurement roughly equal to an acre. As a unit of length, it equalled one side of a square arpent. A *sol* was a monetary unit equivalent to 1/20 of a pound.
21. Joseph Edmond Roy, *Histoire de la Seigneurie de Lauzon*, vol. III, 159-160.
22. Public Archives of Canada, *MG 21, Transcriptions*, Haldimand Collection, series B, vol. 152, 165-168. The style of the original has been preserved.
23. *Ibid.*, vol. 162, 353-354.
24. Eelking, *The German Allied Troops*, 259.
25. DeMarce, *The Settlement of Former German Auxiliary Troops*, 2. This regiment changed names three times, each time a new chief was named.
26. *Ibid.*, 8, 15.
27. Maxwell Sutherland, *"Case History of a Settlement,"* in Dalhousie Review, vol. XLI, spring 1961, 65-74.
28. Public Archives of Canada, *MG, 21, Transcriptions*, Haldimand Collection, series B, vol. 38, 15-16.
29. *Der deuische Pioner*, 13: 317-325, 360-367, 420-441, in Smith, *op. cit.*

28. Public Archives of Canada, *MG, 21, Transcriptions*, Haldimand Collection, series B, vol. 38, 15-16.

30. *Op. cit.*, 28-29.

31. *Op. cit.*, vol. III, 159-160.

32. Public Archives of Canada; Public Record Office archives in London, England; German archives; and lists of names indexed by Dr. Virginia Easley DeMarce in *The Settlement of Former German Auxiliary Troops* and by Herbert Wilhelm Debor in *German Soldiers of the American War*.

33. DeMarce, *op. cit.*, section III, "Annotations to the Lists", 48-50.

34. Public Archives of Canada, archives of the Public Record Office in London, England, German archives, see the muster rolls. Note: although these names belonged to one or several Brunswickers who immigrated to Canada, not everyone with one of these names is necessarily a descendant. For example, a mercenary named Gagné came to Canada at the end of the fighting, but not all the Gagné in Quebec today are his descendants.

35. Gabriel Nadeau, "L'apport germanique dans la formation du Canada français," in Mémoires de la Société généalogique canadienne-française, June 1945, vol. 1, no. 4, 274-277.

36. Public Archives of Canada, *MG21, Transcriptions*, Haldimand Collection, series B, vol. 151, 12. List of the professions of the Anhalt-Zerbst Regiment. Also in Otto Froelich, *Hetrina*, vol. II, III & IV.

37. In 1783 about 35 surgeons and surgeons' mates from the Brunswick and Hesse regiments immigrated to Canada. Herbert Wilhelm Debor, *The Cultural Contributions of the German Ethnic Group to Canada*, 65.

38. F. Murray Greenwood, "Oliva, Frédéric-Guillaume" in the *Dictionnaire biographique du Canada*, vol. 4.

39. Louis Richard, *Bulletin des recherches historiques*, vol. LVI, 1950, 78-89. The following pages on the Loedel family all come from this article, and all quotations marked (Richard) come from the same source.

40. Public Record Office, London, England; a memoir dated January 16, 1946 (Richard).

41. See Abbé Auguste Gosselin, *L'Église du Canada après la Conquète*, part 1, 1760-1775, 380-384. Also, Richard, *op. cit.*, vol. 26, 240.

42. Although the document speaks of "*the parish of St. Mary,*" what it really means is the district of St. Mary, since the only parish in Montreal at that time was Notre-Dame.

43. From a photocopy of the original published in *History of Medicine in the Province of Quebec*, Maude E. Abbotts, B.A., M.D., of McGill University, Montreal, 1931, p. 35 (Richard).

44. Lt. Col. D.-B. Papineau of Quebec City, one of Loedel's descendants, says that the doctor's name appears on a list of commissioners on Feb. 20, 1795 and again on Dec. 15, 1798 (Richard).

45. See the petition from Henry Loedel to His Excellency Sir George Prévost, dated July 22, 1813, preserved in the Public Archives of Canada in Ottawa (Richard).

46. See the statement by Dr. Arnoldi, dated April 1, 1830 and preserved in the Public Archives of Canada, series C206, 36 (Richard).

47. See Maude E. Abbott, *op. cit.*, 44-45 (Richard).

48. *Ibid.*, 45 (Richard).

49. Public Archives of Canada, series C207, 4. Also *La Gazette de Québec*, Nov. 28, 1825 (Richard).

50. Extract of a letter from Doctor Foucher to Canon François Régis Bonin, Oct. 4, 1929, communicated to Louis Richard in 1944 by Abbot O. Valois, secretary of the Historical Society of Joliette.

51. The Faculty of Medicine at McGill University was founded in 1823, not 1829 as mentioned here. Dr. Henry-Pierre Loedel barely saw the launching of this project on which he collaborated (Richard).

52. John Justus Diehl was the tailor who petitioned the governor for payment by the Chasseurs of Hesse-Hanau (see chapter 4) on Aug. 19, 1782. Public Archives of Canada, Haldimand Collection, series B, vol. 151, 307.

53. See Abbot, *op. cit.*, 45-46 (Richard).

54. See Dr. Arnoldi's declaration dated April 1st, 1830. Public Archives of Canada, Series C206, 36. Louis Richard.

55. The death certificate recorded in the register at Christ Church reads: "Henry Nicholas Christopher Loedel of Montreal Physician died on the fourteenth day of January One Thousand Eight Hundred and Thirty. Aged seventy five years, and was buried on the twentieth following by me, (Signed) B.B. Stevens Witnesses Present: (Signed) Wm. Hall Peter Charles Loedel" (Richard).

56. Globensky Yvon, *Histoire de la famille Globensky*, Montréal 1991, 414 pp.

57. Jacques Prévost, *Les Globensky au Canada français*, M.S.G.C.F., vol. XVII, 1966, 158.

58. Yvon Globensky, *La famille Globensky*, family edition, April 1982, Genealogical Society of Quebec, special volume I, 102 pp

59. Herbert Wilhelm Debor, *The Contributions of the German Ethnic Group to Canada*, 36.

60. Pierre-Georges Roy, *Les Besserer de la province de Québec*, B.R. H., vol. XXIII, 1917, 30-3 1.

61. Antoine Roy, *Rapport de l'archiviste de la province de Québec pour 1948-1949*, VG 1798.

62. Pierre-Georges Roy, *Le baron Edmond-Victor von König*, B.R.H., vol. XXIII, 1917, 316-317.

63. Capt.Maurice König, *La famille Koenig au Canada*, M.S.G.C.F., vol. XVI, 1965, 269-270.

64. Raymond Gingras, *Liste annotée de patronymes d'origine allemande au Québec et notes diverses*, "Schiller".

65. Public Archives of Canada, *MG 21, Transcriptions*, Haldimand Collection, series B, vol. 173, 119.

66. Herbert Wilhelm Debor, *op. cit.*, 38.

67. Abbé Couillard Després, *L'histoire de Sorel, de ses origines* à nos jours, 144-145. Also in Public Archives of Canada, *MG 24, C 22*, Théodore de Pincier Papers, 22 pp.

68. Public Archives of Canada, *MG 11, Colonial Office*, series Q, vol. 16, part 2, 486. Muster roll of the troops, Aug. 29, 1779.

69. Debor, *op. cit.*, 28-29.

70. The name was originally spelled Pfotzer, but in Quebec was changed to Pozer, Pauzé, Pausé or Poser. Although the name of Jean Georges Pozer figures in the list drawn up by Virginia DeMarce of German soldiers who immigrated to Canada, we are somewhat skeptical about this information.

71. Extract of *Rameaux de la famille canadienne*, at the Queen's Printer, Ottawa, 6, provided by Roger Gauthier, member of the S.G.C.F.

72. Extract from the *Dictionnaire biographique des musiciens canadiens*, 122-123, Glackemeyer, Frédéric- Henry (Hanover 1751-Québec 1836).

73. Antoine Roy, *op. cit.*, for Reineking; Virginia DeMarce for Rush, 180; Raymond Gingras for Heer.

74. Debor, *op. cit.*, 43

75. *Ibid.*

76. Cyrille Felteau, *La Presse, cahier du centenaire*, Montreal, Thursday, Oct. 20, 1983/100th year, no. 1, 3.

77. Robert Lionel Séguin, "L'apport germanique dans le peuplement de Vaudreuil et Soulanges", in *Bulletin des recherches historiques*, March 1951, vol. LVI 1, 56-58.

78. This spacious home graced the front cover of the 1980 telephone directory for the city of Montreal.

79. Abbé Florian Aubin, *La paroisse de St-Cuthbert*, 1765-1980, vol. II, 113-117.

80. Although there has been no study done on Diehl, there is every indication that he made an active contribution to his adopted country.

81. A minot was old measure of about 39 litres.

82. Antoine Roy, *op. cit.*, 1792 and 1798.

83. Robert Lionel Séguin, *op. cit.*, vol. LXIII, no. 1, 53.

84. Virginia Easley DeMarce, *op. cit*, for Discher and Gudlach; for Spath see Roy, *op. cit.*, 1792.

85. Roland Inkel, *Les familles Henckel-Inkel, 1378-1978*, family edition, 178 pp. and for Pfeiffer, Marcel Longpré de Saint-Jean-sur-Richelieu.

86. Roy, *op. cit.*, 1792.

87. *Ibid.*, for Rath; Schumpff, 1798; Heinllen, see DeMarce, *op. cit.*

88. Roland J.Auger, "L'ancêtre Conrad-Christophe Payeur (Beyer) in *"Mémoires de la Société généalogique canadienne-française"*, 32.

89. DeMarce, *op. cit.*

90. Roy, 1792.

91. *Ibid.*, 1795.

92. DeMarce, *op. cit.*

93. Roy, *op. cit.*, 1792.

94. DeMarce, *op. cit.*, for Gründler; for Kreger, see M.S.G.C. F., 1980, 286 (4296).

95. *Ibid.*

96. *Ibid.*

97. Roy, 1792.

98. *Ibid.*, for Schaeffer. For Conrad and Teffner, see DeMarce, *op. cit.*

99. E.-Z. Massicotte, *Le baron Schaffalisky*, B.R.H., vol .XXIX, 1923, 134-136.
100. *La Presse*, Nov.30, 1981, "The origin of the Christmas tree, a mystery to solve" by Jean-Pierre Wilhelmy.

CONCLUSION

To understand who the German "mercenaries" were, it is important to understand the era. The American Revolution was just beginning and the French Revolution was still fifteen years away. England lacked troops to uphold its authority over its American colonies. King George III, whose forefathers were German, had just learned that Catherine the Great of Russia refused to provide him the military support he needed. He therefore had to sign individual agreements with small German princes, who immediately sensed that they could make some quick money. The German princes therefore jumped at the idea of selling the blood and courage of their small armies, thereby replenishing their coffers and maintaining their courts, patterned after Versailles in France.

The revolution, which the first military encounter was expected to crush, continued nonetheless and required more and more soldiers. Since in most cases the princes' small armies had few "regulars," they used other methods to conscript soldiers. Force was not used at first. However as the King of England's needs grew and as the princes saw the money they could make, new ways were invented including getting peasants drunk or simply kidnapping healthy and able young men. The German army soon became a microcosm of the society from which it came, comprising career soldiers, bandits, and peasants, most of whom had no idea where they were being sent.

They found themselves in a distant land that they did not understand, mixing with the English, Aboriginal nations, and the local Canadian population (including some who wanted to join the rebellion to the south). These groups of people already had long-standing disputes about control of the land. As exiles, they had their own struggle against the isolation they experienced due to cultural, lin-guistic, and political differences.

This German army included people from all walks of life and some elements conducted a wide variety of exactions. Their commanding officer General Friedrich von Riedesel however was inspired by German discipline and justice and was known to have the Germans punished much more severely than the ordinary Canadians or Englishmen.

Other Germans sent directly to war against the Thirteen Colonies, particularly officers who saw this war as a stepping stone towards a higher rank and more prestige, found it difficult to fathom that a col-onial population would rise up against their king and break their own laws. One can therefore imagine the hate that inhabited these German officers and the actions they took, as well as the impact they would have on the American rebels, who saw in them as a bunch of ruffians inspired by Teutonic roughness and arrogance.

From the time of their arrival in 1776, the German mercenaries helped the British defeat the invading armies from the south. Not every soldier saw action, but their sheer numbers daunted the enemy and, for the British, definitely justified their use. During the 1777 campaign, they formed nearly half of Burgoyne's army (although few historians bother to mention this fact), and their performance was of the high level expected from them. Many other German soldiers were watching over the defence of Canada. Their participation was so sig-nificant that Haldimand once wrote to Lord Germain that his "English" army was for the most part German. This was the case for more than two years, from 1779 through 1781.

When winter quarters were first assigned, some problems arose between soldiers and civilians. Carleton and the senior English authorities were well aware of these problems, and deliberately used billeting as a way of punishing those Canadian *habitants* who were not actively supportive of the English cause. This situation fortunately changed with the arrival of the new governor Haldimand, and many close ties were forged between soldiers and *habitants*. The Germans so enjoyed the communal living with their Canadian hosts and host-esses that when the order was given to return to Germany many had already married Canadian girls and chose to settle in Canada.

During their years of service in Canada, the mercenaries were called upon to do the work of policemen and counterespionage agents. This led them to arrest many Canadian and American sympathizers and exposed them to the tongue-lashings of certain historians who, influenced by the Church or others, have spoken scathingly of the Germans as an "army of occupation" or denounced the way they "pressured the peasants." Owing to the lack of exhaustive research, these denunciations are still trotted out when reference is made to the mercenaries and their role.

Some of them did indeed perform unpleasant duties. Others helped rebuild defence works across the country, while still others manned the forts, rebuffing all kinds of attacks, and keeping the invaders at bay.

When the war ended, the many Germans who chose to remain in Canada were assimilated very quickly despite their large numbers. Their names underwent amazing transformations, until they so resembled existing French and English surnames that today very few of their descendants suspect that they have German ancestors. Many Brunswickers benefited from their military experience and lived active lives, greatly contributing to the growth of their new country. Others left traditions that have been so widely adopted that they are considered to be Canadian or Quebec traditions. Their most important contribution however lies in their sons and daughters, grandsons, and granddaughters who simply became part of the French or English-speaking peoples among whom they lived.

Thirty thousand of these German soldiers came to Canada, more than 10,000 lived in Canada for the seven years of the war, and 2400 saw it as a land of opportunity for themselves and their children and their children's children. Yet how many people in Canada, or better yet, how many of their own descendants know nothing of them and their story?

As generations succeed one another, their suffering and their dreams of freedom in a new land lie forgotten. New generations come to the fore who are unaware of the legacy of people whose names over time have been altered beyond recognition, of the country of their ancestors, and of their own roots. This book is a modest attempt to bring bring that legacy back to life.

Appendix A

THE GERMAN MILITARY
CORPS IN CANADA, 1776-1783[1]

As was customary at that time, the regiments of the Holy Roman Empire were differentiated not only by number but by name. They usually bore the name of their honorary "chief." But since he often performed many different functions within the regiment, not to mention other activities not connected with the regiment at all, he was sometimes unable to fulfil them all. In that case, responsibility for the regiment passed to a "commander"; and should he be unable to assume the role of leader (for instance, on a battlefield), the "field commander" would take charge of the regiment.

BRUNSWICK[2]
I - General Headquarters

As the name indicates, General Headquarters oversaw the movements of all the regiments.

The Field Officers of the Corps:

01. **Major General (commander) Riedesel, Frederick Adolphus**, died Jan. 6, 1800, as lieutenant general and commander of Brunswick.
02. **Captain (General Quarter Master) Gerlach, Heinrich** Jan., died Sept. 29, 1798, as lieutenant colonel and commander of the artillery in Brunswick.
03. **Captain O'Connel, Laurentius**, died in 1819, as a pensioned lieutenant colonel in Ireland.
04. **Lieutenant Cleve, Frederick Christian**, died Jan. 6, 1826, as a pensioned major general at Brunswick.
05. **Keeper of the military chest, Godeck, Johann Conrad**, died Dec. 25, 1782, in America.

II - Dragoon Regiment Prinz Ludwig

Raised in 1688, became a dragoon regiment in 1772. Arrived at Quebec, June 1, 1776, served in the Burgoyne campaign, 1777. Lost many men at Bennington, Vermont. Survivors returned to Canada where the regiment's size was strengthened by new recruits from Europe.

CHIEF: **Prince Ludwig, younger brother of the Duke of Brunswick**
COMMANDER: **Col. Friedrich Adolphus von Riedesel**
FIELD COMMANDER: **Lt. Col. Friedrich Baum**.

List of officers:

01. **Lieutenant Colonel Baum, Friedrich** wounded in the battle near Bennington, the 16 of August, 1777, and died two days afterward.
02. **Major von Maibom, Just.Christoph**, died Feb. 17, 1804, as a pensioned major at Wolfenbhttel.
03. **Cavalry officer, Schlagenteuffel III**, Carl, dismissed from the service in 1788.
04. **Cavalry officer, Fricke, Heinrich Christian**, died July 3, 1808, as a pensioned major.
05. **Cavalry officer, Reinking, Carl Friedrich**, killed on August 16, 1777, in the battle near Bennington.
06. **Cavalry officer, Schlagenteuffel IV (Adolph)**, dismissed by request from the army in 1783, as major.

07. **Lieutenant Breva, August Wilhelm**, died the August 16, 1790, as captain of the invalid company at Blankenburg.
08. **Lieutenant von Sommerlatte**, Otto Arnold, became blind in 1783, and placed on the pension list.
09. **Lieutenant Reckrodt, Carl Friederick**, deserted from Wolfenbüttel on August 13, 1784.
10. **Lieutenant von Bothmer, Friederich Wilhelm Dietrich**, dismissed, at his own request, in 1783, with the rank of horse-breaker.
11. **Lieutenant Bornemann, August Friedrich Heinrich**, dismissed in 1788; entered the service of Holland, and died in India.
12. **Cornet Gräfe, August Ludwig Lucas**, remained in America in 1783, by permission; returned in the following year to Germany, and died as governor of Mecklenburg-Strelitz.
13. **Cornet Stutzer, Johann Balthasar**, died on November 29, 1821, as a pensioned lieutenant colonel in Brunswick.
14. **Cornet Schönewald, Johann Friedrich**, died July 5, 1826, with the same rank.
15. **Chaplain Melsheimer, Carl,** deserted from his regiment on May 11, 1779.
16. **Auditor Thomas** remained in America in 1783 by permission.
17. **Regimental Chaplain Vorbrodt**, pensioned in 1783.

III - Regiment Prinz Friedrich (Musketeers)

Raised in 1683, the regiment was divided into two battalions in 1770. The second battalion took the name Regiment Prinz Friedrich in 1776. Arrived at Quebec on the evening of June 1, 1776; during the Burgoyne campaign spent some time at Fort Ticonderoga. Returned to garrison in Canada. A small detachment from the regiment accompanied Burgoyne to Saratoga.
CHIEF: **Lt. Gen. Prince Friedrich August, youngest brother of Karl Wilhelm Ferdinand**
COMMANDER: **Maj. Gen. Eckhard H. von Stammer**
FIELD COMMANDER: **Lt. Col. Christian Julius Prätorius**
List of officers:
01. **Lieutenant Colonel Prätorius, Christian Jullus**, died April 10, 1794, as a pensioned lieutenant colonel at Holzminden.
02. **Major Hille, Freidrich Wilhelm**, died April 29, 1805, as a major general, and named commandant of Wolfenbüttel near Brunswick.
03. **Captain Dietrich, Adolph Lorenz**, died March 10, 1794, as lieutenant colonel at Wolfenbüttel.
04. **Captain Tunderfeld, Carl August Heinrich**, died June 4, 1802, as chamberlain of Brunswick.

05. **Captain Sander, Jacob Christian**, died March 14, 1799, as lieutenant colonel at Wolfenbüttel.
06. **Captain Rosenberg, Friedrich Albrecht**, dismissed at his own request, in 1788, as major.
07. **Captain Zielberg, George Ernst**, died out of service at Horter, Feb. 23, 1797, as captain.
08. **Lieutenant Schröder, Ernst Christian**, pensioned in 1783, and died the same year.
09. **Lieutenant Knesebeck, Friedrich**, dismissed in 1783.
10. **Lieutenant Volkmar, Friedrich Wilhelm**, dismissed in 1783.
11. **Lieutenant Harz, Johann Friedrich**, succeeded in 1787, to the post of secretary of the monastic archives.
12. **Lieutenant Wolgart I, Johann Friedrich**, died Oct. 2, 1825, as a pensioned lieutenant colonel at Brunswick.
13. **Lieutenant Reitzenstein, Gottlieb Christian**, remained in America in 1783 by permission.
14. **Lieutenant Burghoff, Johann Friedrich Heinrich**, dismissed in 1780, in America, and died the same year.
15. **Lieutenant du Roi, August Wilhelm**, after serving the house of Brunswick faithfully for over fifty years, drowned himself in a fit of melancholy, March 23, 1814. At the time of his death he was commissary general, and lieutenant colonel on the general staff.
16. **Lieutenant Wiesener, Christian Friedrich**, discharged in 1783.
17. **Lieutenant von König, Edmund Victor**, remained in America in 1783 by permission.
18. **Ensign Langerjahn, Siegfried Christian**, deserted from his regiment in 1780.
19. **Ensign Adelsheim, Carl Friedrich Christian**, deserted from his regiment in 1780.
20. **Ensign Sternberg, Johann Christian**, died Nov. 16, 1799, as secretary of supplies, at Wolfenbüttel.
21. **Ensign Reinerding, Carl Wilhelm**, died March 14, 1815, as head chamberlain in the service at Blankenburg.
22. **Ensign Kolte, Friedrich**, remained in America in 1783 by permission.
23. **Chaplain Fügerer, Friedrich August**, dismissed in Oct., 1779.
24. **Chaplain Schrader, Friedrich Wilhelm Conrad**, sent in April, 1779, to America with recruits; died Dec. 19, 1792, as pastor at Beierstedt.
25. **Auditor Wolpers, Paul Gottfried Franz**, died May 11, 1802, as chancery clerk at Wolfenbüttel.
26. **Regimental Chaplain Bernt, Johann August**, died Feb. 27, 1807, as city surgeon at Holzminden.

IV - Musketeer Regiment von Riedesel

Raised in 1683, renamed Regiment von Riedesel in 1776. Arrived at Quebec on June 1, 1776, participated in the battles at Ticonderoga, Hubbardton, Freeman's Farm, Bemis Heights and Saratoga.

CHIEF: **Maj. Gen. Friedrich Adolphus von Riedesel**

FIELD COMMANDER: **Lt. Col. Ernst Ludwig W. von Speth**

List of officers:

01. **Lieutenant Colonel Speth, Ernst Ludewig Wilhelm**, died Oct. 27, 1800, as major general and commandant at Wolfenbüttel.
02. **Major Mengen, Otto Carl Anton**, died May 18, 1797, as lieutenant colonel, (retired from service), at Luneburg.
03. **Captain Pöllnitz, Julius Ludwig August,** died March 29, 1805, as major general and commandant at Wolfenbüttel.
04. **Captain Morgenstern, Carl Friedrich**, received his discharge as major in 1817.
05. **Captain Bartling II, Carl Friedrich**, died in 1783, at Munster while on his return journey to Brunswick.
06. **Captain Harbord, Gottlieb Benjamin,** died as a pensioned captain.
07. **Captain Girsewald, Ernst Heinrich Wilhelm**, died Jan. 16, 1818, in time of peace as a major general at Brunswick.
08. **Lieutenant Hoyer, Wilhelm**, died in 1782, in America.
09. **Lieutenant Morgenstern, Johann Carl**, died Dec. 8, 1787, at Brunswick as captain.
10. **Lieutenant Reinking, Friedrich Carl**, died as captain of a regiment.
11. **Lieutenant Burgdorff, Ludwig Traugott**, dismissed in 1786.
12. **Lieutenant Wolgart II, August Theodore Gottfried**, died March 4, 1821, as a pensioned major at Brunswick.
13. **Lieutenant Freyenhagen, Heinrich Julius**, died in 1777.
14. **Lieutenant (de)Pincier, Christian Theodore**, received his discharge in 1784, and returned to America.
15. **Lieutenant Cramm, Heinrich Wilhelm Gottfried**, died Feb. 3, 1784, at Mäestricht.
16. **Lieutenant Meyern, Ludwig Gottlieb**, died 1781, in America.
17. **Ensign Brander, Ernst Christian Heinrich**, dismissed in 1786.
18. **Ensign Unverzagt, Ludwig**, died in 1776, in America.
19. **Ensign Maibom, Carl Christoph**, died April 26, 1794, upon his return journey from Mäestricht to Holzminden.
20. **Ensign Häberlin, Raimund Gottlieb**, died Oct. 6, 1796, at Helmstedt as captain.

21. **Ensign Andree, Carl Conrad,** died as a lieutenant of a regiment.
22. **Ensign Denecke, Friedrich Ludwig,** unknown.
23. **Ensign Forstner, Heinrich Friedrich,** dismissed in 1794.
24. **Chaplain Milius, Johann August,** died Jan. 17, 1819, as pastor at Salder.
25. **General Field Auditor Zinken, Carl Friedrich Wilhelm,** died in the night of August 3, 1806, as counsellor and mayor of Seefen.
26. **Regimental Chaplain Pealle,** died a country surgeon at Jerrheim.

V - Musketeer Regiment von Specht

Raised in 1714, became the Regiment von Specht in 1770 after the Regiment von Rhetz was divided into two battalions. Arrived at Quebec in September 1776, participated in the battles at Ticonderoga, Hubbardton, Freeman's Farm, Bemis Heights and Saratoga.
CHIEF: **Col. Johann Friedrich von Specht**
COMMANDER: **Maj.Karl Friedrich von Ehrenkrook**
List of officers:

01. **Colonel Specht, Johann Friedrich,** died June 24, 1787, at Brunswick as a pensioned colonel.
02. **Major Ehrenkrook, Carl Friedrich,** died July 17, 1797 as a pensioned major in Brunswick.
03. **Captain Plessen, Leopold Franz Friedrich Balthasar,** died Feb. 6, 1808, as captain (retired from military service), at Gandersheim.
04. **Captain Lutzow, August Conrad,** died Nov. 26, 1799, at Brunswick as colonel.
05. **Captain Dahlstirna, Bernhard Rich,** wounded on the 7th Oct., 1777, at the battle of Freeman's Farm, and died the following year in the city of Albany.
06. **Captain von Schlagenteuffel II, George,** died August 15, 1818, as high bailiff at Schöppenstedt.
07. **Captain Yager, Heinrich,** died in 1782, in America.
08. **Lieutenant Meyer, Johann Heinrich,** died Oct. 23, 1800, as postmaster of Helmstedt.
09. **Lieutenant Hertel, Daniel Arnold,** died August 1, 1799, as a pensioned lieutenant at Königslutte.
10. **Lieutenant Papet I, August Wilhelm,** died July 25, 1808, at Brunswick as colonel.
11. **Lieutenant Dove, Heinrich Anton David,** died in 1780, in America.
12. **Lieutenant Milkau, Christian Friedrich,** discharged in 1783.
13. **Lieutenant Oldekopf, Friedrich Ernst,** created secretary in the post office in 1784, and died while holding that position.

14. **Lieutenant Anniers I, Heinrich Daniel**, discharged in 1783.
15. **Lieutenant Kellner, Johann Friedrich Julius**, died November 30, 1808, as commissioner of a monastery at Brunswick.
16. **Lieutenant Roi II, Anton Adolph Heinrich**, died August 19, 1823, at Brunswick, as a pensioned colonel.
17. **Lieutenant Unger II, Friedrich Bodo**, died Nov. 11, 1819, as a magistrate of Salzgitter.
18. **Ensign Bernewitz, Johann Heinrich Carl**, died Dec.13, 1821, as lieutenant general and commandant of Brunswick.
19. **Ensign Redeken, Friedrich**, died in 1777, in America.
20. **Ensign Fromme, Johann Edmund**, died May 8, 1822, at Wolfenbüttel, as a pensioned major.
21. **Ensign Ulmenstein, Samuel Jacob Anton**, died July 9, 1793, a pensioned lieutenant.
22. **Ensign Grimpe**, died as collector of the public gates of Brunswick.
23. **Chaplain Kohle**, unknown.
24. **Chaplain Münchhoff**, unknown.
25. **Auditor Bähr**, unknown.
26. **Regimental Chaplain Bause, Johann Carl**, died Dec. 15, 1814, at Brunswick, as general field surgeon, retired from military service.

VI - Regiment Von Rhetz (Musketeers)

Raised in 1748, divided into two battalions in 1770. The first is named von Rhetz, the second, von Specht. Arrived at Quebec in September 1776, fought at Ticonderoga, Hubbardton, Freeman's Farrn (two companies), Bemis Heights and Saratoga.

CHIEF: **Maj. Gen. August Wilhelm von Rhetz**
FIELD COMMANDER: **Lt.Col.Johann G. von Ehrenkrook**
List of officers:

01. **Lieutenant Colonel Ehrenkrook, Johann Gustavus**, died March 22, 1783, at Trois Rivières in Canada.
02. **Major Lucke, Balthasar Bogislaus**, died as a pensioned major.
03. **Captain Schlagenteuffel I, Ludewig**, placed on the pension list in 1783, and died the same year at Calvörde.
04. **Captain Alers, Conrad Anton**, died Oct. 17, 1810 as major (retired from service), at Brunswick.
05. **Captain Arend, George Philipp**, died Dec. 10, 1803, as lieutenant colonel (though retired from service), and high bailiff at Kl.Biewende.
06. **Captain Cleve, Heinrich Urban**, died Jan. 2, 1808, as lieutenant colonel (retired from service), at Salzgitter.

07. **Captain Fredersdorff, Wilhelm Ludwig**, wounded Oct. 7, 1777, in the battle of Freeman's Farm, and died the following year in the city of Albany.

08. **Lieutenant Bodemeyer, Georg**, died in 1793, at Mäestricht, as captain.

09. **Lieutenant Papet II, Friedrich Julius**, died April 5, 1793, as captain, at Mäestricht.

10. **Lieutenant Hessler, Curt,** discharged in 1783, with the rank of captain.

11. **Lieutenant Meyer, Friedrich Leopold Engelhard**, died Dec. 6, 1802, as inspector of excise at Seefen.

12. **Lieutenant Bielstein, Thedel Wilhelm,** remained by permission in America in 1783.

13. **Lieutenant Conradi, Carl Friedrich**, took his discharge in 1783, and went back to America.

14. **Lieutenant Dobeneck, Hans Philipp Heinrich**, died in 1796, as captain of a land regiment at Holzminden.

15. **Lieutenant Petersen, Carl Ludwig**, died May 7, 1814, as a civil magistrate.

16. **Lieutenant Modrach, Christian Heinrich**, died Aug. 18, 1803, as captain of a land regiment at Bevern.

17. **Lieutenant Unger I, Johann Ludwig**, died May 2, 1805, as counsellor of mines at Salzliebenhalle.

18. **Lieutenant Feichel, Friedrich Wilhelm,** died May 29, 1793, at Brunswick, as captain.

19. **Ensign Bandel, Friedrich**, deserted from his regiment in 1779.

20. **Ensign Frich, Bernhard**, received his discharge in 1783.

21. **Ensign Bode, Johann Friedrich**, died Sept. 19, 1783, at Stade, while on his return from America.

22. **Ensign Gödecke, Johann Heinrich**, transferred to a regiment of the line in 1788.

23. **Chaplain Tögel, Christian Timotheus**, died Oct. 1, 1797, as pastor at Great Twülpstedt.

24. **Auditor Schmidt**, transferred in 1783 to the regiment Riedesel.

25. **Regimental Chaplain Schrader, Johann Friedrich**, died Dec. 16, 1804, at Brunswick.

VII - Grenadier Battalion von Breymann

Raised in 1776, composed of one company from each of the infantry regiments. Arrived at Quebec, June 1, 1776, and in the following months took part in battles at Ticonderoga, Hubbardton, Bennington, Freeman's Farm, Bemis Heights and Saratoga.

CHIEF: **none**

COMMANDERS: **Lt. Col. Heinrich C. von Breymann, Lt. Col.Otto C.A. von Mengen**

List of officers:

01. **Lieutenant Colonel Breymann, Heinrich Christoph**, killed Oct. 7, 1777, in the battle of Freeman's Farm.
02. **Captain Bärtling I, Ernst August**, died Jan. 1, 1793, as lieutenant colonel and commander of a battalion in Mäestricht.
03. **Captain Löhneysen, Albrecht Daniel**, died May 2, 1820, upon his estate at Nemlingen.
04. **Captain Schick, Gottlob Dietrich**, killed August 16, 1777, in the battle near Bennington.
05. **Captain Hambach, August Wilhelm**, dismissed in 1783.
06. **Lieutenant Uhlig, Heinrich Wilhelm**, advanced to captain and transferred to a land regiment in 1783.
07. **Lieutenant Gebhard, Theodore Friedrich**, died June 3, 1810, in Brunswick as a pensioned lieutenant colonel.
08. **Lieutenant Helmecke, August Wilhelm**, dismissed in 1783.
09. **Lieutenant Trott, Christian Wilhelm;** likewise dismissed in 1783.
10. **Lieutenant Rudolphi, Otto Heinrich**, died June 3, 1810, in Brunswick as a pensioned lieutenant colonel.
11. **Lieutenant Wallmoden, Gebhard Thedel**, Friedrich, died Sept. 2, 1807, as major, retired from service.
12. **Lieutenant Muzell, Ludwig Casimir**, died July 28, 1814, as a pensioned colonel of the cavalry of his Serene Highness, Prince George of Brunswick, at Glücksburg.
13. **Lieutenant Meyer, Johann Andreas**, unknown.
14. **Lieutenant Meyern, Johann Jacob**, died July 3, 1802, as captain and chief of the invalid company at Blankenburg.
15. **Lieutenant D'Anniers II, Carl Franz**, died in 1777, while a prisoner at Bennington.
16. **Lieutenant Winterschmidt, Gottfried Jul**, deserted from his battalion in 1779.
17. **Lieutenant Balke, Johann Casper**, died in America in 1777.
18. **Regimental Chaplain Henkel**, died in America in 1778.

VIII - Light Infantry Battalion von Barner

Raised in 1776, composed of the first battalion of Brunswick chasseurs plus light infantry companies from each of the other Brunswick regiments. Arrived at Quebec in September 1776, took part in battles at Ticonderoga, Hubbardton, Freeman's Farm, Bemis Heights and Saratoga

CHIEF: **none**

COMMANDER: **Maj. Friedrich Albrecht von Barner**

List of officers:

01. **Major Barner, Ferdinand Albrecht**, died Oct. 2, 1797, as a pensioned colonel.
02. **Captain Thomä, Georg Ludewig**, died Jan. 10, 1800, at Wolfenbüttel, as captain, retired from service.
03. **Captain Geyso, Carl**, discharged in 1783, as major.
04. **Captain Dommes, August Friedrich**, died in the night of Jan. 5, 1807, as chief commissary at Blankenburg.
05. **Captain Schottelius, Maximilian Christoph Ludwig**, died Dec. 3, 1807, as postmaster at Holzminden.
06. **Captain Gleissenberg, Gottlief Joachim**, died Feb. 20, 1801, as colonel and commandant at Wolfenbüttel.
07. **Lieutenant Hannemann, Johann Caspar**, died as a forest ranger.
08. **Lieutenant Cruse, Philipp Sigesmund**, died as captain in the line.
09. **Lieutenant Kotte, Johann Gottfried**, died in 1776, at Quebec.
10. **Lieutenant Rabe, Albrecht Christian**, died Oct. 18, 1806, as a lieutenant at Königslutter, retired from service.
11. **Lieutenant Gladen, Johann Gottlieb**, died Dec. 14, 1827, at Wolfenbüttel as a pensioned major.
12. **Lieutenant Mühlenfeldt, Carl Anton Ludwig**, killed Aug. 16, 1777, in the engagement near Bennington.
13. **Lieutenant Pflüger, Johann Friedrich**, died in 1777, in America.
14. **Lieutenant Meyer, Andreas**, died Dec. 7, 1795, at the ducal castle at Salzdahlum.
15. **Lieutenant Fricke, George Friedrich Gebhard**, died Nov. 19, 1807 as postmaster at Goslar.
16. **Lieutenant Bode, Johann Andreas**, killed the 7th Oct., 1777, in the battle of Freeman's Farm.
17. **Lieutenant Rohr, Caspar Friedrich**, discharged in 1783.
18. **Ensign Rhenius, Wilhelm Lucas**, died Sept. 30, 1783, at Drangstedt, on his return home from America.
19. **Ensign Specht, Johann Julius Anton**, remained by permission in America, in 1783.

20. **Ensign Begert, Johann,** drowned in 1777, in America.
21. **Ensign Hagemann, George Leopold**, killed August 16, 1777, in the engagement near Bennington.
22. **Ensign Count von Rantzau, Ernst August**, drowned in a schoolyard, while in captivity.
23. **Regimental Chaplain Kunze,** died as a pensioner.

IX - Regiment von Ehrenkrook

Raised in 1778 from the survivors of the Saratoga campaign, and disbanded in November 1781 when the men returned to their original regiments.
CHIEF: **none**
COMMANDER: **Col.Johann Gustavus von Ehrenkrook**

X - Regiment von Barner

Raised in 1778 from survivors of Saratoga and new European recruits, did garrison duty in Canada until the end of the war.
CHIEF: **none**
COMMANDER: **Lt. Col. Ferdinand A. von Barner**

XI - Battalion of Major de Lucke

Raised in New York from survivors of Brunswick regiments in 1781, disbanded upon arrival in Canada in November 1781.
CHIEF: **none**
COMMANDER: **Major de Lucke**

Hesse-Hanau[3]
I - The Hesse-Hanau Regiment (Grenadiers)

Also known as the first battalion of the crown prince, since its chief was Prince Wilhelm of Hanau, eldest son of the Landgrave of Hesse-Cassel and next in line to the throne there as well. Arrived in Quebec on June 1, 1776, took part in the fighting at Ticonderoga, Freeman's Farm, Bemis Heights and Saratoga. Accompanied by the Hesse-Hanau Artillery Company which acquitted itself gallantly during the Battle of Lake Champlain (Valcour Island). After the defeat of Saratoga, one detachment under Capt. Schoell returned to Canada; in 1782 Prince Wilhelm converted it to the Hesse-Hanau Battalion.[4]

CHIEF: **Count of Hesse-Hanau, Wilhelm IX, Erbprinz (crown prince) of Hesse-Cassel.** COMMANDER: **Col.Wilhelm R. von Gall.**
FIELD COMMANDER: **Lt.Col.Johann Christophe Lentz.**
ARTILLERY COMMANDER: **Capt.Georg Pausch.**
List of officers:
01. **Major Luis von Passern**
02. **Major Heinrich Martens**
03. **Capt. Friedrich August von Schacht**
04. **Capt. August Friedrich von Germann**
05. **Capt. Carl August Scheel**
06. **Capt. Friedrich Ludwig von Schoell**
07. **Capt. von Buttlar**
08. **Capt. Friedrich von Geismar**
09. **Capt. Georg von Schoell**

II - Free Corps of Chasseurs of Hesse-Hanau

Recruited in the forests of Europe, this elite corps enjoyed special status because its services were in such demand. Not only were they paid better than most other German soldiers, but the chasseurs were also exempted from all paramilitary duties. The corps, consisting of four companies, arrived in Canada at the end of the spring of 1777, except for Lt. Hildebrandt's company which arrived several months before the others. It was sent to Fort Stanwix. In 1779, another company under Capt. Hugget, arrived to join the others. Their lifestyle was so similar to that of the habitants and Indians of Canada that almost half of these men elected to remain here after the war.
CHIEF: **none**
COMMANDER: **Lt. Col.Carl A. von Kreutzbourg**
Partial list of officers (for complete list, consult Marburg Rep. 15 A, no.205, Library of Congress):
01. **Capt. Hermann Albrecht von Francken**
02. **Capt. Philipp Jacques Hildebrand**
03. **Capt. Ludwig Carl, Count von Wittgenstein**
04. **Capt. Sigmund Hugget**
05. **Capt. Carl Wilhelm Castendyck**
06. **Capt. Adolph Neuburg von Leth**
07. **Capt. Caspar Heinrich Kornrumpff**
08. **Ensign Friedrich von Schaffalisky**
09. **Lt.Wilhelm von Denvelden** (author of the petition to obtain crown lands at Barford and Hinchinbrook, 1800)

Anhalt-Zerbst[5]
The Princess of Anhalt's Regiment

Arrived at Quebec, end of May 1778, forced to spend three months on board ship before being allowed to land by Canadian authorities who had not been officially informed of its arrival. Did not participate in any important battles, did garrison duty in Canada until returned to Germany, summer 1783.
CHIEF: **Princess of Anhalt.**
COMMANDER: **Col. Friedrich von Rauschenplatt**
Other officers:

01. **Maj. Johann Georg von Rauschenplatt**
02. **Capt. Carl Friedrich von Piquet**
03. **Capt. Zacharias Keppenau**
04. **Capt. Joseph Gogel**
05. **Capt. Prince August Wilhelm von Schwarzenburg-Sondershausen**
06. **Capt. Adolph von Wietersheim**
07. **Adjutant of artillery h.q. - Lt.von Möhring**
08. **Adjutant of the first battalion - Lt.Littchau**
09. **Adjutant of the second battalion - Lt.Vierermal**
10. **Quartermaster Pahnier**
11. **Company surgeon - Dr.Pakendorff**
12. **Chaplains: Braunsdorf, Naumann, Backer**

Hesse-Cassel[6]
I - Fusilier Regiment Alt Von Lossberg

Arrived at New York, August 1776, fought at Fort Washington and White Plains. Surprised by rebels at Trenton. Survivors put into combined Regiment von Loos for 1777 Philadelphia campaign. Divided into two battalions in December 1777, reassumed former name upon return to New York in 1778. Sent to Quebec, September 1779. Storm at sea caused great losses, forcing regiment to turn back to New York. May 1780, sent to Canada where they spent the war until returned to Germany.
CHIEF: **none**
COMMANDER: **Col.Johann August von Loos**
Other officers:

01. **Lt. Col. Franciscus Scheffer**
02. **Major Ludwig August von Hanstein**
03. **Capt. Ernst Eberhard von Altenbockum**
04. **Capt. Johann Caspar Reitz**

05. Capt. Friedrich Wilhelm von Benning
06. Capt. Adam Christoph Steding
07. Capt. Constantin von Wurmb
08. Lt. Friedrich Wilhelm Krafft
09. Lt. Georg Christoph Kimm
10. Lt. Georg Wilhelm Hille
11. Lt. Ludwig Wilhelm Keller
12. Lt. Ernst Christian Schwabe
13. Lt. Ernst Wilhelm von Wintzingerode Lt. Jacob Piel
14. Lt. Hermann Henrich Georg Zoll
15. Lt. Wilhelm Christian Moeller
16. Lt. Christian August von Hoben
17. Lt. Henrich Reinhard Hille
18. Lt. Ludwig von Gluer
19. Cadet Franz Friedrich Grebe
20. Cadet Henrich Carl von Zengen
21. Cadet Friedrich Christoph Hendorff
22. Cadet Christian von Waldschmidt
23. Cadet Georg Henrich Kress
24. Cadet Johann Henrich Rathmann
25. Cadet Erns Christian von Hoenningen

II - Fusilier Regiment von Knyphausen

Same history as the Regiment Alt von Lossberg, except that this regiment
returned to the United States in October 1781. Spent the winter in Halifax
before going back to New York.
CHIEF: **Lt. Gen.W.von Knyphausen**
COMMANDER: **Col.Heinrich von Borck**
Other officers:
01. Lt.Col. Friedrich Ludwig von Minnigerode
02. Major Carl Friedrich von Dechow
03. Major Johann Friedrich von Stein
04. Capt. Georg Wilhelm von Loewenstein
05. Capt. Berthold Helfrich Schimmelpfennig
06. Capt. Jacob Baum
07. Lt. Christoph Philipp Reuffurth
08. Lt. Andreas Wiederholk
09. Lt. Johann Nicolaus Vaupel
10. Lt. Henrich Friedrich Zinck

11. Lt. Christian Sobbe
12. Lt. Johann Friedrich Wilhelm Briede
13. Lt. Wilhelm Ludwig von Romrodt
14. Lt. Joachim Hieronymus von Bassewitz
15. Lt. Ernst Philipp Wilhelm Heymel
16. Lt. Carl Ernst Fuehrer
17. Lt. Wener von Ferry
18. Lt. Ludwig Ferdinand von Geysow
19. Cadet Carl Friedrich Fuehrer
20. Cadet Anthon Adolph August von Lutsow
21. Cadet Wilhelm von Drach
22. Cadet Henrich Christoph Zimmerman
23. Cadet Henrich Ritter

III - Garrison Regiment von Stein/Seitz/Porbeck[7]

This regiment changed names three times during the war. Arrived in New York, October 1776, fought at Fort Washington, sent to Halifax in September 1778 where the unit spent the rest of the war, returning to Germany in 1783.
CHIEFS: **Col.F.C.E. von Seitz - Col.F. von Porbeck**
COMMANDERS: **Col.Ludwig von Schallern, Lt.Col.Arnold Schlemmer - Lt.Col.C.von Kitzel**
Other officers:

01. Major Carl Wilhelm Graff
02. Capt. Friedrich Platte
03. Capt. Johannes Neumann
04. Capt. Johann Christoph von Ende
05. Capt. Johann Georg Langenschwartz
06. Capt. Andreas Sandrock
07. Capt. Wilhelm Bode
08. Lt. Carl von Romrodt
09. Lt. Christian Jacob Muench
10. Lt. Peter Bruebach
11. Lt. Johann Erich Vilmar
12. Lt. Wilhelm Justi
13. Lt. Andreas Oelhans
14. Lt. Johann Heinrich Henckelmann
15. Lt. Engelbrecht von Freyden
16. Lt. Arnold von Lahrbusch
17. Lt. Johannes Knies

18. **Cadet Berhard Stunz**
19. **Cadet Georg Albus**
20. **Cadet Georg Heinrich Fenner**
21. **Cadet Reinhard Jungk**
22. **Cadet Adolph Christoph Vieth**

IV - Various Regiments from Hesse-Cassel (Recruited 1781-1783)[8]

Several recruits destined for the United States stayed, for one reason or another, in Halifax and the surrounding region during the last two years of the war. They were under the command of Col. Hatzfeld and Capt. von Münchausen.

Notes

1. Charles M. Lefferts, *Uniforms of the 1775-1783 American, British, French and German Armies in the War of the American Revolution*, Old Greenwich, Conn.; WE Inc., 276-278.
2. Eelking, *Memoirs and Letters, vol. II*, 265-273.
3. German, American, English and Canadian archives.
4. Public Archives of Canada, *MG 21, Transcriptions, Haldimand* Collection, series B, vol. 81, Pt. 2, 86. Letter of July 9, 1782, Adjutant-General to Loos.
5. Max von Eelking, *The German Allied Troops*, 237-238. German and Canadian archives.
6. Otto Frölich, programme HETRINA, vol. II, Marburg, 1974.
7. Otto Frölich, programme HETRINA, vol. II, Marburg, 1974.
8. *Ibid.*

Appendix B

THE NAMES AND COMPANIES OF
THE REGIMENTS OF THE GERMAN CORPS[I]

I - BRUNSWICK

1. REGIMENT PRINZ LUDWIG
A- Colonel company of Prince Ludwig
B- Company Maj. Gen. von Riedesel
C- Company Lt. Col. Baum
D- Company Maj. von Meibom

2. REGIMENT PRINZ FRIEDRICH
A- Colonel company of Maj. Gen. von Stammer
B- Company Lt. Col. Praetorius
C- Company Maj. von Hille
D- Company Capt. Dieterichs
E- Company Capt. Tunderfeld

3. REGIMENT VON RIEDESEL
A- Colonel company of Maj. Gen. von Riedesel
B- Company Lt. Col. Speth
C- Company Maj.v on Mengen
D- Company Capt von Pöllnitz E-Company Capt. Morgens

4. REGIMENT VON SPECHT
A- Colonel company of Colonel Specht
B- Company Maj. Ehrenkrook
C- Company Capt. de Plessen
D- Company Capt. von Lutzow
E- Company Capt. von Dahlstierna

5. REGIMENT VON RHETZ

A- Colonel company of Maj. Gen. von Rhetz
B- Company Lt. Col.von Ehrenkrook
C- Company Maj. de Lucke
D- Company Capt. von Schalenteuffel
E- Company Capt. Alers

NOTE: By the end of the war, there was a significant increase in the number of officers using the "von", sign of nobility.

6. REGIMENT VON BREYMANN

A- Company Lt. Col. Breymann
B- Company Capt. von Bartling
C- Company Capt. von Lohneissen
D- Company Capt. von Schieck

7. LIGHT INFANTRY BATTALION VON BARNER

A- Colonel company of Maj. von Barner
B- Chasseur company of Capt. Schottelius
C- Chasseur company of Ewald Richzet
D- Company Capt. Thomae
E- Company Capt. Geisau
F- Company Capt. Dommes

8. REGIMENT VON EHRENKROOK

A- Colonel company
B- Company Capt. Zielberg
C- Company Capt.v on Schlagenteuffel
D- Company Capt.v on Plessen

9. REGIMENT VON BARNER

A- Colonel company
B- Company Capt. on Hambach
C- Company Capt. von Rosenberg
D- Company Capt. Thomae

II - HESSE-HANAU

1. Hesse-Hanau Regiment (First Battalion Erbprinz)

A- Colonel company of Col. von Gall
B- Company Lt. Col. Lentz
C- Company Maj. Martens

D- Company Capt. von Buttlar
E- Company Capt. von Passern
F- Company Capt. von Schachten
G- Company Capt. von Schöll
H- Company Capt. Schell
I- Company Maj. von Germann
J- Company Lt. Col. Prince Friedrich
K- Artillery company Capt. Georg Pausch

2. Free Corps of Chasseurs

A- Colonel company of Lt. Col. von Kreutzbourg
B- Company Maj. von Franken
C- Company Capt. Count of Wittgenstein
D- Company Capt. Hugget
E- Company Capt. Kastendyck
F- Company Capt. Hildebrandt

III - ANHALT-ZERBST
PRINCESS OF ANHALT'S REGIMENT

A- Colonel company of Col. von Rauschenplatt
B- Company Maj. von Rauschenplatt
C- Company Maj. von Piquet
D- Company Capt. von Wietersheim
E- Company Capt. Prince August Schwartzburg-Sondershausen
F- Company Capt. Gogel
G- Artillery company
H- Chasseur company Capt. Nuppenau
I- Chasseur company Lt. Jaritz

IV - HESSE-CASSEL

1. Regiment Alt von Lossberg

A- Bodyguards
B- Company Lt. Col./Col. Franziscus Scheffer2
C- Company Capt /Maj. Ernst Eberhard von Altenbockum
D- Company Maj. August von Hanstein/Capt. Friedrich Wilhelm Krafft
E- Company Heinrich Anton von Heringen, Col./ Maj. Gen. Johann August von Loos

2. Regiment von Knyphausen

A- Bodyguards
B- Colonel company David Ephraim von Gose/Col. Karl Philipp Heymel
C- Colonel company Karl Philipp Heymel/Maj. Karl von Wurmb
D- Company Maj./Col. Erasmus Ernst Hinte
E- Company Capt./Maj. Christian Mortiz von Kutzleben

3. Regiment von Stein/von Seitz/von Porbeck

A- Bodyguards
B- Company Col. Franz Kar Erdm, von Seltz, Maj./Lt. Col. Ludwig von Schallern
C- Company Col. Arnold Schlemmer, Lt. Col./Col. Karl von Kitzel
D- Company Col. August Ernst Wilhelm von Schreyvo-gel Lt. Col. Karl von Kitzel/Capt. Friedrich Platte/Capt. Johann Christoph von Ende, Capt./Maj. Johann Georg Langenschwartz
E- Company Lt. Col. Wilhelm Graf/Maj. Johannes Neumann

Notes

1. German, English, American and Canadian archives.
2. A / indicates a change in the company's commander or his rank, or the company's name.

Appendix C

ORGANIZATION OF THE HESSIANS
IN THE U.S.A.

The Hessians left for America at the same time as the first division of Brunswickers. They passed Sandy Hook on August 15, 1776 and landed at Staten Island on the 22nd. There were 8,000 men under Lt. Gen. Philip von Heister, divided as follows:[1]

Commander of the first Hessian division: Lt Gen. Philip von Heister

01. Lieb Infantry Regiment, Col. F. W. von Wurmb
02. Fusilier Regiment Erbprinz, Col. F. von Hachenberg
03. Musketeer Regiment Prinz Carl, Col. J. W. Schreiber
04. Fusilier Regiment von Ditfürth, Col. on Bose
05. Musketeer Regiment von Donop, Col. D. von Gosen
06. Fusilier Regiment von Lossberg, Col. von Lossberg
07. Fusilier Regiment von Knyphausen, Col. von Borke
08. Musketeer Regiment von Trhmbach., Col. E. von Bischhausen
09. Musketeer Regiment von Mirbach, Col. Loos
10. Grenadier Regiment von Rall (Rhall), Col. von Rall
11. Ist battalion of Grenadiers von Linsingen, Lt. Col. von Linsingen
12. 2nd battation of Grenadiers von Block, Lt. Col. von Block
13. 3rd battalion of Grenadiers von Minnigerode, Lt. Col. von Minnegerode
14. 2 companies of chasseurs
15. 3 artillery companies, Col. Hans H. von Eitel

The second division, 3,997 men under Lt. Gen. Wilhelm von Knyphausen, landed near New Rochelle. This division was composed as follows:[2]

Commander of the second Hessian division: Lt. Gen. von Knyphausen

First brigade: Col. von Lossberg
Regiments:
01. von Huyn
02. von Stein
03. von Knyphausen
04. Grenadier Battalion Köhler

Second brigade: Maj. Gen. Schmidt
Regiments:
01. von Lossberg
02. von Wissenbach
03. von Bhnau
04. Grenadier Battalion Köhler

This second division of Hessians left Hesse-Cassel in early May, along with the 3rd Waldeck Regiment (670 men) and the second chasseur company under Capt. Ewald.

Notes

1. Charles M. Lefferts, *op. cit.*, 263.
2. *Ibid.*

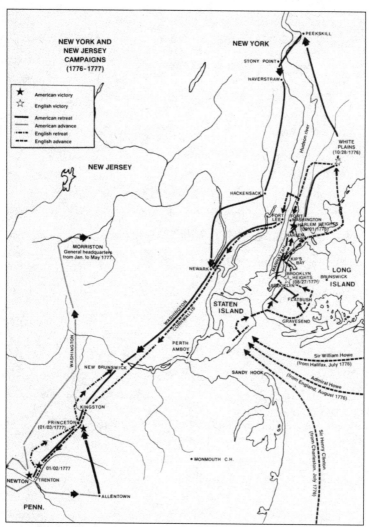

American Campaign.
Map by Jean-Pierre Wilhelmy based on *The American Heritage Pictorial Atlas of U.S. History.*

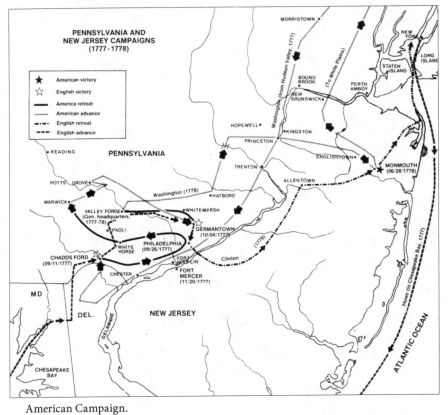

American Campaign.
Map by Jean-Pierre Wilhelmy based on *The American Heritage Pictorial Atlas of U.S. History.*

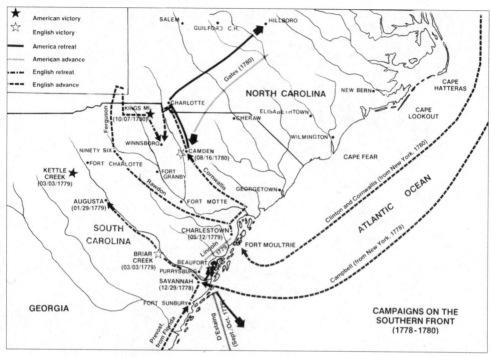

American Campaign.
Map by Jean-Pierre Wilhelmy based on *The American Heritage Pictorial Atlas of U.S. History.*

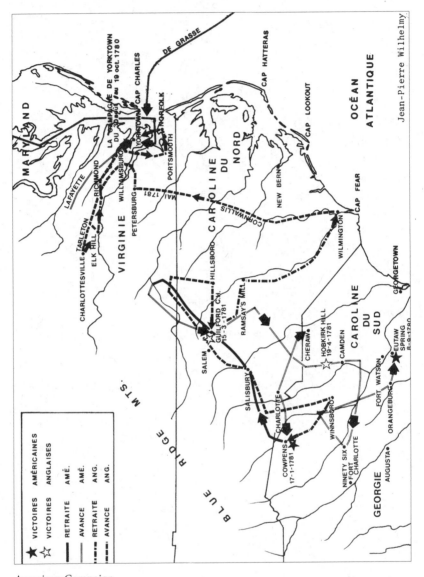

American Campaign.
Map by Jean-Pierre Wilhelmy based on *The American Heritage Pictorial Atlas of U.S. History.*

Appendix D

LIST OF THE MERCENARIES' PROFESSIONS

Businessmen	Carters	Haulers
Apothecaries	Cabinetmakers	Potters
Surgeons	Coopers	Shoemakers
Mechanics	Roofers	Tailors
Clockmakers	Glue makers	Butchers
Painters	Powder makers	Gardeners
Sculptors	Rangers	Millers
Masons	Cloth makers	Bakers
Stonecutters	Drapers	Dyers
Horse grooms	Serge makers	Tobacconists
Blacksmiths	Weavers	Cauldron makers
Locksmiths	Cloak makers	Tool grinders
Nail makers	Button makers	Chaplains
Brush makers	Chamois makers	Cooks
Pewterers	Comb makers	Tanners
Tinsmiths	Bonnet makers	Needle makers
Carpenters	Wig makers	Hatters

The Riedesel house in Sorel where the first Christmas tree was illuminated by Baroness von Riedesel on December 25, 1781. Photo: Jean-Pierre Wilhelmy.

The Jean-Josepht Troestler house. Photo published by Kent Inc. The house was built in three stages (1708, 1805, and 1806) and has been classed as a historic monument. It is located on chemin de la Commune, in Vaudreuil-Dorion and is the finest monument left by on the the German "mercenaries."

Appendix E

LIST OF THE MERCENARIES
BY COUNTRY OF ORIGIN

Austria
Belgium
(Austrian Low
Countries)
Brandenburg
(outside East
Germany)
Canada
Denmark
Spain
France
Great Britain

Hungary
Ireland
Iceland
Switzerland
Czechoslovakia
(Bohemia and
Moravia)
Italy
Luxemburg
Norway
Holland
Poland

Pomerania
(outside East
Germany)
Portugal
East Prussia
Germany
Silesia
Sweden
Countries from the
former U.S.S.R.
United States
West Indies

Grenadier from Hesse-
Hanau, drawn by Jean-Pierre
Wilhelmy from the original
Embleton/Osprey.

Musketeer from the Anhalt-
Zerbst Regiment, drawn by
Jean-Pierre Wilhelmy from the
original Embleton/Osprey.

Appendix F

GENERAL DESCRIPTION OF THE GERMAN UNIFORMS WORN IN NORTH AMERICA, 1776-83[1]

"(...) German coats were made of coarse, heavy blue wool, lined with a slightly lighter-weight red wool. Buttons were plain brass or pewter. As with British coats, the wool was heavy enough for the coats to be unhemmed. They were usually made without collars, the cuffs, the single shoulderstrap on the left shoulder, and the lapels being made of a facing colour cloth – red, yellow, white, black, or orange. Garrison regiments, of which Hesse-Cassel sent four, had no lapels but small, turn-down collars of the facing colour. Collars were also used by some regular regiments, as well, and exact cuff designs differed from state to state, and from regiment to regiment. Wool lace, sometimes plain and sometimes with a woven design, was used by some but not all regiments.

An important feature of the German coat was the shortness of the sleeves, which exposed a great deal of shirtsleeve. Frederick of Prussia[2] thought such short sleeves made his men look taller.

The shirt was white linen, made without a collar. The black or red stock, depending on the regiment, had a white strip along its top to look like the top of a shirt collar. Waistcoats and breeches were of white or pale yellow wool, again depending on the regiment, with the breeches tied at the bottom rather than buckled or buttoned like British ones. In the field in Canada, Germans cut up old tents and made long gaitered trousers which were more comfortable than breeches. In the winter in New York both Germans and British received similar gaitered trousers made of blue, green, red, and brown wool. Otherwise, thigh-length black linen gaiters, fastened with plain brass buttons, were worn over shoes, stockings, and breeches.

Dragoon from the Regiment
Prinz Ludwig (Brunswick)
drawn by Jean-Pierre Wilhelmy
from an original of Embleton/
Osprey.

Footsoldier of the
3rd Waldeck Regiment
drawn by Jean-Pierre
Wilhelmy from an original of
Embleton/Osprey.

Sergeants had their uniforms laced with silver, and carried halberds. Spontoons, much like British ones but elaborately engraved, were carried by officers. Officers were also set apart by their large, ornate gorgets, often enamelled with different colours, worn usually under their coats. Officers had sashes of different colours, often in stripes, according to their states. Boots, rather than gaiters, were preferred by officers.

German and British regiments had many weapons and accoutrements in common because of their shared Hanover heritage. The German musket, a copy of the Prussian one, was also of 0.75 calibre, pin-fastened, with brass furniture. Slings were of red-dyed leather, buckled at both ends. Unlike British troops, all ranks of German regiments carried short, brass-hilted hangers, mostly like the so-called pattern 1742 of the British. These were carried in black scabbards worn on a white waistbelt which was fastened with a frame brass buckle. Buckles were often false, the clasp inside the frame being what actually fastened the belt. Waterbottles were the same as those of the British.

From his left shoulder the German carried his cartridge box on an extremely wide whitened leather sling. The box was equally large, usually bearing his prince's cypher on a large oval pewter plate fastened to the flap's centre. A small pocket on one end held the musket-pick.

From his other shoulder he slung his knapsack, a hairy cowhide affair closed with three buckles and leather straps. It was carried on a plain brown strap with a brass buckle to adjust its length and worn on the centre of the chest.

Battalion men wore cocked hats bound with white wool tape like the British, but usually with different coloured pompons worn over the black cockade and at the edge of the left cock. Small pewter or brass-fronted caps, like those of British light infantry, bearing the prince's cypher, were worn by battalion men in fusilier regiments. Grenadiers wore much larger metal-fronted caps, with a worsted tassel on top and a bag of the regimental facing colour showing from the back. On fatigue duty, it would appear, they wore wool caps quite similar to those worn by the French in the last war.

Although German-made uniforms were quite good, the troops, when in the British service, were to be supplied by the British government, and quality was much poorer. Lapels were often simply pieces of coloured wool sewn down, in contrast to the German types which could be buttoned across the chest for warmth. One shipment of shoes sold to a German regiment turned out to be nothing but ladies' slippers."

Corporal in the corps of
chasseurs of Hesse-Cassel,
drawn by Jean-Pierre
Wilhelmy from an original
of Embleton/Osprey

Soldier with the 1st Anbach-
Bayreuth regiment, drawn by
Jean-Pierre Wilhelmy from an
original by Foncken/Casterman

GERMAN UNIFORMS DURING THE AMERICAN REVOLUTION[4]
(Canada and the United States)
Hesse-Cassel

	Coat	Collar and cuffs	Lapels	Buttons	Button-holes	Vest and breeches	Hats or caps
Du Corps	blue	yellow	yellow	white	white	yellow	Silver fusileer caps
Erb Prinz	blue	crimson	crimson	white	plain	white	Silver fusileer caps
Prinz Carl	blue	red	red	gilt	yellow	white	Hat bound white
Dittfurth	blue	yellow	yellow	white	white	white	Hat bound white
Donop	blue	straw	straw	gilt	plain	straw	Hat bound white
Lossberg	blue	orange	orange	gilt	plain	white	Brass fusileer caps
Knyphausen	blue	black	black	gilt	plain	straw	Brass fusileer caps
Trümbach	blue	white	white	gilt	plain	white	Hat bound white
Mirbach	blue	red	red	white	white	white	Hat bound white
Rall	blue	red	red	gilt	plain	straw	Brass fusileer caps
Wutgenau	blue	red	none	gilt	plain	straw	Hat bound white
Wissenbach	blue	white	white	white	plain	white	Hat bound white
Huyne	blue	yellow	yellow	white	plain	blue	Hat bound white
Büneau	blue	crimson	crimson	white	plain	blue	Hat bound white
Stein	blue	orange	orange	white	plain	blue	Hat bound white
Chasseurs à pied	green	crimson	crimson	gilt	plain	green	Hat bound black
Chasseurs montés	green	crimson	crimson	gilt	plain	green	Hat bound black
Corps d'artillerie	blue	crimson	crimson	gilt	plain	straw	Hat bound white

Hesse-Hanau

	Coat	Collar and cuffs	Lapels	Buttons	Button-holes	Vest and breeches	Hats or caps
Regiment Erprinz	blue	red	red	white	plain	yellow	Silver fusileer caps
Artillery Corps	blue	red	red	gilt	plain	white	Hat bound white
Corps of chasseurs	green	crimson	crimson	gilt	plain	green	Hat bound black

Ansbach-Bayreuth

1st regiment	blue	red	red	white	plain	white	Hat bound white
2nd regiment	blue	black	black	white	plain	white	Hat bound white
Corps of chasseurs	green	red	red	gilt	plain	white	Hat bound black
Artillery Corps	blue	crimson	crimson	gilt	plain	white	Hat bound white

Waldeck

3rd infantry	blue	yellow	yellow	gilt	plain	white	Edged with wide yellow scallop

Anhalt-Zerbst

Infantry Regiment	white	red	red	gilt	plain	white	Hat bound white

Brunswick

Dragoon Regiment	blue	yellow	yellow	white	plain	yellow	Hat bound black with white feather
Grenadier Battalion	blue	yellow	none	white	plain	white	Silver fusileer caps
Prince Friedrich	blue	yellow	none	white	plain	white	Hat bound prince white
Von Riedesel Infantry	blue	yellow	yellow	white	plain	white	Hat bound white
Von Specht Infantry	blue	red	red	gilt	plain	white	Hat bound white
Von Rhetze Infantry	blue	white	white	gilt	plain	white	Hat bound white
Light Infantry Batt.	blue	black	none	gilt	plain	white	Hat bound white
Yager Company	green	red	red	white	plain	green	Hat bound chas- black

Artillery officer from
Hesse-Cassel drawn by
Jean-Pierre Wilhelmy
from an original by
Embleton/Osprey

Chasseurs of Hesse-Hanau[3]

The chasseurs, sometimes called Jaegers or Feldjaegers, were men recruited from the forests, used to hunting, and armed with short, European rifles, firing large balls. As the rifles were made by individual gunsmiths, not according to set patterns, they differed in detail. Generally, however, they were three feet ten inches long, with a wooden patchbox, pin-fastened, and made with brass furniture. The rifles took no bayonet so the Jaegers carried short, straight-bladed hunting swords. Game wardens, foresters or simple hunters, they shared the honour of belonging to the elite of the British army in North America.

Oddly, for men whose main duty would be in woods, their cocked hats had brims cut much larger than those of battalion men. Otherwise the Jaegers were rather sensibly dressed in dark green coats. Facings and linings were red, although those of Hesse-Cassel were crimson, while those of Brunswick were plain red with green linings. Details such as waistcoat, breeches, and gaiter colour would also differ from state to state. Their sergeants had gold lace on their cuffs and a white feather topped red on their hats, while officers had gold lace both on lapels and cuffs and a plain white feather.

Both mounted and foot Jaegars units were used in America, both originally wearing tall boots. Boots were pretty uncomfortable to wear when on foot in America, and most foot Jaegars switched to long brown or grey linen gaiters and often to gaitered trousers made from ld tents.

He Jaeger coat was cut similar to all German coats, which were largely based on those worn n the Prussian Army.

Notes

1. Philipp Katcher, *Armies of the American Wars, 1753-1815*, Hasting House Publishers, New York, Germans and Provincials 1775-1783, 65-69.
2. Frederick II of Prussia's army set the pace in military questions in the German Empire.
3. Philip Katcher, *Armies of the American Wars, 1753-1815*, Hasting House Publishers, New York, Germans and Provincials 1775-1783, 65-69.
4. These tables come from Lieutenant Charles M. Lefferts, *Uniforms of the 1775-1783 American, British, French and German Armies in the War of the American Revolution*, Bicentennial Edition, 1776-1976, 252-268.

Appendix G

NAMES OF GERMAN SOLDIERS
WHO REMAINED IN CANADA AND
THEIR MAIN QUARTERS DURING
THE AMERICAN REVOLUTION

Much of the research for this books stems from curiosity to know more about the roots of the people of Quebec and of Canada. Here are some names of German mercenaries who immigrated to Canada more than two hundred years ago followed by a table locating the German soldiers' main quarters during the American Revolution:

A
Abbesté Jno.
Abraham Daniel
Abraham David
Abt Friedrich
Abt Johann
Achilles Heinrich
Ackermann Carl, Johann
Adam/Eidam
Adelsheim Hans
Adenstedt/Ahdenstel Georg
Adlon Johann
Adolph Christoph
Aeneke/Heineck/Heinert
Aernerd/Ahearned/
  Erdner
Ahl Johann
Ahrenns Johann
Albert Conrad

Alberti Christoph
Albrecht Heinrich
Albrecht Johann Heinrich
Albus Georg
Aldorff François
Allé Jean-François
Almis Christian
Alsdorff Ervin
Alter Friedrich
Amberg/Hemberg Georg
Americh/Hommerich
Amman(n)/Hamann Conrad
Ammon Godefroid
Angel/Engel
Angenant Karl
Angerer/Angever Andreas
Appel Johann
Arens Johann
Armbrecht

Arnold Sigismund, Friedrich
Arnold Thomas
Asmus Michel
Assmer Bernhard
Astman Georg
Astmann Jacob
Aul Heinrich
Aussem/Aussen/Hosseme
Aut

B
Baacke Heinrich
Babe/Pape Johann
Bach Georg
Bader Jacques
Baehr/Baehr Gaspar
Bähr
Baier/Beyer
Bail Jean
Baker/Becker Adam
Baker/Becker August
Baker/Becker Heinrich
Baker/Becker Jacob
Baker/Becker Johann
Baker/Becker Johannes
Baldau Bernhard
Bangert/Pangart Conrad
Barban Lucas
Barnickel Jacob
Barth Adam
Barth Johann
Barthel Antoine
Barthel Thomas
Bartholomae/Bartholomaei Andreas
Bartholomae/Bartholomaei Johann
Bartholomae/Bartholomaei Georg
Bartram Andreas
Bartram Heinrich
Batz Joseph
Bauer Adam
Bauer Christian
Bauer Conrad
Bauer Friedrich, Wilhelm
Bauer Godefroid
Bauer Johann
Bauer Leonhard
Bauernfeind Jacob
Bauernfreund/Baugert Adam

Baumann/Bowmann Johann
Baumbronn/Baumbrun/Pambrun
   Dominique
Bawl/Buhler Andreas
Beauclair Simon
Bebendorff Valentin
Becker/Baker Adam
Becker/Baker August
Becker/Baker Heinrich
Becker/Baker Jacob
Becker/Baker Johann
Becker/Baker Johannes
Beddiger Franz
Behr Georg
Behrbom Ludwig
Behrens Gottlieb
Beichert Gottlieb
Beithnitz Georg
Bellhard/Billhard Johann, Friedrich,
   Wilhelm
Bemanne Adam
Bender/Binder François-Xavier
Bender/Binder Georg
Bender/Binder Johann
Benecke Conrad
Benecke Friedrich
Bengle/Bingle/Beingle/Pingle Johannes
Benoth
Benther Johann
Benty/Bonte
Bentz Joseph
Beom/Behm Heinrich
Berck Johann
Berg Christian
Berger/Nunberger/
   Nünrberger Friedrich, Wilhelm
Berghalser
Berglasen Karl, Bogislaus
Bergstraeser Justus
Berk Andreas
Berling Johann
Berner Georg
Bernhard/Bernoth/Benoth Andreas
Bésette/Beyssert Wilhelm
Besner
Besselmann Johann, Karl
Bethge Andreas
Beukert/Beuckert Joseph

Beuschill Leonhard
Beust Phillip, Otto, Heinrich
Beuter Johann
Beutz/Peutz
Beyer/Baier/Payeur/Payer Albert
Beyer/Baier/Payeur/Payer Christophe
Beyer/Baier/Payeur/Payer
    Georg, Albert (Antoine)
Beyer/Baier/Payeur/Payer Johann,
    Wilhelm
Beyer/Baier/Payeur/Payer Nicolaus
Beyssert
Bickell Gaspar
Bicker Gaspar
Biehler/Biehl/Biehle/Piehl/Buhler
    Andreas
Bielefeld Johann
Bielstein Thedel, Wilhelm
Biennommé Jacques
Biller Georg
Billhard Johann, Friedrich Wilhelm
Billion Jacob
Binder/Bender François-Xavier
Binder/Bender Georg
Binder/Bender Johann
Birscher/Birschire Georg
Bischoff Jacob
Bishop Wilhelm
Blech
Bleck Martin
Bleich Elias
Blimel/Blummell/Oslimel
Block Johann
Blödecker
Blum(e) Nicolaus
Blümberg Jurgen
Blümchen Johann
Blüminell
Blumke Johann
Blummell Friedrich
Böbe Chretien
Böbe Friedrich
Böbe Simon
Bödecker Johann
Bödecker Johann, Friedrich
Bodenbinder Conrad
Boehm(e) Friedrich
Boehm(e) Heinrich

Boehmreüther Johann
Böetger Godefroid
Bohle David
Böhling Heinrich
Bohnsack Johann, Georg
Bojack Martin
Boland
Bollmann Johann, Heinrich
Bonckell Andreas
Bonde
Böning Johann
Bonnan/Bormann Karl
Bonnan/Bormann Georg
Bonnan/Bormann Sigmund
Bonnan/Bormann Simon
Bonse/Bonte
Bonte/Bonse Augustin
Boos Gaspar
Bosse/Bossé Andreas
Böttcher Johann, Christian
Bottmann Heinrich
Boulman/Bolmann/Bollmann Johann,
    Heinrich
Braatz Friedrich
Brandan Conrad
Brand(t) Christophe
Braun/Brown Balthazar
Braunbronn
Braune/Brown Andreas
Braune/Brown Georg
Braune/Brown Phillip
Braune/Brown Martin
Brecht Georg
Breltenbach Heinrich
Breitschuh Heinrich
Brendel Franz
Brennecke Johann
Brennecke Johann, Christ.
Brennecker
Briel Heinrich
Brown/Braun(e)
Bruchhausen Chretien
Bruckhof Georg
Brückner Johann, Christ
Bruder Adam
Brum/Blum(e)
Bruns Christian
Brunsteidell Barthell

Büchs Johann
Buckell/Buckle/Puckel
Buhler/Biehler/Biehl/Biehle/Piehl
  Andreas
Buhler/Biehler/Biehl/Biehle/Piehl Jacob
Bungar Conrad
Bunty/Buntey/Bonte
Burchard Paul, Gebhard
Burchhard
Burckard Christophe
Burgy Gaspar
Busch Gaspar
Busch Ludwig
Büttner Christophe
Butz/Pads

C
Calessteing/Calestagne/Kellerstein
Calnec Jacob
Cappay/Coppey Friedrich
Carl/Karl Adam
Carl/Karl Friedrich
Carl/Karl Gottfried
Catchhof
Catmann/Cattemann
Caux/Koch
Chaum/Schaum
Chambel
Champier/Schambier
Chayte/Scheid
Cheffer/Scheffer/Scheffler
  Cheffvre/Schaeffer/Scheffer
Cheit/Scheid/Scheed Valentin
Cheling/Schelling/Schilling Wilhelm
Childley/Gescheidle
Chink/Schink/Schenck
Choulz/Schultz
Chretien-de-Fitzienstin
Christ Jacob
Christa Martin
Chrystler/Griessser
Ciliac/Ziliac
Claick Gaspar
Clan/Clang-Lens Gaspar
Claprood/Klapproth Ernst
Claude/Claus Gaspar
Claude/Claus Heinrich
Clearla

Cleing/Klein(g) Albert
Clengenbruner/Klingenbrunner
Clerge/Ehlers
Cline/Klein
Clodius August
Coache/Kuwatsch/De Kovadchy
Coll/Kohle Nicolaus
Cölling Franz
Collius Daniel
Collon Abraham
Condelack/Gundlach/Kundlach
Conrad Georg ·
Conrad Stephan
Conradi Karl, Friederich
Cook/Koch
Coppay Friedrich
Cossart/Gossart
Couterman/Gunterman
Cragle/Kroekel
Cramer/Kramer Daniel
Cramer/Kramer Heinrich
Cregheur/Kruger
Cretschmann/Graettchmann Christian
Creutzbourg Simon
Creutznacher Johann, Friedrich

D
Daffner/Teffner/Deffner
Dahler/Dallaire Conrad
Dahler/Dallaire Johann
Daldelshiem/Adelsheim Dalwingh
Dantz Jean
Daphner/Teffner
Daudorf/Dandoff/Dondoff/Dandorff
  Johann
Daudorf/Dandoff/Dondoff/Dandorff
  Heinrich
Dauth Gaspar
David Heinrich
De Beust/Beust
De Bold Christophe
Decker Joseph
Dederick/Dietrich Johann
Deffner/Daffner/Teffner Johann
Degen/Dengen
Degenhardt/Degenhard Friedrich
De Heer/Heer
Dehne Matthias

Dehnert Jacob
Dehnhardt Ernst
Deissinger Georg
Deissinger Gernhard
De Kovadchy/Coache Johann
Dell Jacob
De Molithe/Demolitor/Molithor
   Christian
Demuth Ludwig
Dengen Gaspar
Denhart/Dehnert Jacob
De Pencier Theodore
Deschmer Georg
De Schoell/Schoell
Des Coudres Ludwig
Deseindre Johann
Desider Martin
Desselberger/Dosselberger
Dessinger
Detrie/Detrui Heinrich
Dettmer/Dittmer Heinrich
Deülher Phillip
Dhoren Johann
Dickhaut Heinrich
Dickner Johann
Diedrich/Dietrich Johann
Diehl Johann
Dieler Johann
Dietrich/Diedrich Michel
Dietzel/TittselDiller Leonhard
Dillmann/Dillemann Sebastian
Dillman(n)/Dillman Christophe
   Dillman(n)/Dillman Friedrich
Discher Gaspar
Dittlie Martin
Dittmer/Dettmer Henrich
Ditzel Johann
Döenges Gernhard
Dohmprobst Friedrich
Dohren Friedrich
Dondoff/Daudorf/Dandoff/Dandorff
   Johann
Dondoff/Daudorf/Dandoff/Dandorff
   Heinrich
Donny Anton
Dorder Martin
Dören Christian
Dörffer/Dörffler Friedrich

Dörffler/Dörffer Friedrich
Dörge Johann, Daniel
Döring Heinrich
Dormeyer Friedrich
Dorsch Christophe
Dosselberger/Desselberger Christ.,
   Friedrich
Drechsler Johann, Georg
Dreher Johann
Dreyer Conrad, Heinrich
Drill Conrad
Duchscher/Tuchscheer Georg
Dudloff Gottlieb
Duff(t) Conrad
Duff(t) Johann, Adam
Dümmler Chistophe
Dümmler Conrad
Duniess Martin
Dupenack
Durdÿ Matthias
Duvinet(t) Baptiste
Duynes Martin
Dyce/Dyer Georg

E
Eckhard Gottfried
Ebacher Johann
Ebbinger/Elbinger/Eppinger Christophe
Ebenhardt/Eberhard/Everhard Christian
Ebert/Eberths/Hébert Gaspar
Ebert/Hébert/Eberths Hermann,
   Melchior
Eckhard(t) Georg
Effland/I(f)fland/Ifflandt/Adam
Effland/I(f)fland/Ifflandt/Johann
Egell Gaspar
Egner Erhard
Ehlers Johann, Conrad
Ehlers Johann, Ludwig
Ehrecke Georg
Ehrensperger Laurent
Ehrenstein
Eichenberg Georg, Gottlieb
Eidam/Adam Johann
Eidman Johann
Eigell Joseph
Eimecke Georg
Eisenkolben Heinrich

Ekemberg/Heckenberg Wilhelm
Eldam Laurent
Elebrante/Hildebrant Wilhelm
Elleure/Heller Ludwig
Elsner
Eltzer
Emmerich Brenhard
Emong Johann
Engel Georg
Engelhard/Angelhard/Ingelhard(t)
 Bernhard
Ensenberger Johann, Friedrich
Eppinger/Ebbinger/Elbinger Christophe
Erck Andreas
Erdmann Johann, Peter
Erdner/Aernerd/Ahearned Joseph
Eschenbach Andreas
Essleur/Hessler
Estdo Jacob
Etzner Nicolaus
Euler(s) Conrad
Euler(s) Johann
Everhard/Ebenhardt/Eberhard/
 Frantz
Eyberts/Hébert/Ebert/Eberths Gaspar
Eyberts/Hébert/Ebert/Eberths Hermann
Eydam/Eidam Johann
Ewaldt Martin

F
Fabricius Karl, August
Fail/Faille Heinrich
Fasnacht Johann
Fatchell Heinrich
Faulstroth/Falstro Heinrich
Fausel Johann
Fausse/Faust/Fost Andreas
Fausse/Faust/Fost Friedrich
Febvre/Froebe Frantz
Feith/Veuth Frantz
Felge/Voelger
Felz Heinrich
Femme/Temme Julius
Femmeling Heinrich
Ferbitz Johann
Ferdinand Johann, Heinrich
Ferries/Ferry
Ferry/Ferries Johann, Daniel

Fessner Georg
Fetter Johann
Fiedler/Fideler Andreas
Fiffre/Pfeiffer
Filsoffer Johann
Fink Karl
Finsterer Georg
Finsterwalt/Finsterwald Johann Baptiste
Firy/Tiry/Siry/Liry Wolfgang
Fischer Bernhard
Fischer Gaspar
Fischer Chretien
Fischer Francis
Fischer Georg
Fischer Heinrich
Fischer Johann, Christophe
Fischer Johann, Friedrich
Fischer Phillip
Fischer Wilhelm
Fitzhofen
Fleckstein Rudolph
Fleischer Andreas
Fleischman/Heischman/Flacshaman
 Jacob
Flemme Christophe
Flonius
Florer Johann
Flührer Conrad
Föhr Hans
Foss/Winkelvoss
Foser/Pfotzer/Pausé/Pauzé Sebastian
Francisca Gaspar
Franck(e) Johann, Heinrich
Franck(e) Michel
Franck(e) Peter
Franisco Christofore
Frantz/Franz Baptiste
Franz/Frantz Johann
Franz/Frantz Johann, Ernst
Fratschell
Frazer Donald
Frédéric/Friedrich Johann, Baptiste
Freel Conrad
Frees Heinrich
Freund Daniel
Frey David
Freyenhagen Karl
Freyenhagen Wilhelm

Freyensoner Georg
Freymuth Sigmund
Frewe/Froebe
Frick/Fricth Johann, Baptiste, Friedrich
Fricke Eberhard
Fricke Friedrich
Fricke Heinrich
Fricke Karl
Fride(l) Eberhard
Friderici Salomon
Friedemann Jacob, Chretien
Friedrich/Frédéric Johann, Baptiste
Frinbrecht Johann
Friser
Froebe/Frewe Johann, Wilhelm, Franz
Fromme Gottfried
Fröstler Frunsteidell/Fuchs Johann
Fuhrmann Johann
Fuhrmann Georg, Samuel
Fust/Just
Fütterer Georg

G
Gabriel Ferdinand
Gabriel Friedrich
Gagné Louis
Galland(t) Joseph
Gammerdinger Ludwig
Gans Christophe
Gastens Christian
Gauers Andreas
Gause/Gohse Christophe
Gebel/Kaeble
Geffre/Schaeffer/Scheffer
Geiger/Gelpke Gottlieb
Genaud/Jenot Adam
Genaud/Jenot Jacob
Genthaler Anton
George Friedrich
Gerbig Wilhelm
Gerecke Christian
Gerger Georg
Gerhard/Guérard Ernst
Gerhard/Guérard Phillip
Gerke/Gerecke Christian
Gerlach Johann, Georg
Gerlig/Gertig
Gerner Friedrich

Gerthmann/Gertman Conrad
Gervais/Servais/Service Jean
Gescheidle Johann
Geschke Michel
Gessler Samuel
Giesler/Gisler Johann, Joseph
Gildner Simon
Gille Friedrich
Gimble Heinrich
Gislow Wilhelm
Glackemeyer Friedrich
Glaser Johann
Gleissenberg Gottlieb, Joachim
Globenskindt/Globensky August, France
Göbell/Kebel(l) Theodore
Gödecke Heinrich
Godiché
Godschal Stephan
Goeckell/Gokell/Goekel Anton
Goedick(e) Friedrich,
Goedick(e) Rudolphe
Goëtz/Gotze/Goëtz Andreas
Goëtz/Gotze/Goëtz Benjamin
Goëtz/Gotze/Goëtz Gottfried
Gohse Christophe
Gorman/Bormann Sigmund
Gossart Karl
Goutcher/Gutcke Friedrich
Gräeff August, Ludwig, Lucas
Gräeff Johann
Gräeter Friedrich
Graetsch Friedrich
Graetschmann/Cretschmann Christian
Grau Nicolaus
Grauling Heinrich
Greben Johann
Gref Johann
Greger/Kruger/Cregheur Christophe
Grennwats Johann
Gress(e) Karl
Gress(e) Heinrich
Grichel Johann
Griesinger Karl
Griesman(n) Georg
Griesser August
Grimm Johann, Georg
Grimming Johann, Andreas
Grimpe Andreas

Grope Christophe
Gross Georg
Grossman Georg
Grothe/Grothé Christian
Grubenstein
Gruber
Gruendler/Gründler Anton
Gründler/Gruendler Friedrich
Gründler/Gruendler Jacob
Grüne Jacob
Grünewald Gaspar, Friedrich
Grutschmit Francis
Grysingher/Griesinger
Gschwind Friedrich
Gue/Guhe Johann
Guérard/Gerhard Ernst
Guérard/Gerhard Philipp
Gullery Nicolaus
Gundlach Christian
Gundt/Hund/Gunn Georg
Günter Johann
Guntermann Johann
Gutcke Johann, Friedrich
Guttschmitt

H
Habermann Jurgen, Paul
Hachenberger/Hatschenberger Johann
Haeberlein Matthias
Haemel/Hamel/Hammell Johann
Haemel/Hamel/Hammell Heinrich
Hagemann Arnold
Hagen Heinrich
Hahn(e) Anton
Hahn(e) Georg, Friedrich
Hahn(e) Friedrich
Hail/Heil
Hailman/Heillmann
Haller Wilhelm
Halm Andreas
Ham/Hamm/Stam Martin
Hamann/Amman(n) Conrad
Hamburg/Amberg
Hamerla Johann
Hamm/Ham/Stam Peter
Handell Johann
Hanekratt Christian
Haner David

Harbec/Harbique/Herbecke Georg
Harbord/Harborth Ernst
Harbord/Harborth Friedrich
Harlowe Wilhelm
Harman Heinrich
Harnekratt
Harnick David
Harries Heinrich
Hartline Adam
Hartman(n) Anton
Hartman(n) Christopher
Hartman(n) Ludwig
Hartman(n) Wilhelm
Hartog Johann
Harton Felix
Hartung Joseph
Has/Hao Georg
Hasselmann Andreas
Hasslinger Joseph
Hasstinger
Hatschenberger Johann
Haue Georg
Hauf Johann
Hauffmeister/Hoffmeister
Haumann Nicolaus
Haveline Mathew
Hayn Phillip
Hébert/Ebert/Eberths/Eyberts Gaspar
Hébert/Ebert/Eberths/Eyberts Herman
Heckenbert/Ekemberg/Hegenberg
  Joseph
Heckenroth/Heckenroth/
  Heckerott Conrad
Heer/De Heer Ludwig, Christophe
Heh Gottfried
Heil/Heill Dietrich
Heil/Heill Phillip, Friedrich
Heill/Heil Matthias
Heillmann Peter
Heidelbach Julius, Jeremias
Hein(e)/Heyne Christian
Hein(e)/Heyne Heinrich
Hein(e)/Heyne Phillipe
Hein(e)/Heyne Maximilien
Heineck/Heinert Tobias
Heinecker Anton
Heineman(n)/Heynemand/Hennemann
  Christophe, Friedrich

Heineman(n)/Heynemand/Hennemann Friedrich
Heineman(n)/Heynemand/Hennemann Heinrich
Heineman(n)/Heynemand/Hennemann Karl, Friedrich
Heiniger Joseph
Heinllein Andreas
Heintze/Hintze
Heinze Gottfried
Heischman Jacob
Heise August
Heise Johann
Heiss Michel
Held Johann, Gottfried
Hellberg Johann
Heller Ludwig
Hellmuth Georg
Hemann Samuel
Hemberg/Amberg Georg Georg
Hemmerle Thadeus
Henaider/Riemenschneider
Henckel/Inkel/Henkel Gottfried
Henckel/Inkel/Henkel Jacob
Henkelman/Hinkleman
Hendorf Friedrich
Hengel Georg
Henning Chretien
Henning Georg
Henschell
Henss(e)/Henss Friedrich
Henss(e)/Henss Heinrich
Henssell Andreas
Henzell Conrad
Herbecke/Harbec/Harbique Georg
Herchfield Friedrich
Herchner August
Herdt Paul
Hermann Johann
Hermsdorff Karl
Herner Friedrich
Herricke Karl, F.
Hertel/Oertel Christophe
Herterich/Hederiche Johann, Conrad
Herth
Hertlein Adam
Hertz Lieborius
Hespeden

Hesper Friedrich
Hesse Johann
Hessing
Hessler Christophe
Hessler Friedrich
Hessler Peter
Hettig Johann
Hettler Christophe
Hetzer Francis
Hetzler Pancrat.
Heuer August
Heusse
Heydefuss Johann, Heinrich
Heynert Johann
Hiep Bernhard
Hildebrant/Elebrant Wilhelm
Hildner Friedberg
Hille Christophe
Hiller Michel
Hind Johann
Hinderkarker Jacob
Hinderkirchen
Hirschmann Johann, Heinrich
Hintze Jacob
Hirschbach Friedrich
Hirschmann Johann, Jacob
Hitlaire/Egner
Hittel Sigmund, Georg
Höber Diedrich
Hock Georg
Hoefer Johann
Hoehn Chretien
Hoen Friedrich
Hoffenrath Friedrich
Hoffman(n) Adam
Hoffman(n) François
Hoffman(n) Friedrich
Hoffman(n) Godfried
Hoffman(n) Gottlieb
Hoffman(n) Jacob
Hoffman(n) Johann, Lebrecht
Hoffman(n) Just.
Hoffman(n) Kraft.
Hoffman(n) Thomas
Hoffmeister Friedrich
Höh Gottfried
Holland Johann
Holle Godfried

Holle Gottlieb
Hollwege Gottfried
Holtögel Christophe
Holzberger Leonhard
Holzer François
Holzhausen Heinrich
Holzmeister Friedrich
Holzwerter Gottfried
Homann Gottfried
Homermar Heinrich
Hommerien/Hommerich/
    Hommelmann/Hommeriche
    Christian
Hommerien/Hommerich/
    Hommelmann/Hommeriche Georg
Hopffenrath/Hoffenrath
Hoppe Johann
Horn Johan
Hornburg Christ.
Horneber Andreas
Hort/Orth Johann
Hortus Georg
Hottelmann/Hotte Hans
Houff/Hough Christian
Hoyer Wilhelm
Hubert/Huberth Jacob
Huck Francis
Hufschmidt Francis
Hufschmidt Jacob
Hull/Ohl(e) Gottfried
Hull/Ohl(e) Joseph
Hull/Ohl(e) Ludwig
Hummerich/Hommerich Christ.
Hummerich/Hommerich Georg
Hund/Hundt Joachim
Hunstedt Heinrich
Hunter/Jaeger Friedrich
Hupenden Phillip
Huppert Jacob
Hurd Joachim
Hutner Godfried
Hütting Michael
Hüttinger Adam
Hüttner August

I
Ifland/Iffland/Ifflandt/Effland Adam
Ifland/Iffland/Ifflandt/Effland Johann

Immenthal Christophe
Immhoff Ludwig
Inderkerber/Hinderkarker
Ingelhart/Engelhard(t) Bernhard
Inkel/Henckel
Iserhof Gustavus
Ist/Iot/Iol
Isten

J
Jacobs/Jacques Johann
Jäeckell Johann
Jaeger/Hunter Friedrich
Jahn Johann
Jatscheck Johann
Jean/John(s) Wilhelm
Jecker Johann, Christian
Jenot/Genaud Adam
Jenot/Genaud Jacob
Jockell/Yockell Andreas
Jockell/Yockell Johann, Heinrich
Jockell/Yockell Peter
Jocks Johann
John(s)/Jean Wilhelm
Jomphe/Schumpff Christian
Jordan Johann
Jordan Heinrich
Jost/Just Conrad
Juinque/Schenck/Schink Heinrich
Juncker/Younker Conrad
Jung/Young Georg
Jürgens/Yurgens
Just/Jost Conrad

K
Kaeble/Goebell
Kahmann Heinrich
Kalb Johann, Conrad
Kalck Ernst, Ludwig
Kalkoff Johann
Kannaps/Knapp
Kappe(s) Adam
Kappey/Coppay/Karpey Friedrich
Karpe(s) Nicolaus
Karpey/Kappey/Coppay Friedrich
Karsch Joseph
Karweil Andreas
Kascho/Kescho

Kassmann Johann
Kauffmann/Kaufman Anton
Kaufholtz Johann Christof
Kaune Julius
Kayser Melchior
Keaning Johann
Kebel(l)/Goebell Theodore
Keenig/Konig Friedrich
Kegle Ludwig
Keldermyer Johann, Christophe
Kellarmann/Kellermann Johann,
    Friedrich
Keller Karl
Keller Phillip
Kellermeir/Keldermeyer
Kellerstein Gottlieb
Keny/King/Ko(e)nig Friedrich
Keny/King/Ko(e)nig Johann
Keny/King/Ko(e)nig Julius
Kenns Augustus
Kerm Nicolaus
Kerth/Kersch
Kertzner Johann
Kescho Jacob
Kes(s)ler Michael
Kes(s)ler Laurent
Ketler Ludwig
Kettner Johann, Andreas
Kiebonitz
Kiehron/Kuhron
Kielburg Johann
Kinstler/Kiltoner Wilhelm
Kirsch Ludwig
Kirsch Melchior
Kizer Gaspar
Klahold Gaspar
Klapper/Klauber
Klapproth/Claprood Ernst
Klatterer Conrad
Klauber Jacob
Klebonitz Johann
Kleemann Adam
Klein(g)/Clein(g) Adam
Klein(g)/Clein(g) Johann, Phillip
Kleinert Karl
Kleinschmidt Gaspar, Friedrich
Klengenbrummer/Klingenbrunner
Klenzmann Daniel

Kletcher/Kletscher Johann
Kling(e) Albert
Kling(e) Arend.
Kling(e) Theodore
Klingenbrunn Nicolaus
Klinger Philippe
Klingsoerh Christian
Klosterbauer Sebastian
Kludius/Clodius
Kluge August
Klusmann/Klussmann Daniel
Knab Friedrich
Knabenschube Georg
Knap Heinrich
Knauff Gottfried
Knipschild Heinrich
Kniratsch
Knoblauch
Knust Andreas
Koch/Caux Anton
Koch/Caux Balthazar
Koch/Caux Gerbert
Koch/Caux Heinrich
Koch/Caux Johann
Koch/Caux Johann, Ernst, Heinrich
Koch/Caux Johann, Heinrich
Kock Andreas
Köehler Georg
Köelscher Dietrich
Koenig/Konig
Kohle/Kouel
Kohlep Adam
Köhler Christian
Köhler Georg
Köhler Nicolaus
Kohlmeyer Andreas
Koll/Kouel/Coll/Kohle Nicolaus
Koller Phillip
Koller Wilhelm
Kolmyer/Kohlmeyer
König/King Edmund, Victor
König/King/Friedrich
König/King/Johann
König/King/Justin
Kopp(e)/Ropp Georg, Heinrich
Kopp(e)/Ropp Johann
Kopp(e)/Ropp Friedrich
Körber Johann

Korn Johann
Köscher
Kotte
Kouel/Koull Michael
Koutash/DeKovadchy/Kovash Johann
Kowald Johann
Kraatz Johann, Christophe
Krafft Franz
Krafft Nicolaus
Krahane/Krehaan
Kraig Wagner
Kraigie Johann
Kramer/Cramer Daniel
Kramer/Cramer Heinrich
Krass Karl
Krässane
Kratikofsky/Kradikowsky Friedrich
Kratz Wilhelm
Krauss Georg
Krautwurst Johann
Krebs Nicolaus
Kreckel/Kroeckel
Kreissler Casimir
Krendel/Kreudel Heinrich
Krepper Christophe
Krepper Johann
Kreutzer Christophe
Krickel/Kroeckel
Krieg Johann, Adam
Krieg Johann, Gottfried
Kroekel Johann, Nicolaus
Kroeser
Krug Johann, Adam
Krüger/Creger/Cregheur Christophe
Krull Heinrich
Krum Georg
Kruse Georg
Kuffener Johann, Ludwig
Kugeler Gaspar
Kuhlman Johann
Kühn(e) Conrad
Kühn(e) Heinrich
Kühn(e) Johannes
Kühron Johannes
Kulong Jacob
Külp Karl
Kümmel Friedrich
Kummerle/Kurnerle

Kumpff Christophe
Kunckell Friedrich
Kunckel Johann
Kundelach/Gundlach
Kunigers
Künstler/Kinstler Wilhelm
Kunstmann Bernhard
Kunz Georg
Kupffer Georg
Kurnerle Jacob
Küten Conrad
Kuttman Christophe
Kuwatsch/Coache Johann

L
Laick/Lake Adam
Lainzee/Lentze
Lamar/Lamarre Nicolaus
Lamarre/Lamar Nicolaus
Lambert Nicolas
Lander/Sander
Landerman/Lentremanm/
　　Laterman/Lentremann Augustin
Landseygner/Lanzinger Johann
Landwehr Jacob
Lang(e) Christophe
Lang(e) Conrad
Lang(e) Jacob
Lang(e) Martin
Lang(e) Matthias
Langemeyer Heinrich, Karl
Langerjahn Siegfried, Heinrich
Lángins Valentin
Langkop Heinrich
Lans Jacob
Lanzinger/Lantzinger Johann
Laparé/Neuberger August
Larsch Johann
Lasse/Sasse
Laterman/Lentremann Augustin
Lattmann Heinrich
Latz
Lauer Andreas
Lauer Johann, Conrad
Launhard Heinrich
Lauter Michel
Laws Jacob
Lebrecht Johann

Lederer Michel
Leffert/Lessert/Lessard
Lehincter Nicolaus
Lehn Kark, Friedrich
Leibenrider
Leibenzeder Johann
Leight Gustavus
Leilman Daniel
Leitz Johann
Lemaire Chretien
Lemberger Andreas
Lenhard Johann
Lentz(e) Friedrich
Lentz(e) Jacob
Lentz(e) Johann
Lentzinger/Lanzinger Johann
Léonard/Leonhard Gaspar
Leonhard/Léonard Jacob
Lerche Heinrich
Lessert/Lessard/Lessart/Leffert Johann,
  Phillip
Ley/Leydolff Johann
Leyer Johann, Anton
Lichtenwalter Michel
Liebau Christian
Liebegott Heinrich
Liebenhaar
Liedel/Lidell Jacob
Lieder Gottlieb
Lielouiter/Lauter/Lichtenwalter
Lieffert/Liesert Laurent
Lilly Gotthelf
Linch Friedrich
Lindau Johann, Heinrich
Lindgrün Johann
Lindner/Dickner Johann, Christophe
Lindworm Wilhelm
Lindwurm
Linne Johann
Liry/Firy/Siry/Tiry Georg, Wollsgany
Lishler/Lishlar Georg
Löde Gottlieb
Lödell/Loedel Christian
Lödell/Loedel Heinrich, Nicolaus,
  Christophe
Loeter/Loeder/Loeder/Lettre/Laître/
  Letter Georg
Löfferer Karl

Löfferer Johann
Löhmann Johann
Loiseau/Vogel
Long/Laing
Lotherer Karl
Lotz/Loz/Lodz/Lotz Johann
Louth/Lonx Johann
Löw(e) Chretien
Löw(e) Johann
Löw(e) Joseph
Loyd Johann
Lucht Gustavus
Lückel Georg
Ludecke Johann, Phillip
Luders Johann, Baptiste
Ludgeradt Johann, Gaspar
Lüters Gottlieb
Lüttge Johann
Lutz Johann

M
MacGraw
Mack/Mauk
Maher/Mayer/Maillé/Maheu/Meyer
  Johann, Chretien
Maillé/Mayer/Maheu/Maher Johann,
  Chrétien
Maigal/Mikel/Mogel
Maisch Joachim
Major Georg
Manck/Mauck Gottlieb
Manecke/Manike Friedrich
Marreck Godefroid
Martin Christian
Martin Johann
Maschweg Michael
Matthaes Johann
Mauck/Mauk Gottlieb
Mayer/Maillé/Maheu/Maher Johann,
  Chrétien
Mayne Christy.
Mayonnet/Minoni
McDonald David
McGraw Duncan
Mebius Heinrich
Mecker Franz
Meffert Franz
Meinecke/Mnecke/Manike Friedrich

Meinecke/Mnecke/Manike Johann
Meinen
Meinone/Minoni
Meir/Maher/Meyer
Meixner Michel
Melsch Jacob
Melschenske
Meneky/Monekay/Menekai/Monnecke/
  Meinekey Johann, Friedrich
Menske Johann
Mentze
Mentzel Johann
Mentzer Johann
Merckel Heinrich
Merckel Johann
Mertens Jacob
Messenger Christophe
Messing
Metch/Metsch Jacob
Metch/Metsch Johann
Metzdorff Gottlieb
Metzger Lorenz
Metzler Wilhelm, Sebastian
Meyer(s)/Mayer/Meir/Maher Christian
Meyer(s)/Mayer/Meir/Maher Christophe
Meyer(s)/Mayer/Meir/Maher David
Meyer(s)/Mayer/Meir/Maher Friedrich
Meyer(s)/Mayer/Meir/Maher Georg
Meyer(s)/Mayer/Meir/Maher Georg,
  Wilhelm
Meyer(s)/Mayer/Meir/Maher Heinrich,
  Wilhelm
Meyer(s)/Mayer/Meir/Maher Jacob
Meyer(s)/Mayer/Meir/Maher Johann,
  Christian
Meyer(s)/Mayer/Meir/Maher Leonhard
Meyer(s)/Mayer/Meir/Maher Mathieu
Meyer(s)/Mayer/Meir/Maher Nicolaus
Meyer(s)/Mayer/Meir/Maher Theodore
Meyer(s)/Mayer/Meir/Maher Wilhelm,
  Nicolaus
Meyn(e)/Mayne Christian
Meyn(e)/Mayne Georg
Meynone/Minoni Michael
Michael/Mittchell Friedrich
Michaelis Friedrich
Mikel Godlove
Miller/Müller/Moller Andreas

Miller/Müller/Moller Heinrich, Wilhelm
Miller/Müller/Moller Johann, Christophe
Millon Johann
Milton Johann
Mines Georg
Minicke/Meinecke
Minoni/Meynone Michael
Mittchell/Michael Friedrich
Mogel/Mongel/Mikel/Mongel/Mogl
  Andreas
Molithor Christian, Theodore, Sigmund
Molithor Stephan
Molle Michel
Mö(e)ller Andreas
Mönnecke/Meinecke
Montreal Joachim
Mordt/Moro/Moreau/Morr August
Moro/Moreau/Morr/Mordt Heinrich,
  August
Moses Johann
Most Anton
Most Johann
Mouché Antoine
Muess Heinrich
Mukodell/Schffalisky
Müller/Miller/Moller Andreas
Müller/Miller/Moller Christian
Müller/Miller/Moller Conrad
Müller/Miller/Moller Franz
Müller/Miller/Moller Friedrich
Müller/Miller/Moller Georg
Müller/Miller/Moller Heinrich
Müller/Miller/Moller Johann
Müller/Miller/Moller Johann, Christian
Müller/Miller/Moller Jurgen
Müller/Miller/Moller Leonhard
Müller/Miller/Moller Nicolaus
Müller/Miller/Moller Paul
Müller/Miller/Moller Peter
Müller/Miller/Moller Samuel
Müller/Miller/Moller Ulrich
Müller/Miller/Moller Wilhelm
Mund Karl
Munich/Meinecke/Manike Friedrich
Myer/Schmidtmeyer Wilhelm

N
Naacke/Nack Gaspar
Naacke/Nack Gottfried
Nanaimer Georg
Nebel Johann
Nehrengardt Joseph
Neisele Gaspar
Neitz Johann
Neisele/Neizell Gaspar
Neuburger/Laparé August
Neuheimer Georg
Neumeister Georg
Neuwald Friedrich
Newmann
Nickel Johann
Nickner/Nichner/Dickner Chrysostome
Nieding Gaspar
Nietz Johann
Nisski/Nissky Anton
Nix Johann
Noe Leonhard
Noigh/Nol
Nongesser Wilhelm
Noth/North Christophe
Nunberger/Berger/Laparé Friedrich,
  Wilhelm

O
Obrick Mathias
Oelschlager Johann
Oertel/Hertel Christophe
Offeney Wilhelm
Offman/Hoffmann Johann
Offmestre/Hoffmeister
Ogleman/Heinman/Heinemann
Ohl(e)/Hull Gottfried
Ohl(e)/Hull Joseph
Ohl(e)/Hull Ludwig
Ohme Friedrich
Oldendorf Karl
Oliva Friedrich, Wilhelm
Opennrat/Hopfenrath
Opitz Michael
Oppermann Andreas
Orbel/Orbell/Ornal Conrad
Orpet Johann, Arnold
Orterott/Osterott
Orth/Hort Johann

Orthner/Ortner Franz
Orthner/Ortner Leonhard
Oslimel Friedrich
Osterott/Orterott Heinrich
Osterwald Gaspar
Ostman/Othamann/Ottman/Astma
  Hausmann Johann
Ostman/Othamann/Ottman/Astma
  Hausmann Joseph
Otto Gottlieb
Otto Karl
Otto Tobias
Ottobusch Jacob

P
Paar Georg
Page/Pagé Karl
Pambrun/Baumbrun/Baumbronn
  Dominique
Pangart Conrad
Pape/Bape Johann
Pasche Karl
Paster Georg
Pattingall Jacob
Pätzel Johann, Christ.
Paul/Poll Friedrich
Paul/Poll Jacob
Paul/Poll Johann, Georg
Paul/Poll Johann, Christophe, Friedrich
Paul/Poll Joseph
Paulsen Christian
Pauser/Pauzer/Pfotzer/Foser Sebastian
Payeur/Baier/Beyer/Payer Albert
Payeur/Baier/Beyer/Payer
  Christophe
Payeur/Baier/Beyer/Payer Georg, Albert
  (Antoine)
Payeur/Baier/Beyer/Payer
  Johann, Wilhelm
Payeur/Baier/Beyer/Payer Nicolaus
Peitsch Heinrich
Pelz
Penz Martin
Perlinger Paul
Peters Daniel
Peters Friedrich
Peters Julius
Peters Ludwig

Petersdorff Tobias
Peterson/Petersen Johann
Peutz/Beutz Ferdinand
Pfänder Christophe
Pfanner Peter
Pfannkuchen Conrad
Pfaud(t) Friedrich
Pfeiffer/Fiffre/Pieper/Fiffle Christian
Pfeiffer/Fiffre/Pieper/Fiffle Ernst
Pfeiffer/Fiffre/Pieper/Fiffle Heinrich
Pfeiffer/Fiffre/Pieper/Fiffle Johann
Pfitzer F.
Pforius Friedrich
Pfotzer/Pauser/Pauzer/Foser/Sebastian
Pfuhl Gottlieb
Phenider/Riemenschneider
Phevre/Weber Phillips
Pickell Georg
Picket/Piquet/Piquette Conrad
Picket/Piquet/Piquette Johann
Picket/Piquet/Piquette Karl, Friedrich
Pisand/Piscand Nicolaus
Pitre/Vivisse
Plangert/Pangart Conrad
Plasse/Plat/Platz/Plate Bernhard
Plasse/Plat/Platz/Plate Christian
Platner/Plettner Heinrich
Pleich/Bleich
Plimel/Oslimel/Blummel
Poetner Wilhelm
Pohle/Bohle/Poll/Paul
Porth Chretien
Power/Bauer
Poyer Nicolaus
Prach
Preller/Presser Ludwig
Prerea Ph.
Presser/Preller Johann
Presson Johann
Prosig
Prossmann
Prosy Georg
Proth Mathieu
Prusse Heinrich, Johann
Puckel/Puckell/Pückel Buckle Georg
Puckel/Puckell/Pückel Buckle Johann
Puckel/Puckell/Pückel/Buckle Jean,
  Baptiste
Putz/Padz Joseph

Q
Quedhatte/Gerhardt
Quequell/Goekel
Querl/Quert Christian
Quert

R
Raabe Johann
Rach Rudolphe
Raimond/Raymond/Raymondt Peter
Rakman/Rahman Herman
Ramler Friedrich
Rapp Heinrich
Raquepas/Reichenbach
Rasch Heinrich
Rasehorn Christ.
Rath Georg
Ratzmann Hermann
Raubenheimer Adam
Rauch/Rausch Adam
Rauch/Rausch Joseph
Raul/Raull Heinrich
Rauschenberg Johann
Regenbogen Anton
Regenbogen Joseph
Reges Wilhelm, Andreas
Reichenbach/Reinchenback Conrad
Reichenback/Reinchenbach Ludwig
Reichenberg Ludwig
Reiffert Heinrich
Reill Peter
Reimschneider/Rheimschneider/
  Riemenschneider Heinrich
Reinboth Johann
Reineck(e) Friedrich
Reineck(e) Johann
Reinhard/R(h)einhart/Reinhard/
  Rennert Heinrich
Reinhard/R(h)einhart/Reinhard/
  Rennert Jacob
Reinhard/R(h)einhart/Reinhard/
  Rennert Joseph
Reinhard/R(h)einhart/Reinhard/
  Rennert Michael
Reinhole Friedrich
Reissig Heinrich
Reit(z) Vitus
Reither/Ritter
Reitzenstein Gottlieb Chr.

Remeck/Remmeck Francis
Remhoff/Reimphoff Heinrich
Remler Friedrich
Ren Anton
Resh/Resch(e)/Reiche/Riech Phillip
Ressing Andreas
Reussing Georg
Reussner Karl
Rhein Conrad
Rhein Friedrich
Rholing/Roehling
Richter August
Richter Christian
Richter Johann
Ridschefsky
Riech Johann
Riede
Riesenkirch Andreas
Rimmerman/Roemerman
Ringe Karl
Ringeling E., Karl
Rinier Jacob
Rinne Karl
Rittberg Wilhelm
Ritter/Ritzer/Ritaie Bernhard
Ritter/Ritzer/Ritaie Friedrich
Ritter/Ritzer/Ritaie Hieronymus
Ritter/Ritzer/Ritaie Johann, Franz
Röbbel Christian
Robin Louis
Rocktreschler Gaspar
Roderfeld Conrad
Roehling Phillip
Roerer Heinrich
Roese Andreas
Roge/Rogge/Roggie Karl
Roge/Rogge/Roggie Johann
Rohde Friedrich
Rohmann Adam
Rolfs Conrad
Rolshaussen
Römerman Heinrich
Romm Johann
Roose/Rose Godfried
Roose/Rose Heinrich
Rooth/Roth
Ropp Georg, Heinrich
Roppert/Ruppert Johann
Roppert/Ruppert Godfried

Rörer
Rosencrantz Johann
Rosenthal Christ.
Rosshausen Heinrich
Rossmann Jacob
Rost/Rush/Rouche/Rust Georg
Rost/Rush/Rouche/Rust Johann
Roth/Rath/Proth Edmund
Roth/Rath/Proth Mathieu
Roussell/Russel Heinrich
R(ö)over Heinrich
Rullmann/Roullmann Johann
Rupert/Roppert
Rusk
Russel/Roussel Heinrich
Rust/Rouche Rutzenstine/Reitzenstein
Gottlieb

S
Sabora/Safferra Joseph
Sagus Heinrich
Saillie Heinrich
Salmon/Zellmann
Sander Christophe
Sander Heinrich
Sandhagen Friedrich
Sangerhausen August
Sarges Heinrich
Sasse Erdman
Saterman/Laterman/Lentremann
Sauer/Sawer/Sayer Johann
Sauer/Sawer/Sayer Johann, Gottlieb
Sauer/Sawer/Sayer Gottlieb
Sauer/Sawer/Sayer Heinrich
Saupe Gottlieb
Saust Christian
Sawer/Sauer/Sayer
Scalaipahe Friedrich
Schabash Peter
Schacht Johann
Schade Johannes
Schaeffer/Schefer/Schafer/Geffre
Andreas
Schaeffer/Schefer/Schafer/Geffre Gaspar
Schaeffer/Schefer/Schafer/Geffre
Christian
Schaeffer/Schefer/Schafer/Geffre
Christophe
Schaeffer/Schefer/Schafer/Geffre Conrad

Schaeffer/Schefer/Schafer/Geffre
  Ditmars
Schaeffer/Schefer/Schafer/Geffre
  Friedrich,Wilhelm
Schaeffer/Schefer/Schafer/Geffre Georg
Schaeffer/Schefer/Schafer/Geffre
  Gerhard
Schaeffer/Schefer/Schafer/Geffre
  Gotthard
Schaeffer/Schefer/Schafer/Geffre Jacob
Schaeffer/Schefer/Schafer/Geffre Johann
Schaeffer/Schefer/Schafer/Geffre Johann,
  Franz
Schaeffer/Schefer/Schafer/Geffre Michel
Schaffalisky Friedric
Schambier Heinrich
Schammel Karl
Schaper Heinrich
Schaphardt Jurgen
Schaphardt Johann, Heinrich
Schaudt Heinrich
Schaum Johann
Schawack
Schedleur/Sheidley/Gescheidle
Scheidt Martin
Scheid/Sheede/Scheidt Martin
Scheid/Sheede/Scheidt Valentin
Scheinemann Friedrich
Schel(l)/Schoell Anton
Schel(l)/Schoell Georg
Schellhammer Conrad
Schelsted Georg
Schenaille/Chenaille
Schenck/Schink/Juinque Heinrich
Schentzell Gottlieb
Schepner Heinrich
Scherkoffsky Adam
Scherman Heinrich
Scherneck Heinrich
Scherrer/Scherer Adam
Scherrer/Scherer Joseph
Scheuerlein Leonhard
Schiebel Franz
Schiller/Sceller August
Schiller/Sceller Karl
Schiller/Sceller Johann
Schilling Wilhelm
Schinck/Schenck

Schipper Georg
Schirelant Johann
Schlabaum Franz
Schlamilch Heinrich
Schlauderbeck Michel
Schlechtleitner Johann
Schleiffer Sebastian
Schleiter Johann
Schlerett Adam
Schliecker Andreas
Schliephake/Schliphache Heinrich
Schlirff/Schlirth/Schlierf Michael
Schloczmacher/Schlossmacher Michael
Schlüter Andreas
Schmid/Schmidt/Schmitt/Schmith/
  Smith Andreas
Schmid/Schmidt/Schmitt/Schmith/
  Smith August
Schmid/Schmidt/Schmitt/Schmith/
  Smith Christian
Schmid/Schmidt/Schmitt/Schmith/
  Smith Friedrich
Schmid/Schmidt/Schmitt/Schmith/
  Smith Georg
Schmid/Schmidt/Schmitt/Schmith/
  Smith Heinrich
Schmid/Schmidt/Schmitt/Schmith/
  Smith J.C.
Schmid/Schmidt/Schmitt/Schmith/
  Smith Jacob
Schmid/Schmidt/Schmitt/Schmith/
  Smith Johann, Christophe
Schmid/Schmidt/Schmitt/Schmith/
  Smith Johann, Balthazar
Schmid/Schmidt/Schmitt/Schmith/
  Smith Johann, Georg
Schmid/Schmidt/Schmitt/Schmith/
  Smith Michael
Schmid/Schmidt/Schmitt/Schmith/
  Smith Nicolaus
Schmid/Schmidt/Schmitt/Schmith/
  Smith Phillip
Schmid/Schmidt/Schmitt/Schmith/
  Smith Valentin
Schmidtmeyer Wilhelm
Schmiedel Wilhelm
Schmoll Christophe
Schmorr Johann, Benjamin

Schmotter Johann, Heinrich
Schmut Johann
Schnabel Johann
Schnaebill
Schnee Anton
Schneider Christian
Schneider Elias
Schneider Ernst
Schneider Gottlieb
Schneider Johann
Schneider Valentin
Schneider Wilhelm
Schnitter Nicolaus
Schnödler Johann
Schnurr Johann, Conrad
Schoell Georg
Schoenbier/Schambier
Schoepner/Schepner
Schollhammer
Schomberg Heinrich
Schonberger Johann
Schondorff Johann
Schonecker Elias, Gottlieb
Schönecker
Schott/Shutt Friedrich
Schott/Shutt Wilhelm
Schrader Heinrich
Schrader Magnus
Schrankemüller Michael
Schreiber Andreas
Schreiber Heinrich
Schreiber Johann
Schrempf Andreas
Schröder/Schroeder Johann
Schröder/Schroeder Thomas
Schrodt Franz
Schroot Heinrich
Schroth Heinrich
Schubart/Schubert/Shoubert August
Schubart/Schubert/Shoubert Johann
Schubart/Schubert/Shoubert Peter
Schudlett Jacob
Schukard Paul
Schuler/Schüler Johann
Schueltes Nicolaus
Schultz(e)/Shoults Andreas
Schultz(e)/Shoults Christian
Schultz(e)/Shoults Conrad

Schultz(e)/Shoults Friedrich
Schultz(e)/Shoults Gottlieb
Schultz(e)/Shoults Heinrich
Schultz(e)/Shoults Joachim
Schultz(e)/Shoults Johann
Schultz(e)/Shoults Johann, Georg
Schultz(e)/Shoults Johann, Gottlieb
Schultz(e)/Shoults Karl
Schuman/Shumann Georg
Schumann/Shuman Friedrich
Schumpff/Jomphe Christian
Schünemann/Scheinemann Johann
Schuoter/Schuster August
Schut(t)/Schott Friedrich
Schut(t)/Schott Wilhelm
Schütz/Schut Leopold
Schütz/Schut Wilhelm
Schwaab Stephan
Schwack Peter
Schwalm Chretien
Schwan Johann
Schwan Johann, Heinrich
Schwarz(e)/Schwartz Friedrich
Schwieger
Schwimmer Georg
Scidleir
Scolle/Coll
Seelander Chretien
Seibert Balthazar
Seidenzahl Johann
Seidler Andreas
Seissner
Seitz/Seiz Jacob
Seitz/Seiz Johann
Semler Johann
Semmigen Christophe
Sempf Lucas
Senuke E.
Sereny Jacob
Servet/Servais/Gervais Jean
Severin Johann
Severt Johann
Seitz/Seiz Jacob
Seitz/Seiz Johann
Shabash
Shamben/Schambier
Shaver/Schaeffer
Sheilheimer

Shirelant
Shools/Schoell/Schultz/Choults Georg
Shrenell
Shumann
Sicman/Si(e)ckmann/Silckmann/
    Siegmann/Sigouin Andreas
Sicman/Si(e)ckmann/Silckmann/
    Siegmann/Sigouin, Christophe
Sicman/Si(e)ckmann/Silckmann/
    Siegmann/Sigouin Heinrich,
    Christophe
Sidner Johann
Siebenhaar
Siebenhaar Franz
Siebetslie
Siebetslie Georg
Siesert/Liessert
Sigouin/Siegman/Sicman/Sickmann/
    Silckmann
Simonie/Simony Christian
Singer Friedrich
Singer Wilhelm
Sirestere/Finsterer
Siry/Tiry/Liry/Firy Wolfgang
Skine/King
Skinner Johann
Slieneman Heinrich
Small Christian
Smith/Schmidt/Schmid
Snyder Heinrich
Soldow Friedrich
Söllig Ernst
Sommer(s) Friedrich
Sonnerthat Christophe
Spahn Adam
Spahn Ferdinand
Spath/Spatz Johann
Spath/Spatz Gottlieb
Specht Johann, Julius, Anton
Spitter Christophe
Spoeder Johann
Springer Christophe
Spulit Anton
St-Pierre Jean-Marie
Stadermann Johann
Staggmann Johann
Stainger Philipp, Jacob
Stam Martin

Stamin
Stangell Georg
Stanze Christian
Stanze Johann, Wilhelm
Starch Philipp
Stauber Johann
Staughmill Heinrich
Steckhane Johann
Steger/Steiger Johann
Steger/Steiger Ludwig
Steger/Steiger Michel
Stegle/Kegle/Tegle/Steger
Stegmann/Staggmann
Stein/Stone Karl
Stein/Stone Heinrich
Stein/Stone Theodore
Steinbruck Heinrich, Christian
Steinert Tobias
Steinmann Johann, Heinrich
Steinmetz Chretien
Stengel Georg
Stenger Philipp
Stenzell Sammuel
Sterne Diedrich
Sterner Johann
Stenke Christian
Stiber Philipp, Heinrich
Stiern Johann
Stilling Georg
Stirner
Stock Andreas
Stolzenberg Friedrich, Christian
Storr Friedrich
Straderick Johann
Strafsman Heinrich
Straub Gaspar
Stricker Johann
Stringue/Stengel
Strope/Straub
Strötz Friedrich
Struve Christophe
Stubenhauer Johann
Stübenitzky Karl
Stüber Christian
Stübinger Georg
Suh Friedrich
Summer/Sommer Michael
Süss(e) Georg

Süss(e) Heinrich
Süss(e) Johann
Süss(e) Johann, Paul
Süss(e) Paul
Sussner Georg
Sweet Philipp
Szass/Sasse

T
Täger Andreas
Talham/Thalham
Tappe Heinrich
Tarlouse Johann
Tauschmann Gottfried
Teffner/Thavener Georg
Tegle/Kegle/Goekel
Tehtmeyer/Thatmeyer Ludwig
Temme Julius
Terries/Ferries
Teshneur/Teffner
Thanweber Johann, Heinrich
Thavener/Teffner
Theilheimer Georg
Thesser
Thevener/Teffner
Thiele David
Thiele Friedrich
Thielebein Friedrich
Thienel/Thenel/Thunel Karl
Thiess Johann
Thisser/Tyssère Martin
Thoene Heinrich
Thomae/Thomas Daniel
Thomae/Thomas Karl
Thun
Tieckman Heinrich
Tielecke/Tieleke Andreas
Tillert Christophe
Tip Wilhelm
Tiry/Siry/Liry/etc. Wolfgang
Tisser/Thisser
Titley/Dittlie
Tittsel/Dielzel
Töelle Johann
Tornier Karl
Tost Christian
Trauth Christophe
Trautner Peter

Treller Johann
Trestler/Troestler Johann, Joseph
Treutz Gaspar
Triff/Trith August
Triff/Trith Friedrich
Troestler/Trestler Johann, Joseph
Trottmann Anton
Trümper Georg
Tuchscheer Georg
Tude Heinrich
Tulft/Duff
Turger Johann
Turnau Bened.
Tyssère/Thisser Martin

U
Ulrich Peter
Unschück Conrad

V
Vachestein/Weissenstein
Vatterott Johann, Valentin
Veith/Veuth François
Velling/Welling/Walling
Venert Jacob
Verdries Christophe
Vernau Johann, Christian
Verner Jacob
Vevre/Vevres/Weber
Viano Andreas
Vicario Johann, Baptiste
Vieth Adolphus
Viger Gaspar
Vodine Joseph
Voelger Heinrich
Vogel/Loiseau Johann, Georg
Vogel/Loiseau Stephan
Vogeler/Vogler Francis
Vogelsberg Christophe
Voges Johann, Heinrich
Vohl/Vaul
Voigt Harthmann
Volchmann/Vollmann Sigmund
Volmer Nicolaus
Vondenvelden Wilhelm
Voss Christian
Voul/Vaul
Voulph/Wolf

W
Wacker/Walker Johann
Wagemann Laurent
Wagenknecht
Wagner/Wagener Christian
Wagner/Wagener Conrad
Wagner/Wagener Friedrich
Wagner/Wagener Heinrich
Wagner/Wagener Johann
Wagner/Wagener Johann, Andreas
Wagner/Wagener Johann, Christophe
Wagner/Wagener Johann, Georg
Wagner/Wagener Matthias
Wagner/Wagener Nicolaus
Wagner/Wagener Philipp
Wahl Johann, Michael
Walch/Walsh Bernhard
Walch/Walsh Franz, Emmanuel
Walling/Walling Christophe
Warleck/Warleck Adam
Warnecke Heinrich
Warnecke Johann
Warnecke Johann, Ludwig
Weber Georg
Weber Johann
Weber Johann, Georg
Weber Peter
Weckesser/Weickerssen/ Vickerson
   Georg
Weddig/Wedding Johann, Peter
Wegelein/Wegelin Georg Peter
Wegelein/Wegelin Matthias
Wegener Gaspar
Wehling Ernst
Wehmeyer/Wehrmeyer Christian
Wehr Hugo
Weibell Friedrich
Weigand Oswald
Weihte Johann
Weiland Heinrich
Weinem Leonhard
Weinküber Johann
Weipert Siriac
Weiss(e) Georg
Weiss(e) Johann, Georg
Weissenborn Johannes
Weissenborn Johann, Friedrich
Weissenstein Karl

Weithe/Weihte/Withe
Welfret/Wolfart
Welling Augustus
Welling Christophe
Weltz/Wells
Wendel Wilhelm
Wenderich Chretien
Wepper/Wipper
Werner Johann, Daniel
Werner/Verner Jacob
Werneri Johann, Christian
Wesche Johann
Westerkamp Rudolph
Wetter Georg
Wettig/Weddig
Weyand/Waeigand Conrad
Weyand/Waeigand Nicolaus
Weyguiver Joseph
Whitsack/Withsack Samuel
Whitsell Nicolaus
Whittaker Andreas
Wideman Johann
Wieg Ferdinand
Wiegman J.
Wiesell Conrad
Wiesener/Wiesner Chretien
Wiesener/Wiesner Ludwig
Wiesener/Wiesner Sebastian
Wilhelmi/Wilhelmy Ernst, Christian,
   Diedrich
Will Laurent
Willner Heinrich
Wilment Wolmand
Wimmer Friedrich
Winckelmann/Winkelmann Johann,
   Heinrich
Winckelvoss Andreas
Winckler Johann
Windill
Winkeifer Joseph
Winterbergt Ernst
Withsack Samuel
Wittemann Karl
Witthun Friedrich
Wittig Ernst
Wittlacken Heinrich
Wittlacker Heinrich
Woberich Johann

Wolf(e)/Wolff August, Ludwig
Wolf(e)/Wolff Emmanuel,
  François-Emmanuel
Wolf(e)/Wolff Johann
Wolf(e)/Wolff Ludwig
Wolf(e)/Wolff Michael
Wolf(e)/Wolff Philipp
Wolf(e)/Wolff Wilhelm
Wolfart/Wolfert/Welfret Sebastian
Wöllendorf Daniel
Wollmann/Wolmand Anton
Wolss/Wolls/Wolz/Wolf Bernhard
Wriland H.
Wull/Wolf
Würfel/Würtel Johann, Michael
Wyley Wyndel

Y
Yockell/Jockel Andreas
Yockell/Jockel Johann, Heinrich
Yockell/Jockel Peter

Young/Jung Georg
Yurgern/Jurguns Friedrich

Z
Zaust/Saust
Zehnert Paul
Zeillmann/Zellmann Daniel
Zeillmann/Zellmann Ludwig
Zick Anton
Ziegenhain/Ziegenhyin Peter
Ziegenstiel/Ziegelstiel Georg
Ziegler Andreas
Ziegler Johann
Ziermann Johann, Heinrich
Ziliac/Ciliac Georg
Zips Valentin
Zischler Georg
Ziten Laurent
Zollenger Sebastian
Zorn Johann
Zwicker Chretien
Zyprian Heinrich

List of patronyms of Brunswickers who might have immigrated to Canada as German mercenaries.

A
Adam/Eidam/Raubenheimer
Adel Friedrich
Adrian
Aernerd/Aherned Johann, Thomas
Ahanns Johann
Ahl/All/Hall
Aiot/Ayotte
Alberg
Albrecht Johann
Alin/Alain
All/Ahl/Hall
André
Angelhart Johann, Baptiste
Appel Christian
Aprenant Peter, Alexis
Arnoldi
Ayotte/Aiot

B
Back Karl
Bampf

Baner
Baour Johann, Conrad
Barck Thomas
Beaher/Beaker Johann, Daniel
Beck
Becker Christian
Becker Georg
Becker Johann
Benecke Johann
Benedict Johann
Benick Baptiste
Benther/Benth
Berger Johann
Bergspaer/Spaer Johann, Georg
Bernard/Bernhard
Beschard/Béchard
Besré/Besserer Friedrich
Besré/Besserer Ludwig
Besré/Besserer Théodore
Bittner Georg
Blumhardt Johann, Georg
Bobart

Bode Johann, Christophe
Bolt
Bonge
Boutton
Bleneau/Brennecki
Braunn Luke
Brenegal Heinrich
Brotmeyer Christian
Byer Johann

C
Camerer Jacob, Christophe
Carpenter/Zimmerman
Casselman(n)
Chattoni
Chemonte Johann, Marie
Chrisman Georg, Wilhelm
Christ
Christian Anton
Christian Johann
Christiny
Ciliak(c)/Ziliac
Claprood Ernst
Claprood Johann, Friedrich
Classen
Cleman Adam
Clousdepas Gabriel
Coje
Cordes
Corneli
Cronne Johann, Christophe
Crouppe/Grouppe Christian, Heinrich

D
Dahle
Dangerro
Dehue
Delamarre
Dion Pierre
Ditzel Johann
Disle Johann
Donné
Dorlord Thomas
Dufais
Durr
Duttloff Johann, Baptiste

E
Eckel/Eykel
Eichelmann Bernhard
Ekemberg Christian, Friedrich
Emmert Johann, Joseph

F
Faber
Fabet
Feltalsade J.B.
Feve Pierre
Fisbach Dominique
Fisher Heinrich
Fisher Joseph
Fix
Fleischmann
Fleurant Sebastian
Forcade Johann, Baptiste
Forest/Forrest
Fredemberg/Fridemberg
Frederick Johann, Heinrich
Futre Johann, Julius

G
Gahbert
Garst-Pitre Peter
Gärtner
George
Gerhart Andreas
German
Glass
Goetze Johann
Gottsschalck/Gottsshall/Gottsschalck
Grass Nicolaus
Grein Paul
Grey
Gürtler/Gürttler
H
Habich
Hall/Ahl/All
Hamburger
Harl Johann, Friedrich
Hartt Paul
Hass/Haws/Hawse Georg
Hegner Philipp, Jacob
Heil Johann
Hein Heinrich
Henforth Johann

Henrick Sebrecht, Lebrecht
Henss Joseph
Herforth Johann, Godfroy
Herguener Franz
Herport
Hess Andreas
Hess Johann
Hesse Johann
Hibo
Himm Heinrich
Hoffmann Godfried
Hoffmann Heinrich
Hoffmann Thomas
Hoffmeister Friedrich
Hoffmeister Nicolaus
Hoopstadt Leonhard
Hooseme Joseph
Hubuk
Hugo
Hyeinemann/Heynemand Christophe,
    Friedrich

J
Jacobi
Jansen
Jarosh
Jasper
Jean Jean-Baptiste

K
Kabitzky
Kamerla
Kastner Johann
Kaufholtz, Johann Christof
Kebenhar/Kibeham
Keisler Mickel
Keller J.B.
Kenner
Kepper Johann, Christophe
Kers Philipp
King Friedrich
Knobloch/Konoblau Johann
Koch Gerbert
Koenig Just.
Koller Nicolauss
Kolp Jacob
Krafft
Kratz Georg

Küchenthal
Kukn Simon
Kuoth

L
Laing Philipp
Lang Johann
Laurenceau/Moncourt Joseph
Leard/Lessard Johann, Karl, Ignace
Leb Friedrich
Leffler Gustavus
Lehman
Leimer/Lemmert
Leinss Johann, Christian
Leipold
Leitenfieth J.B.
Lentremann Augustin
Léo
Liemon
Lime
Lobbes
Loffard Jean, Laurent
Lohr/Lorensen/Lorenzen
Lucas
Lucke
Ludwick Friedrich
Lutter/Luther

M
Mahler/Maller
Mahlo/Malo/Mahlo
Maller/Mahler Christian
Maller/Mahler Felix
Malacie Johann
Maouk Godefroid
Mardefeldt
Marchand
Marx Ignace
Maurer
Meiners
Melcher(s)
Merckel Johann
Meyer Johann, Christian
Michel
Milker Conrad
Mischky
Miskaner Johann
Moche

Modell
Moly
Muller Leonhard
Munich Jean-Baptiste
Myers Christian
Myers Mikel

N
Nantel Nicolaus
Nappert/Nopper Johann, Franz
Nicolai/Nicolas
Nimer Franz
Noaere Ignace
Noel
Nohra
Nolte
Norman(n)
Noster

O
Oberman Joseph, Friedrich
Ohlman/Ullman
Olrich/Ulrich
Outerhart Ezkel

P
Padz Joseph
Pannier
Panst Bonaventure
Paull/Poll/Paul Joseph
Paro
Penser
Pétri(e)/Pettry
Pfaff
Pfeiffer Peter
Pierri
Pousse Jean
Power Johannes
Pozer Johann, Georg
Presse
Prussien Nicolaus
Pulver

Q
Queuliche Friedrich
Quintal Antoine

R
Rainking
Reese
Reiche/Resche Johann, Baptiste
Reinath Johann
Remi/Remy/Remmy
Robert
Roch
Rochenbard/Montagne Joachim
Rochenberger
Roman(n)
Romel Jacob
Romer/Rosemeyer
Rosenberger
Rotger Ben.
Ryner Gaspar

S
Sabbner Johann
Sasse Johann, Andreas
Sauer Johann
Sauter
Sceller Johann
Seltzer
Selye/Silliez Andreas
Schaeffer/Schaper Johann
Scheffler Ferdinand
Schene Johann
Schetky/Scheltry/Schetky Friedrich
Schmidd Wilhelm
Schmitz Johann
Schmoutz Karl
Schneider/Scheider J.B.
Schob Heinrich
Schoecke Nicolaus, Johann
Schoulz/Choulz Joseph
Scusse Paul
Seiz Andreas
Sheling Johann, Nicolaus
Shreader Michel
Shreiter Michel
Shriber Johann
Shribert Johann
Shrider Christophe
Shrite Johann
Shroader Johann
Siebert Godefroid
Siegmund

Simon
Smith Johann, Rodolphe
Snider/Snyder Tobias
Spaer/Bergspaer Despar.
Spuck
Stande
Steger Johann, Baptiste
Stein Johann
Steinhoff Johann
Steinmetz/Stemetz Goltier
Steineck
Suder
Suzor Franz

T
Tauge
Tegle Johann
Tell Adam
Telle Jacob
Thalham Joseph, Alexandre
Theopold
Trabant Johannes
Tutite Theodore
U
Ullman/Ohlman
Ulrich/Olrich
Unger

V
Vachausky Joseph
Vagner Fr.
Vaul Paul
Verwerth Johann, Christophe
Vesel Nicolaus

Viane/Vianne
Vianne/Viane
Vivisse/Pitre Ludwig

W
Wagner Andreas
Walker
Walter
Waltz
Weber Bernhard
Weber/Weiber Johann
Weber/Weiber Johann, Baptiste
Wegger Jacob
Welter Jacob
Wentzel Johann
Werre Johann
Wert Mathieu
Werther Johann, Baptiste
Westphal
Wik Johann, Martin
Wikof Joseph
Wilhelm
Wilhem Johannes
Winter
Wintzel Adam
Wisigard Conrad
Wulffe/Wolf Georg

Z
Zacharia
Zimmerman/Carpenter
Zoo
Zorbach

MAIN WINTER QUARTERS FOR GERMAN SOLDIERS FOR 1776

Regiments	Date	Places
Grenadiers Battalion Lt.Col Von Breymann	1St June To 4Th June	On Board of Pallas
	June 20Th	In Laprairie
	July 1St	In Laprairie
	August 1St	In Laprairie
	September 1St	In Laprairie
	October 1St	In The Camp of St-Jean
	November 1St	St-Denis
	December 1St	St-Sulpice
Musketeers Von Riedesel Lt.Col. Von Speth	1St June To 4Th June	On Board of Pallas
	June 20Th	In Laprairie
	July 1St	In Laprairie
	August 1St	In Laprairie
	September 1St	In Laprairie
	October 1St	In St-Jean
	November 1St	In Three Rivers
	December 1St	In Three Rivers
First Battalion of Hesse-Hanau Lt.Col. Johann Lentz	1St June To 4Th June	On Board of Pallas
	June 20Th	In Laprairie
	July 1St	In Laprairie
	August 1St	In Laprairie
	September 1St	In Laprairie
	October 1St	In St-Jean
	November 1St	Berthier
	December 1St	Berthier
Musketeers Prince Frederic Lt.Col. Präetorius	1St June To 4Th June	On Board of Pallas
	June 6Th	Disembark In Quebec
	July 1St	In Quebec
	August 1St	In Quebec
	September 1St	In Quebec
	October 1St	In Quebec
	November 1St	In Quebec
	December 1St	In Berthier
Dragoons Prince Ludwig Lt.Col. Baum	1St June To 4Th June	On Board of Pallas
	June 6Th	Disembark in Quebec
	July 1St	In Quebec
	August 1St	In Quebec
	September 1St	In Quebec

Regiments	Date	Places
	October 1St	Goellette Basaite Union
	November 1St	In Three Rivers
	December 1St	In Three Rivers
Musketeers Maj.Gen. Von Rhetz	October 6Th	Maskinongé
	November 1St	In Ste-Anne
	December 1St	In Ste-Anne
Musketeers Von Specht Col. Specht	October 6Th	In Maskinongé
	NoVember 2Nd	In Batiscan
	December 1St	In Batiscan
Light Infantry Battalion Maj.Von Barner	October 6Th	In Maskinongé
	November 2Nd	In St-Jean
	December 1St	In St-François

MAIN WINTER QUARTERS FOR GERMAN SOLDIERS FOR THE YEAR 1777

Regiments	Date	Places
Grenadiers Battalion Lt.Col Von Breymann	January 1St	In St-Sulpice
	February 1St	In St-Sulpice
	March 1St	In St-Sulpice
	April 1St	In St-Sulpice
	May 1St	In St-Sulpice
	June 1St	In St-Sulpice
	July 1St	In St-Sulpice
	July 30Th	In L'assomption
	August 1St	In L'assomption
	September 1St	In L'assomption
	October 1St	In L'assomption
	November 1St	In L'assomption
	December 1St	In L'assomption
	September 1St	In L'assomption
Musketeers Von Riedesel Lt.Col. Von Speth	January 1St	In Three Rivers
	February 1St	In Three Rivers
	March 1St	In Three Rivers
	April 1St	In Three Rivers
	May 1St	In Three Rivers
	June 1St	In Three Rivers
	July 1St	In Three Rivers
	August 1St	In Three Rivers

Regiments	Date	Places
	September 1St	In Three Rivers
	October 1St	In Three Rivers
	November 1St	In Three Rivers
	December 1St	In Three Rivers
First Battalion Of Hesse-Hanau Lt.Col. Johan Lentz	January 1St	In Berthier
	February 1St	In Berthier
	March 1St	In Berthier
	March 8Th	No Data
	April 1St	No Data
	May 1St	No Data
	June 1St	No Data
	July 1St	No Data
	August 1St	In Berthier
	September 1St	In Berthier
	October 1St	In Berthier
	November 1St	In Berthier
	December 1St	In Berthier
Yagers Corps Of Hesse-Hanau Lt.Col. Von Kreutzbourg	July 1St	No Data
	August 1St	No Data
	September 1St	No Data
	October 1St	No Data
	NoveMber 1St	No Data
	December 1St	In L'assomption
	December 23Th	In L'assomption
	December 23Th	In Lachenaie
	December 23Th	In Mascouche
	December 23Th	In Repentigny
	December 23Th	In Terrebonne
Musketeers Prince Frederic Lt.Col. Präetorius	January 1St	In Berthier
	February 1St	In Berthier
	March 1St	In Rivière Aux Loups
	April 1St	In Rivière Aux Loups
	May 1St	In Rivière Aux Loups
	June 1St	In Rivière Aux Loups
	July 1St	In Rivière Aux Loups
	August 1St	In Rivière Aux Loups
	September 1St	In Rivière Aux Loups
	October 1St	In Rivière Aux Loups
	November 1St	In Rivière Aux Loups
	November 22Th	In St-Antoine
	December 1St	In St-Antoine

Regiments	Date	Places
	December 23Th	In St-Sulpice
		In Lavaltrie
		In Lanoraie
		In Berthier
		In St-Antoine
		In St-Esprit
		In St-Cuthbert
		In St-Jean
		In Fort York ?
Dragoons Prince Ludwig Lt.Col. Baum	January 1St	In Three Rivers
	February 1St	In Three Rivers
	March 1St	In Three Rivers
	April 1St	In Three Rivers
	May 1St	In Three Rivers
	June 1St	In Three Rivers
	July 1St	In Three Rivers
	August 1St	In Three Rivers
Lt.Col. Maibaum	September 1St	In Three Rivers
	October 1St	In Three Rivers
	November 1St	In Three Rivers
	November 22Th	In Three Rivers
	December 1St	In Three Rivers
Musketeers Maj.Gen. Von Rhetz	January 1St	In Cap Santé
	February 1St	In Cap Santé
	March 1St	In Cap Santé
	April 1St	In Cap Santé
	May 1St	In Cap Santé
	June 1St	In Cap Santé
	July 1St	In Cap Santé
	August 1St	In Cap Santé
	September 1St	In Cap Santé
	October 1St	In Cap Santé
	November 1St	In Cap Santé
	November 22Th	In Cap Santé
	December 1St	In Cap Santé
Musketeers Von Specht Col. Specht	January 1St	In Ste-Anne
	February 1St	In Ste-Anne
	March 1St	In Ste-Anne

Regiments	Date	Places
	April 1ˢᵗ	In Ste-Anne
	May 1ˢᵗ	In Ste-Anne
	June 1ˢᵗ	In Ste-Anne
	July 1ˢᵗ	In Ste-Anne
	August 1ˢᵗ	In Cap De La Magdeleine
	September 1ˢᵗ	In Cap De La Magdeleine
	October 1ˢᵗ	In Cap De La Magdeleine
	November 1ˢᵗ	In Cap De La Magdeleine
	December 1ˢᵗ	In Cap De La Magdeleine
Light Infantry Battalion Maj. Von Barner	January 1ˢᵗ	In St-François
	February 1ˢᵗ	In St-François
	March 1ˢᵗ	In St-François
	April 1ˢᵗ	In St-François
	May 1ˢᵗ	In St-François
	June 1ˢᵗ	In St-François
	July 1ˢᵗ	In St-François
	August 1ˢᵗ	In Yamaska
	September 1ˢᵗ	In Yamaska
	October 1ˢᵗ	In Yamaska
Light Infantry Battalion Maj.Von Barner (More)	November 1ˢᵗ	In Yamaska
	December 1ˢᵗ	In Yamaska

MAIN WINTER QUARTERS FOR GERMAN SOLDIERS FOR THE YEAR 1778

Regiments	Date	Places
Musketeers Prince Frederic Lt.Col. Präetorius	January 1ˢᵗ	In Berthier
	February 1ˢᵗ	In St-Charles
	March 1ˢᵗ	In St-Charles
	April 1ˢᵗ	In St-Charles
	May 1ˢᵗ	In St-Charles
		In St-Charles
	May 6ᵀʰ	In St-Antoine
		In St-Denis
		In Quebec
		In Berthier (Keep A Close Watch Of The Stores)
		Montreal=The Patiens
	December 1ˢᵗ	In St-Charles
Dragoons Prince Ludwig Lt.Col. Meibaum	January 1ˢᵗ	In Quebec
	February 1ˢᵗ	In Quebec
	March 1ˢᵗ	In Quebec
	April 1ˢᵗ	In Quebec

Regiments	Date	Places
	May 1St	In Quebec
	May 6Th	In Quebec
		In Three Rivers (Bagages)
	June 1St	In Quebec
	July 1St	In Quebec
	August 1St	In Quebec
	September 1St	In Quebec
		In Three Rivers (Bagages)
	October 1St	In Quebec
	November 1St	In Quebec
	December 1St	In Quebec
Grenadiers Battalion Lt.Col Von Mengen	January 1St	In Fort Sorel
	February 1St	In Fort Sorel
	March 1St	In Fort Sorel
	April 1St	In Fort Sorel
	May 1St	In Fort Sorel
	May 6Th	In Fort Sorel
		In Three Rivers (Bagages)
	June 1St	In Fort Sorel
	July 1St	In Fort Sorel
	August 1St	In Fort Sorel
	September 1St	In Fort Sorel
		In Three Rivers (Bagages)
	October 1St	In Fort Sorel
	November 1St	In Fort Sorel
	December 1St	In Fort Sorel
Musketeers Von Riedesel Lt.Col. Von Speth	January 1St	In Quebec
	February 1St	In Quebec
	March 1St	In Quebec
	April 1St	In Quebec
	May 1St	In Quebec
	May 6Th	In Quebec
		In Three Rivers (Bagages)
	June 1St	In Quebec
	July 1St	In Quebec
	August 1St	In Quebec
	September 1St	In Quebec
		In Three Rivers (Baggages)
	October 1St	In Quebec
	November 1St	In Quebec

Regiments	Date	Places
	December 1St	In Quebec
Musketeers Maj.Gen. Von Rhetz	January 1St	In Three Rivers
	February 1St	In Three Rivers
	March 1St	In Three Rivers
	April 1St	In Three Rivers
	May 1St	In Three Rivers
	May 6Th	In Three Rivers
		St-Pierre (Some Men)
	June 1St	In Three Rivers
	July 1St	In Three Rivers
	August 1St	In Three Rivers
	September 1St	In Three Rivers
		St-Pierre (Some Men)
	October 1St	In Three Rivers
	November 1St	In Three Rivers
	December 1St	In Three Rivers
Light Infantry Battalion Maj. Von Barner	January 1St	In Yamaska
		In St-François
		In Nicolet
	February 1St	In Yamaska
		In St-François
		In Nicolet
	March 1St	In Yamaska
		In St-François
		In Nicolet
		In Yamaska
	April 1St	In St-François
		In Nicolet
	May 1St	In Yamaska
		In St-François
		In Nicolet
	May 6Th	In Yamaska
		In St-François
		In Nicolet
		In Three Rivers
	June 1St	In Yamaska
		In St-François
		In Nicolet

Regiments	Date	Places
	July 1St	In Yamaska
		In St-François
		In Nicolet
	August 1St	In Yamaska
		In St-François
		In Nicolet
	September 1St	In Yamaska
		In St-François
		In Nicolet
		In Three Rivers
	October 1St	In Yamaska
		In St-François
		In Nicolet
	November 1St	In Yamaska
		In St-François
		In Nicolet
	December 1St	In Yamaska
		In St-François
		In Nicolet
Yagers Corps of Hesse-Hanau Lt.Col. Von Kreutzbourg	January 1St And 12Th	In L'assomption
	February 1St	In St-Antoine
	March 1St	In St-Antoine
	April 1St	In St-Antoine
	May 1St	In Terrebonne
	May 6Th	In Terrebonne
		In Mascouche
		In Lachenaie
	June 1St	In Terrebonne
	July 1St	In Terrebonne
	August 1St	No Data
	September 1St	In Terrebonne
		In Mascouche
		In Lachenaie
		In Repentigny
	October 1St	In Terrebonne
	November 1St	In Terrebonne
	December 1St	In Terrebonne
Detachement of Capt. Georg Von Schoell	January 1St	In St-Antoine
	February 1St	In St-Antoine

Regiments	Date	Places
	March 1St	In St-Antoine
	April 1St	In St-Antoine
	May 1St	In St-Antoine
	May 6Th	In Rivière du Chêne
		In Three Rivers
	June 1St	In Terrebonne
	July 1St	In Terrebonne
	August 1St	No Data
	September 1St	In Rivière du Chêne
		Mascouche
	September 5Th	In Terrebonne
	October 1St	In Rivière du Chêne
	November 1St	In Rivière du Chêne
	December 1St	In Rivière du Chêne
Hesse-Hanau Artillery Capt. Georg Pausch	June 28Th	In Quebec
	August 1St	In Quebec
	September 1St	In Quebec
	September 5Th	In Terrebonne
	October 12Th	In St-Jean
		In Île-Aux-Noix
		In Sorel
	November 1St	In Sorel
		In St-Jean
	December 1St	In Sorel
		In St-Jean
The Princess of Anhalt's Col. Friedrich Von Rauschenplatt	September 5Thand 12Th	In Quebec
	September 28Th	In Quebec
	November 1St	In Quebec
	December 1St	In Quebec
Regiment Von Barner Lt.Col. Ferdinand A. Von Barner	October 1St	In Three Rivers
	November 1St	In La Baie
	December 1St	In La Baie
Regiment Von Ehrenkrook Col. Johann G. Von Ehrenkrook	October 1St	In Three Rivers
	November 1St	In Three Rivers
	December 1St	In Three Rivers

MAIN QUARTERS FOR GERMAN SOLDIERS FOR AUGUST 1779

States	Regiments	Companies	Places
Hesse-Hanau	Yagers Corps of Hesse-Hanau	Lt.Col. Von Kreutzbourg	In L'assomtion
Hesse-Hanau	Yagers Corps of Hesse-Hanau	Maj. Von Franken	In Lachenaie
Hesse-Hanau	Yagers Corps of Hesse-Hanau	Capt. Count of Wittgenstein	In Terrebonne
Hesse-Hanau	Yagers Corps of Hesse-Hanau	Capt. Kastendyck	In Repentigny
Hesse-Hanau	Yagers Corps of Hesse-Hanau	Capt. Hugget	In Beauport

MAIN QUARTERS FOR GERMAN SOLDIERS FOR FALL 1779

States	Regiments	Companies	Places
Hesse-Hanau	Yagers Corps of Hesse-Hanau	No Data	In Fort Niagara
			In Carleton Island
			In Montreal
Brunswick	Regiment Von Barner	Capt. Von Hambach	In Montreal
Hesse-Hanau	Some Men of First	Capt. Frederic	In St-Martin
	Battalion Crown Prince	Louis Von Schoell	In Ste-Rose
		223 Soldiers	In St-François
Hesse-Hanau	Some Men of Artilery	81 Soldiers	In St-Jean
			In Sorel
			In Île-Aux-Noix

MAIN QUARTERS FOR GERMAN SOLDIERS FOR WINTER 1780

States	Regiments	Companies	Places
Brunswick	Part of The Regiment Prince Frederic	No Data	In St-Jean
			In Iberville
Hesse-Hanau	Yagers Corps of Hesse-Hanau	No Data	In La Prairie
			In St-François du Lac
Hesse-Hanau	First Battalion Crown Prince	Capt. Schoell	In Quebec
Brunswick	Staff And Some Soldiers From Differents Regiments	No Data	In Berthier

MAIN QUARTERS FOR GERMAN SOLDIERS FOR SUMMER AND FALL 1780

States	Regiments	Companies	Places
Hesse-Hanau	Yagers Corps of Hesse-Hanau	No Data	In Camp In Pointe de Lévis
			In Belœil
			In Lavaltrie
			In St-Matias
			In Baie St-Paul
			(La Baie St-Paul)

MAIN QUARTERS FOR GERMAN SOLDIERS FOR WINTER 1781

States	Regiments	Companies	Places
Brunswick	Some Soldiers From	No Data	In L'assomtion
	Differents Regiments		In Bécancour
			In Pointe-Au-Fer
Hesse-Hanau	First Battalion Crown Prince	No Data	In Ste-Anne
Hesse-Hanau	Hesse-Hanau Artillery	No Data	In Kamouraska
Hesse-Hanau	Yagers Corps of Hesse-Hanau	No Data	In St-Vallier
			In Châteauguay
Anhalt-Zerbst	Princess of Anhalt-Zerbst Regiment	No Data	In Rivière-Ouelle
Hesse-Kassel	Alt Von Loosberg	No Data	In Berthier
			In New York
Hesse-Kassel	Alt Von Loosberg	No Data	In Île D'orléans

MAIN QUARTERS FOR GERMAN SOLDIERS FOR SUMMER 1781

States	Regiments	Companies	Places
Hesse-Hanau	Yagers Corps of Hesse-Hanau	No Data	In Quebec
Hesse-Hanau	One Officer and 50 Soldiers	No Data	In Carleton Island
	of Yagers Corps of Hesse-Hanau		
Brunswick	Some Soldiers	No Data	In Montreal
			In Quebec
			In Berthier
			In Three Rivers
Hesse-Kassel	Alt Von Loosberg	No Data	In Quebec
Hesse-Hanau	First Battalion Crown Prince	No Data	In Quebec
Anhalt-Zerbst	Princess Of Anhalt-Zerbst Regiment	No Data	In Quebec
Brunswick	Some Soldiers	No Data	In Quebec

MAIN QUARTERS FOR GERMAN SOLDIERS FOR WINTER 1782

States	Regiments	Companies	Places
Brunswick	Some Soldiers of	No Data	In L'assomption
	Differents Regiments		In Montreal
			And Scattered From
			Bécancour to Pointe-au-fe
Hesse-Hanau	Hanau Infantry Regiment	No Data	In Ste-Anne
	(First Battalion Crown Prince)		
Hesse-Hanau	Hanau Artillery Regiment	No Data	In Kamouraska
Hesse-Hanau	Yagers Corps of Hesse-Hanau	No Data	In St-Vallier
			In Châteauguay
Anhalt-Zerbst	Princess of Anhalt-Zerbst Regiment	No Data	In Rivière-Ouelle

| Hesse-Kassel | Von Knyphausen Regiment | No Data | Return To New York |
| Hesse-Kasse | Alt Von Loosberg Regiment | No Data | In Île D'orléans |

MAIN QUARTERS FOR GERMAN SOLDIERS FOR SUMMER 1782

States	Regiments	Companies	Places
Brunswick	Dragoons Prince Ludwig	No Data	In St-Antoine
			In St-Charles
Brunswick	Musketeers Prince Frederic	No Data	In Ste-Famille
			In Ste-Anne
			In Château-Richer
			In L'ange-Gardien
			In St-Joachim
Brunswick	Grenadiers Battalion	No Data	In Berthier
Brunswick	Musketeers Von Rhetz	No Data	In Sorel
			In St-Denis
			In St-Charles
			In Iberville
Brunswick	Musketeers Von Riedesel	No Data	In Sorel
Brunswick	Musketeers Von Specht	No Data	In St-François
Brunswick	Regiment Von Barner	No Data	In St-Sulpice
			In Montreal
Hesse-Hanau	First Battalion Crown Prince	No Data	In Lévis
	(Hanau Infantry)		
Hesse-Hanau	Yagers Corps	No Data	In Île-Aux-Noix
			In Lacolle
Anhalt-Zerbst	Princess of Anhalt-Zerbst Regiment	No Data	In Rivière-Ouelle

View of the western tip of the promontory where, partly girdled by the Avenue du Cap-aux-Diamants, the remains of the advanced works of the temporary citadel can be seen clearly. (NBC Photo)

The square shows the location of the plaque, and the circle, the location of the descriptive panel. The arrows indicate the ends of what is believed to be a masonry wall, which was discovered accidentally in 2001 during maintenance work.

Appendix H

A CITADEL CALLED TEMPORARY...

The promontory of Cap-aux-Diamants (west of the current citadel in Quebec City) is a tourist attraction and a place familiar to many Quebecers. Many have admired the magnificent panorama from these heights? It is also a historical site where, in the early 1780s, a temporary citadel was built that protected Quebec for nearly half a century. Vestiges remain but unfortunately have not been identified or developed. As a result, most Quebecers are unaware of the site's historical significance (see photo).

Identifying places

A commemorative plaque erected on this site by the National Commission Battlefields (NBC) in the late 1930s reads as follows:

> (The excavations at Cap-aux-Diamants were done during the American Revolutionary War after the attack on Montgomery in 1775. They were the only fortifications erected there at any time.)

It seems that when that plaque was erected no in-depth research had yet been made on this construction.[1] What exactly does "excavation" mean? The answer can be found in an excellent book: *QUÉBEC, The Forified City Seventeenth to nineteenth Century*, published in 1982 by Parks Canada and Les Éditions du Pélican, and written by historians André Charbonneau, Yvon Desloges and Marc Lafrance. It provides a detailed review of all the fortifications that protected Quebec since its founding, including the temporary citadel. It also offers the general public a wealth of information unknown to the general public. The magnitude of this construction as illustrated by the relief plan of Quebec.[2] In addition to the fortifications themselves, several buildings for both housing the troops and storing war materiel can be identified. This appendix is largely drawn from that book, except the conclusions.

Some fifty years later after the plaque was erected in the late 1980s, the Commission installed a more explicit interpretation panel on the grounds of the municipal reservoir (south-east corner). The panel includes an etching by James Peachey dated 1784 depicting the temporary citadel and its advanced works. Visitors can compare the etching to what they see and learn about the old citadel and its advanced works built before the current temporary citadel was built. The same visitor, however, after reading the explanation on the panel, will not necessarily visit the site of these fortifications to verify the presence of vestiges that remain:

> TEMPORARY CITADEL (1779-83). Quebec: entrance to the new world, rich in natural resources, mainly in furs, is coveted by France and England both seeking new territories for their economic expansion. For this reason, the defence of New France has always been a concern for governments. Since the very beginning of the colony, the idea of establishing a citadel on the Cap-aux-Diamonds was considered. Yet it was only after the failed U.S. invasion in 1775 that Governor Haldimand requested that the engineer William Twiss establish a temporary citadel. The British feared another attempt on the part of Americans as well as a popular uprising. In addition, France was perhaps still hoping to retake the newly conquered territory. Due to lack of manpower and money, the citadel was temporary, i.e. it was made of earth and wood. The construction began in 1779 but the signing of peace between England and the USA in 1783 led to interruption of work, leaving the citadel incomplete. Later (1820-31), the military authorities ordered that this structure be replaced by a temporary structure of masonry, i.e. the citadel that we know now.

On this same panel is the reproduction of a watercolor by James Peachy which gives an overview of the temporary citadel in 1784. (See photo)

Why build a citadel?

For nearly two hundred years, from Phips' attack in 1690 until the departure of the English garrison in 1871, Quebec was a stronghold, a garrison town, protected by fortifications. Upon his arrival in 1716, Chaussegros de

Duberger Model

Léry recommended the construction of a citadel, but the fortress of Louisbourg was the priority at that time. In the aftermath of the Conquest, the British saw how precarious the existing walls were. Rather than restore them, Governor Murray prefered to build a citadel. From experience, the military knew that the military occupation of a conquered city entails a risk of a popular uprising, perceived to be suspicious. This risk was increased with the possibility of a French attempt to return to Canada; or the arrival of an enemy fleet before Quebec City haunted the British military.

Other factors supported construction of a citadel: the lack of barracks for soldiers, their dispersion in the city, and the lack of storage weapons and other materiel. During the first years after the Conquest, the soldiers occupied the New Barracks, the Dauphine Barracks, and the Palace of the Intendant.[3] Others were billeted among inhabitants of the city, which caused discontent. Part of the Jesuit College was then transformed into barracks and officers' quarters. There were not enough powder houses and warehouses and they were poorly located. These problems were solved with a citadel.

Since 1762, at Murray's behest, the engineer Samuel Holland submitted a draft for the citadel to the British authorities, who only acknowledged reception. Despite that refusal, the following year Murray took over the land on the heights of Cap-aux-Diamants. Five years later, Carleton renewed the request for a citadel but the austerity program in effect forced the city to postpone the decision again. During the American attack in December 1775, the walls of Quebec were in poor condition since they had not been repaired since 1760. Fortunately, those who laid siege only had artillery with low-calibre bullets that only ricocheted off the frozen walls. Carleton took advantage of the arrival of 3,000 German soldiers [4] in June 1776 and sent 800 of them to repair the walls. In February 1778, France's commitment to support the United States made the British realize the need for new defensive works in Quebec City and they resumed the citadel project.

Decision to build

In May 1778, the British authorities accepted the idea of building a fortress on the heights of Cap-aux-Diamants. The military budget was already heavily taxed by the fight against the rebel Americans. Their reluctance to invest large sums in building a permanent citadel which could not be completed until the end of hostilities is therefore understandable. To minimize costs, the engineer Twiss proposed to use the military manpower available. They therefore opted for a temporary construction made mostly of earth and wood but that would be able to resist an assault. Eventually, this construction could be replaced by a permanent citadel, which in fact was the case half a century later.

While Twiss prepared plans for the citadel, Governor Haldimand built a series of barracks on the heights of Cape Town that could accommodate 1600 soldiers, warehouses for military equipment, a powder house, a workshop, and water reservoirs. The defensive work started in October 1779, continued even in winter, and was interrupted in the summer of 1783 when peace was reached. It should be added that the bulk of the work was carried out on the site of the current citadel. On the other hand, a significant part of fortifications (advanced works) was built on the promontory where vestiges can still be seen.

The project

The size of the project is demonstrated by the larger number of workers, both military and civilians. On average, there were 300 during the summer of 1780, 500 and 700 during the next two summers, reaching a peak of 900 in August 1782. This does not include people from surrounding parishes forced to work and who were obliged to deliver materials to the site. Despite the rigours of winter and the strong winds, work continued with about 300 men during the winters of 1780-81 and 1781-82. Contrary to what one would might believe, only twelve percent of the workforce were civilians, the policy of the army being to minimize the involvement of civilians on military construction sites. The majority of these civilians were employed as craftsmen, nearly two-thirds of them being Canadians.

The workforce, both military and civilian, included craftsmen and unskilled workers. Craftsmen were divided into about twelve groups, including carpenters, wheelwrights, coopers, miners, bricklayers, etc.. Unskilled daily workers included labourers, carters, and botchers.[5] It is not surprising to note that in summer, the unskilled workers constituted about seventy percent of the workforce, while in winter, the same percentage applied to craftsmen. As everything was done by hand, it can be assumed that the excavation and transportation of fill employed a large number of day workers and carters in the summer only. Another surprising fact is that nearly two thirds of military personnel who worked there were German soldiers recruited to support the British against the American revolutionaries.

German soldiers

During the American War of Independence, the presence of German soldiers with General Friedrich von Riedesel in Canada made it possible to replace a some of the British soldiers whose services were required to fight in the American colonies. In fact, during these years of war, the garrison of Quebec City had a high proportion of German soldiers. In addition to them, soldiers were detached from regiments in garrison elsewhere in the province, which meant that they represented the majority of military personnel on site, both craftsmen (70%) and unskilled workers (60%).

According to the foreman, James Thompson, the foreign builders were slow, but he did not complain because "their work is much preferable to any done in this Country by the hands of a Canadian; besides they are constant and do not require much looking after, but they must have Profiles to work by. "[6] Although these soldiers were mostly recruits, they nevertheless constituted a skilled workforce but whose experience was limited. In addition, these soldiers could never have foreseen that some 160 years later, in 1940, at a stone throw from their workplace, several hundred of their compatriots would be interned as prisoners of war and enemy aliens.

The bondsmen

By definition, bondsmen work for free whether they are volunteers or not. Under the English, craftsmen are paid for work they are assigned to and are only ones allowed to work on site. The unskilled workers, usually from surrounding parishes, were responsible for supplying materials to the site for which they are paid, but at prices generally below market value. They receive no pay for their services. The materials they were required to provide to Cap-aux-Diamants included fascines, all kinds of wood, stone, and lime.

Trips were made to as far as Nicolet and Grondines for certain types of wood such as cedar pilings, which were assembled into cages and floated to Quebec City by bondsmen from parishes along the river. The parishes between Pointe-Lévis and Saint-Vallier were called upon to provide squared logs while those further inland had to contribute harnesses and horses for transportation to the river. Lime-kiln operators from Beauport, despite their many complaints, were forced to deliver their lime on site at prices fixed by the government. More fortunate, the bondsmen from St. Augustine and Lorette provided charcoal at the market price.

The usefulness of the temporary citadel

The citadel was almost complete when the German soldiers left in August 1783. In subsequent years, other structures were added so that during the Anglo-American war of 1812-1814, the barracks could accommodate more than 3000 soldiers. The usefulness of the temporary citadel became obvious, both for housing the military and providing a sense of security. Thus, for almost fifty years before completion of the citadel that we now know, this so-called temporary citadel was the linchpin of the defence of Quebec City and of Canada.

What remains…

What remains today of the work that occupied so many men for almost five years? For the most part, structures built on the site of the current citadel were demolished or rebuilt and incorporated in the new construction. As a result, the few elements still in place are virtually inaccessible to the public. As for advanced works, the construction of a new citadel rendered them obsolete, so that those built on the side of Grande-Allée have been razed, while those discussed at the beginning of this appendix were left to the abandonment. Whereas these works accounted for between fifteen and twenty percent of the total area covered by the temporary citadel, what remains represents only six percent of the same area. More than two hundred years after their construction, the vestiges are still visible, but less and less with the passage of time.[7]

Archaeological digs

No systematic digging program has never been conducted on the location of the advanced works, except on the site of Blockhaus No. 1[8] at the west end of the promontory. That two-storey building erected by Governor Murray after the capitulation of Quebec could accommodate sixty men. It was the largest of the five bunkers erected in front of the walls between the Battle of the Plains in 1759 and the attempt to take back Quebec at the end of April 1760. It was integrated with advanced works when they were built. Archaeological digs carried out in connection with stabilization work of some works in the current citadel revealed the presence of elements of the temporary citadel, and even components of old fortifications dating back to the French regime, buried under the current works.[9]

Conclusions and hopes

Although the fact that these vestiges have been abandoned to the wear of time for so long is to be deplored, it is comforting to know that the National Battlefields Commission announced plans in 2009 to continue digging in bunker No. 1. Hopefully this program will continue in the future so that possibly some of the other components of advanced works will be brought forth, such as what is believed to be a masonry wall designated by the arrows on the photo whose top is very close to the current ground surface. In this regard, the reconstruction of the Royal Battery in Old Quebec thirty years ago could be used as an example to follow.

It would be easy to improve the identification of places. First, the text of the current commemorative plaque could be reformulated to be more explicit and it could be moved to a place that could be seen by a larger number of visitors. Interpretive signs of the kind mentioned in the text could be installed at strategic locations where vestiges are still visible.

In summer 2009, at the initiative of Société historique de Québec and under the auspices of the Commission on Historic Sites and Monuments

View of the temporary citadel by James Peachy in 1784. Blockhouse 1 can be seen at the far right. (Photo: Parks Canada)

Board of Canada, a plaque was unveiled commemorating the arrival in the land of 10,000 German soldiers to support the British defence of Canada. The National Battlefield Commission is receptive to the suggestion made by the Société historique to install the plaque on the site where German soldiers worked to build the temporary citadel. It is planned to make this unveiling a milestone in Quebec, given the VIP guests and the expected presence of hundreds or even thousands of descendants of 2400 soldiers who chose to settle in Canada after the war, including nearly 1400 in Quebec. This event should be an incentive to implement the above suggestions?

Paul Fortin, mars 2008

Notes

1. Here's what tends to confirm this hypothesis. In 1976, when the Société organized and held the WEEK OF HISTORY, which covered the period from 1800 to 1835, no member of the Board of Directors, of which the author was a member, made any reference to the temporary citadel or its advanced works. These members included people with a significant background in history, including the abbot Honorius Provost, a well-known archivist and historian, and Mr. Georges-Henri Dagneau, president of the Société and a specialist in the history of British rule.

2. Commonly known as the Duberger Model. It was made between 1806 and 1808 by the surveyor Jean-Baptiste Duberger and Captain John By. It is exposed has been exposed in Artillery Park since 1980.

3. Destroyed in December 1775 during a U.S. attack.

4. Jean-Pierre Wilhelmy, *Les mercenaires allemands au Québec*, 1776-1783, Septentrion, 1997, p. 6.

5. Plaster and cement plunger and mixer.

6. James Thompson, foreman, worked under the orders of William Twiss, the king's engineer.

7. The author recalls that in mid 1940s enjoying a bicycle ride on the "roller coaster" i.e. on parapets where the remains of gun embrasures still showed significant depressions, a century and a half after their construction. Sixty years later, traces of these embrasures have completely disappeared, apparently the result of more intense human activity on this site.

8. Archaeological digs carried out in 2006 and 2007 led by archaeologist Louis-Philippe Picard, suggest that this building was occupied until the start of construction of the current citadel. These digs continued in 2008.

9. Surprisingly, the British have forgotten what they themselves built. A proof is this excerpt from the book byJacques Mathieu and Eugen Kedl: *The Plains of Abraham, The Search for the Ideal,* p. 262: "The most important vestiges are those of the temporary citadel at Cap-aux-Diamants, built between 1779 and 1783. However, from the middle of the nineteenth century, the British military authorities refer to them as old French fortifications. They had even forgotten their own work, leaving it to others." The author thanks historian Yvon Desloges, Parks Canada, and archaeologists Robert Gauvin, Parks Canada, and Louis-Philippe Picard, and also Héleène Quimper, historian and ethnologist with the National Battlefields Commission, and Marie-Claude Belley, Parks Canada, for their collaboration.

BIBLIOGRAPHY
(with supplementary notes)

A- MANUSCRIPTS

I- BRITISH AND CANADIAN SOURCES

A) General Sources

1- *MG11, Colonial Office, London*
This group is composed of copies (transcript and microfilms) of documents from the Colonial Office, 1580-1922. For this book, we consulted specifically section C.o.5, America and West Indies, 1638-18-7, and C.o.42, Canada, Original Correspondence. There is a transcription of the latter in the Public Archives of Canada, in series Q.

2- *MG13, War Office, London*
This group consists of transcript, photostat and microfilm copies of War Office records in the Public Record Office, dated 1755-1913.
We consulted:
a-W.O. 1 o, Muster Book and Pay Lists: Artillery b-W.O. 12, Muster Book and Pay List: General
c-W.O. 17, Monthly Returns
d-W.O.28, Headquarters Records

3- *MG14, Audit Office (London)*
This group consists of transcripts, photostat and microfilm copies of papers, 1749-1837, of the various offices which eventually comprised the Exchequer and Audit Departments.
We consulted:
a-A..O.12, Loyalists' claims, series
b-A.O. 13, Loyalists' claims, series II

4- *MG21, Transcripts.from papers in the British Museum*
This group consists of copies of manuscripts held by the British Museum. The papers of Sir Frederick Haldimand have been copied in their entirety into series B in 232 volumes in Ottawa. A full inventory of their contents can be found in Records of the Public Archives of Canada. For this book,

we consulted the following volumes: 39, 40, 45, 56, 62, 80, 81, 82, 83, 84, 86-1, 86-2, 86-3, 87, 111, 117, 129, 130, 131, 133, 136, 137, 138, 139, 147, 148, 151, 152, 153, 162, 164, 171, 173, 174, 177-2, 178, 189, 191, 196, 204, 207, 217, 218.

5- *MG23, Late Eighteenth Century Papers of political and military leaders and colonial administrators predominate in this group.*
We consulted:
a-B- American Revolution.
b-B-1: . British Headquarters Papers or Carleton's Papers or Dorchester's Papers. Similar in nature to the Haldimand's Collection, this is a collection of correspondance with the Brunswickers and lists of names in several volumes. The originals are found in 61 volumes in London. Ottawa owns a partial transcript in 12 volumes dating from WWI.
c-B-42: Unpublished officers'journals, including that of C. de Kreutzbourg, in German (Gothic), 199 double pages.The original is conserved in the departmental archives of arburg.
d-B-44: Unpublished officers' journals, including J.H.C. Benewitz, 1776-1783. Transcript of a document belonging to A.V. Koch, 25 pp.

6- *RG1 - Executive Council, 1764-1867*
Archives of the Executive Council of Quebec, Lower and Upper Canada as well as the Province of Canada, divided into two sections: "for matters of state and" for land matters. We consulted especially vol.108 concerning the period from Aug. 17, 1775 to Feb. 5, 1783; and papers 94203-94-221 in the territorial documents section (RGI-L- 3L, vol. 199, demands for lands).

7- *RG8 - British Military and Naval Records*
This group consists of records of British military and naval forces serving in Canada.

8- The National Archives of Quebec contains manuscripts of letters, memoirs and other documents relating to New-France for the period 1492 to 1789.

9- The Archives of the Seminary of Quebec contain the Viger-Verreau Collection; in carton 17 no. 28 are found the document entitled Informations et procédés de la milice de Berthier (en haut) concerning the German troops and Arnold's papers from Sept. 1775 to Oct. 1776. There are also some items of interest concerning the Brunswickers in Cartons 9-39 and 9-49.

B) Sources Relating to Individuels

1- Badeaux, Jean-Baptiste, notary. Journal. *See Invasion du Canada.*
2- Burgoyne, John. *A State of the Expedition.from Canada*, London, 1780, VIII-140 XLII pp.

3- Carleton, Guy. See the Haldimand Collection and other volumes in series Q.

4- Haldimand, Frederick. Sec the *Haldimand Collection.*

5- Sanguinet, M. Journal: Le témoin occulaire du Canada de l'invasion du Canada par les Bastonnais. See Invasion du Canada.

6- Verreau, Invasion du Canada, Collection de mémoires recueillis et annotés, by Verreau Abbé, priest, Montreal, 1873. Contains journals of Badeaux, Sanguinet and Lamier as well as letters written during the American invasion.

7- Verreau, Hospice Anthelme. Sec Invasion du Canada.

II- AMERICAN AND GERMAN SOURCES AA-GERMANY

1- *Anhalt-Zerbst (Staatsarchiv Magdeburg)*
   a- List of deserters during the march to Philipsburg.
   b- Recruits sent to America.
   c- Soldiers whose wives and children were at Zerbst, Coswig, Rosslau and Jever and who received subsidies (wheat, wood, rye or money).
   d- Officers who stayed in Canada.
   e- Deaths on the ships between Stade and Quebec.
   f- Reports of the régiments in Quebec and recruits ordered from Jever.
   g- Troops ordered to America.
   h- Men, women and children who died from the start of' the march from Zerbst.
   i- N.C.O.'s and soldiers in Quebec who deposited money for their parents.
   j- Recruits who embarked from Stade.
   k- Troops, garnissons and infantry regiments with notes on the places where they served.

2- *Brunswick (Niedersächisisches Staatsarchiv, Wolfenbüttel)*
   a- Akten und Briefschaften Riedesels aus dem amerikanischen Kriege, 1776-1783, NiedersBchsisches Staatsarchiv, Wolfenbüttel.
   b- Amerikanische Briefe an den Herrn Erbprinzen Hochfürstl. Durchl. 1776-1777. Niedersächsisches Staatsarchiv, Wolfenbüttel.
   c- Amerikanischer Feldzug, 1776-1779, Niedersächsisches Staatsarchiv, Wolfenbüttel.
   d- Aufzeichnungen des Feldscher Julius Friedrich Wasmus, iedersächsisches Staatsarchiv, Wolfenbüttel.
   e- Briefe von meinen Bruder J.C.C. Dehn und zwar von der Abfahrt von Portsmouth und seinen Aufenhalt in Nord Amerika bis dei Jahr 1782. Staatsarchiv Braunschweig.
   f- Journal der Seereise nach Nord A merika wie auch von denen darin emachien Campagnen... aufge zeichnet von Friedrich Julius von Papet jun: Premier Lieutenant. Staatsarchiv Braunschweig.

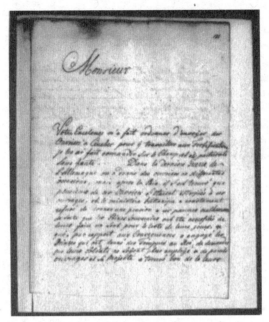

Example of a German letter (in French). The Haldimand
Collection contains thousands of such letters in both
French and English.

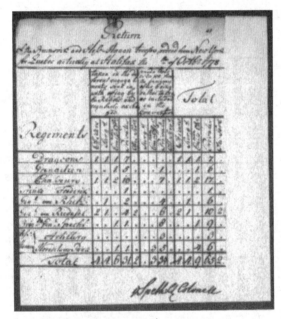

Example of a retun, Oct. 1778.

g- Marsch Route von Braunschweig bis Amerika. Nebst den nehmsten Gegebenheiten der Herzoglichen Braunschweigischen Truppen. Die 1ste Division. Von Johann Bense. Niedersächsisches Staatsarchiv, Wolfenbüttel.

h- Nachrichten und Tagebuch des Regiments-Adjutanten A nton Adolf Heinrich du Roi, 1776. Niedersächsisches Staatsarchiv, Wolfenbüttel.

i- Tagebuch des in Herzogl. Brschw. Diensten Stehenden Lieutenants und Adjutanten du Roi des älteren, 1776-1777. Staatsarchiv Braunschweig.

j- Tagebuchüber den Feldzug der Brauschw. Truppen in Amerika vom 29. Aug. 1777 bis zum 15. Jan. 1779 von dem Hauptmann (nachmals Generalmajor) Cleve. Staatsarchiv Braunschweig.

k- Tagebuch von Braunschweig bis America von Johan Conrad Ruff. Staatsarchiv Braunschweig.

3- *Hesse-Cassel (Staatsarchiv Marburg)*

a-Amerikana im Staatsarchiv Marburg, Allgemeine Aktenverzeichnisse, Verz. 9. Hessisches, Staatsarchiv, Marburg.

b-Auerbach, Inge, et Fro'lich, Otto, Hessische Truppen im Amerikanischen Unabhängigkeitskrieg (Hetrina), 4 Bde. Veröffentlichungen der Archivschüle Marburg, Nr. 10, Marburg, 1974-1976.

c- Waldecker Truppen im Amerikanischen Unabhängigkeitskrieg (Hetrina), Veröffentlichungen der Archivschüle Marburg, Nr. 10, Bd. V. Marburg.

d- Journal des Grenadier Bataillons Block nachher Lengercke, Hessisches Staatsarchiv, Marburg.

e- Journal des Hochfürstl. Hessischen Grenadier-Bataillon von Bischhausen, Hessisches Staatsarchiv, Marburg.

f- Journal des Hochlöbl Fuselier Regiments v.Alt Lossberg, Hessisches Staatsarchiv, Marburg.

g- Journal des Leib-Inf.Rgts von Kospoth, Hessisches Staatsarchiv, Marburg.

h- Journal Geführt Bey dem Hochlöblich Hessischen Feld-Jäger Corps während denen Campagnen der Könogl. Brittanischen Armee in Nord Amerika, Hessisches Staatsarchiv, Marburg.

i- Journal Regiment von Knyphausen, Hessisches Staatsarchiv, Marburg. Journal uber die merkwurdigen Vorfälle bey dem Hochlöbl. Leib Infanterie Regiment modo Erbprinz, Hessisches Staatsarchiv, Marburg.

k- Journal vom Hochfürstlich Hessischen Grenadier-Bataillon Platte, Hessisches Staatsarchiv, Marburg.

l- Journal vom Hessischen Corps in A merika unter dem General von Heister, 1776-1777, Hessisches Staatsarchiv, Marburg.

m- Journal vom Hochlöbl. Regiment Prinz Carl, 1776-1784, Hessisches Staatsarchiv, Marburg.

n- Journal vom Jäger Corps Hanauisches Jäger Corps, Hessisches Staatsarchiv, Marburg.

o- Journal vom Löbl. Garnisons-Regiment von Huyn nachher von Benning, Hessisches Staatsarchiv, Marburg.

p- Journal von dem Hochfuerstlich-Hessischen Hochlöbl. Infanterie Regiment von Trümbach modo General-Lieutenant von Bose, Hessisches Staatsarchiv, Marburg.

q- Journal vom dem Hochfürstlich Hessischen des General Major von Knoblauch Löbl. Garnisons Regiment, Hessisches Staatsarchiv, Marburg.

r- Journal vom dem Hochlöbl. Hessischen Grenadier Bataillon olim von Minnigerode modo von Lowenstein, Hessisches Staatsarchiv, Marburg.

s- Journal von dem Hochlöbl. Regiment von Donop modo v. Knyphausen, Hessisches Staatsarchiv, Marburg.

t- Journal von der Campagne in Amerika. Tome I-VIII, Hessisches Staatsarchiv, Marburg.

u- Journal von Sr. Hochfüstl Durchlaucht Prinz Friedrichs Hochlöblichen Infanterie Regiment von 1776 bis Ende 1783, Hessisches Staatsarchiv, Marburg. Militärberichte und Relationen von den Operationen der Hessischen Korps im A merikanischen Kriege, 1776-1782, Hessisches Staatsarchiv, Marburg.

v- Order Buch vom HochlöbL Regiment von Mirbach, Hessisches Staatsarchiv, Marburg.

w-Relationen vom Artilleriekorps 1776-1784, Hessisches Staatsarchiv, Marburg.

x- Relationen vom Nord-A merikanischen Kriege, VoL I- V, Hessisches Staatsarchiv, Marburg.

y- Tagebuch eines Teilnehmers am Feldzug des General Burgoyne in Albany, 1776, Museumsverein Lüneburg.

z- Tagebuch des Friedrich Wilhelm von der Malsburg, Regiment von Dittfurth, Hessisches Staatsarchiv, Marburg.

aa-Tagebuch des Hauptmans Wiederhold, 1776-1780, Landesbibliothek Kassel.

bb- Tagebuch des Regiments Jung von Lossberg antes von Mirbach, Landesbibliothek Kassel.

4- *Hesse-Hanau (Staatsarchiv Marburg)*

a- Diarum aller Mir Ernst Philipp Theobald bey dem Hochfürstl. Hesse Hanauischen Infanterie Regiment Erbprinz, Feldprediger, vom 15ien MB'riz bis den 10ten Aug. 1776 ayf meiner americanischen Reise vorgefallenen, und von mir beobachteten merkwürdigkeiten, Landesbibliothek Kassel.

b- Journal über die merkwhrdigen Vorfälle bey dem Hochlöbl. Leib Infanterie Regiment modo Erbprinz, Hessisches Staatsarchiv, Marburg.

c- Journal vom Jäger Corps (Hanauisches Jäger Corps), Hessisches Staatsarchiv, Marburg.

d- Orders für das Hessen-Hanauische Feld-Jäger-Korps, Hessisches Staatsarchiv, Marburg.

e- Tagebuch eines Grenadiers vom Fürsilich Hessen Hanauischen Infanterie Regiment Erbprinz, Compagnie des ObristLieutenants Lenz, Burschen beim Stabs Capitan späteren Brigade Major Friedrich Wilhelm von Geismar, Hessisches Staatsarchiv, Marburg.

5- *Ansbach-Bayreuth*

a- Döhla, Johann Konrad, A merikanische Feldzüge, 1777-1783; Tagebuch von Johann Konrad Dohla.

b- Tagebuch des Markgräflichen Jäger- Lieutenants Carl Philipp von Frelitzsch Historischer Verein for Oberfranken, Bayreuth.

c- Wörtgetreue Abschrift des Tagebuchs eines Markgräflichen Soldaten über den Aufenhalt in Amerika, 1777-1781. Historischer Verein for Mittelfranken. Ansbach.

6- *Waldeck*

a-Curtze, L., Geschichte und Beschreibung des Fürstenthums Waldeck. Arolsen Speyer'sche Buchhandling 1850 XIII, (2) 664S.

b-Waldeck, A., Waldeck's Diary of the Revolution, 1776-1780. Ed M.D. Learned and Rudolph Cronau.

7- *U. S. A. (Public Library of Congress. Containing many photocopies of documents in the German archives)*

a- Jungkenn Paper, 1775-1784. William L. Clements Library, Michigan University, Ann Arbor, Michigan.

b- Peter Force Papers, Letters qf Heinrich Urba Cleve, 17771778. Library of Congress, Washington, D.C.

c- Orderly Book of Frederick Baum, 1777. Library of Congress, Washington, D.C.

d- Anspach Papers, 1776-1785, New York Public Library, New York.

B- BOOKS

Anburey, Thomas, *With Burgoyne from Quebec*. Toronto Macmillan, 1963, 220 pp.

Arndt, Karl, J.R., *The Voyage of the First Hessian Army from Portsmouth to New York in 1776* (A.Pfister's Report), German-Canadian Yearbook III, Toronto, Historical Society of Mecklenburg Upper Canada Inc., 1976, pp. 129-139.

Apel, Karl, *Regiment Prinz Karl im Amerikanischen Unabhängigkeitskrieg, 1776-1783*, Mein Heimatland (Monatsbeilage zur Hersfelder Zeitung), XVII, Nr. 6,23 Aug. 1956, pp. 21-23.

Atwood, Rodney, *The Hessians, Mercenaries from Hessen-Kassel in the American Revolution,* Cambridge, Mass., 1980.

Aubin, Florian ptre. *La paroisse de St- Cuthbert,* 1776-1980, Vol. 2, 113-117.

Bardeleben, Heinrich von, *Tagebuch eines Hessischen Offiziers, Heinrich von Bardeleben,* Hrsg. von Julius Göbell, Deutsch-Amerikanische Geschichtsblätter, XVII-XVIII, 1927-1928, pp. 7-119.

Benoît, Pierre, *Lord Dorchester,* Montréal 1961, 203 p.

Bezzel, Oskar, *Ansbach-Bayreuther Miettruppen im Nordamerikanischen Freiheitskrieg,1777- 1783,* Zeitschrift für bayerische Landesgeschichte, VIII (1935), pp. 185-214 et 377-424.

Bowie, Lucy Leigh, *The German Prisoners in the American Revolution,* Maryland Historical Magazine, XL, 1945, pp. 185-200.

Brown, Marvin L., *Baroness von Riedesel and the American Revolution,* Chapel Hill, University of Carolina Press, 1965.

Butterfield, Lyman H., *Psychological Warfare in 1776: The Jefferson-Franklin Plan to Cause Hessian Desertions,* American Philosophical Society Proceedings, XCIV, 1950, 233- 241.

Canniff, William, *History of the Province of Ontario.* Toronto, 1872.

Caux, Arthur M.D., *Les colons de Saint-Gilles et leurs descendants dans Lotbinière.* Bulletin des Recherches Historiques. Volume LVII, No. 1, 1951, 50-60.

Carrington, Henry B., Battles of the American Revolution, 1775-1781, New York 1877. Reissued by the New York Times in 1968.

Charland, Thomas (M.o.1.), *Histoire de St-François-du-Lac,* Ottawa 1942, 132-149.

Chittenden, Hon. Lucius Eugène, The Capture of Ticonderoga, Annual speech to Vermont Historical Society, Vermont Rutland, 1872, 127 pp.

Collins, Varnum Lansin, Hrsg., *A Brief Narrative of the Ravages of the British and Hessians at Pinceton in 1776-1777,* Princeton, N.J., 1906.

Couillard, Després, Abbé Azaire-Etienne, *Histoire de Sorel, de ses origines à nos jours,* Montréal, 1926, 343 pp.

Cruickshank, Ernest Alexander, *The Settlement of the United Empire Loyalists on the Upper St-Lawrence and Bay of Quinte in 1784,* A documentary record, Toronto, Ontario Historical Society, 1934 (reprint 1966), 188 p.

Debor, Herbert Wilhelm, Deutsche Jäger in Kanada, Der Nordwesten (Winnipeg), 19 May 1966.

—, Das Regiment Prinz Friedrich, DerNordwesten, 31 March 1966.

—, Deutsche in der Stadt und Festung Quebec, Der Nordwesten, 8 Aug. 1966.

—, German Regiments in Canada, 1776-1783, German Canadian Yearbook II, Toronto, Historical Society of Mecklenburg Upper Canada Inc., 1975, pp. 34-49.

—, *German Soldiers of the American War of Independence as Settlers in Canada,* German-Canadian Yearbook III, Toronto, Historical Society of Mecklenburg Upper Canada Inc., 1976, pp. 71-93.

DeMarce, Virginia Dr., *The Settlement of Former German Auxiliary Troops in Canada after The American Revolution,* Family edition, Arlington 1982, 223.

—, *The Anhalt-Zerbst Regiment in the American Revolution*, "Musters Rolls", 18 sept. 1982. 60 p.

Dippel, Horst, *Germany and the American Revolution, 1770-1800: A Sociohistorical Investigation of Late Eighteenth Century Political Thinking*, Translated by Bernhardt A. Uhlendorf, Chapel Hill, University of North Carolina Press, 1977.

—, *Sources in Germany for the Study of the American Revolution*, Quarterly Journal of the Library of Congress, XXXIII, 1976, pp. 199-217.

Döhla, Johann Konrad, *Tagebuch eines Bayreuther Soldaten aus dem Nordamerikanischen Freiheitskrieg, 1777-1783*, Archiv for Geschichte und Altertumskunde von Oberfranken, XXV, 1912-1914, Nr. 1, pp. 81-202, Nr. 2, pp. 107-224.

Döllner, Max, Erlebnisse der ansbach-bayreuthischen Hilfstruppen im Kriege Grossbritanniens gegen die Vereinigten Staaten von Nordamerika (1777-1783), Neustadt an der Aisch, 1933.

Donne, W. Bodham, *The Correspondence of King George the Third with Lord North from 1768 to 1783*, 2 vol., Londres, 1867.

Dörnberg, Karl Ludwig, Freiherr von, Tagebuchblätter eines hessischen Offiziers aus der Zeit des nordamerikanischen Unabhängigkeitskriege, 1779-1781, Hrsg. von Gotthold Marseille, Pyritz: Backesche Buchdruckerei, 1899-1900.

Dufebvre B. (Emile Castonguay), *La baronne de Riedesel ou le modèle des épouses*, Dans *Cinq femmes et nous*, Québec 1950, 59-110.

Du Roi, August Wilhelm, *Journal of Du Roi the Elder, Lieutenant and Adjutant in the Service of the Duke von Brunswick, 1776-1778*, translated by Charlotte S.J. Epping, Americana Germanica XV, New York, D. Appleton & Co., 1911.

Du Roy, Anton Adolf, *Tagebuch der Seereise von Stade Nach Quebec in Amerika, 1776*. Deutsch und Englisch Übertragen und Herausgegeben von Gerhart Teuscher, German-Canadian Historical Association, Toronto, 1983.

Eelking, Max von, Lebven und Wirken des Herzoglich Braunschweigschen General- Lieutenants Friedrich Adolph Riedesel, Freiherrn zu Eisenbach, nebst Original- Correspondenzenund historischen Aktenstücken aus dem siebenjährigen Kriege, dem nordamerikanischen Freiheits-Kampfe und französischen Revolution-Kriege, Bd. II und III, Leipzig, Verlag Otto Wigand, 1856.

—, *The German Allied Troops in the American War of Independence, 1776-1783*, translated and abridged by J.G. Rosengarten, Albany N.Y. 1893.

—, *Memoirs and Letters and Journals of Major-General Riedesel during His Residence in America*, 2 vol., translated by William L. Stone, Albany, J. Munsell, 1868.

Ehlers, Karl, Der Soldatenverkauf Karl Wilhelm Ferdinands von Braunschweig während des nordamerikanischen Freiheitskrieges, Niedersachsen XXXI, 1926, pp. 601-604.

Eisentraut, G., Johan Gottfried Seumes Rekruntenzeit, 1781-1783, Hessenland, XXV, 1910, pp. 57-59, 89-91, 107109, et 122-124.

Elster, O., *Geschichte der siehenden Truppen im Herzogtum Braunschweig-Wolfenbuttel Zweiter Band, von 1714-1806*, Leipzig, 1901.

Elting, John R., *The Battles of Saratoga*, Monmouth Beach, Philip Freneau Press, 1977.

Ewald, Johann, *Diary of the American War.- A Hessian Diary*, Translated and edited by Joseph P. Tustin, New Haven and London, Yale University Press, 1979.

Ferron, Madeleine, *Les Beaucerons, ces insoumis. Petite histoire de la Beauce*, 1735-1867, Montréal, 1974.

Fortescue, John, *The Correspondence of King George the Third, from 1760 to December 1783*, London, 1927-1928.

Friedrich II und die neuere Geschichtsschreibung, Ein Betrag zur Wiederlegung der Märchen Überangeblichen SoldatenHandel hessischer Fürsten, 2 vol. Melsungen, W. Hopf, 1879.

Fritsch, W.A., *Stimmen deuischer Zeitgenossen über den Soldatenhandel deutscher Fürsten nach Amerika, DeutschAmerikanisches Magazin*, I, 1887, pp. 589-593.

Gilroy, Marion, *Loyalists and Land Settlement in Nova Scotia*, Publication no. 4 of the Genealogical Committee, Royal Nova Scotia Historical Society, 1980.

Gingras, Raymond, *Liste annotée de patronymes d'origine allemande au Québec et notes diverses, 1975*.

Gradish, Stephen Francis, *The German Mercenaries in Canada, 1776-1783*, M.A. thesis, Western University London, Ontario, September 1964, 174 pp.

—, *The German Mercenaries in North America during the American Revolution.- A Case Study*, Canadian Journal of History, IV, 1969, pp. 23-46.

Green, Samuel, Abbott, ed. and trans, *My Campaigns in America:* A Journal Kept by Count William de Deux Ponts, 1780-1781, Boston, J.K. Wiggin & Wm. Parsons Lunt, 1868. *311*

Greenwood, Murray F., Oliva, Friedrich Guillaume, in the *Biographical Dictionary of Canada*, volume 4, Oliva.

Handlow, Hermann, et Carl Kämpe, *Braunschweigische Offiziere als Freimaurer in Nordamerika und Holland*, Braunschweig, 1931, Sonderdruck aus dem "Freimaurer-Museum", Bd.6, Seulenroda, o.I.

Heintz, G., *German Immigration into Upper Canada and Ontario from 1783 to the Present Day*, thesis, Queens University 1938, 147 pp.

Hess, Anna K., *A Voyage of Duty: The Riedesels in A merica*, German-Canadian Yearbook I, Toronto, Historical Society of Mecklenburg Upper Canada Inc., 1973, pp. 131-139.

Herrmann, Friedrich, *Die Deutschen in Nordamerika. In drey Schulderungen entworten*, Lübben, 1806.

Hudleston, F.V., *Gentleman Johnny Burgoyne. Misadventures of an English General in the Revolution*, Indianapolis, 1927.

Huth, Hans, *Lettersfrom a Hessian Mercenary*, Pennsylvania Magazine of History and Biography, LXII, 1938, pp. 488-501.

Janssen-Sillenstede, Georg, *Eine Verlustliste verkaufter deutscher Soldaten während des nordamerikanischen Frelheitskrieges, 1778-1783*, Oldenburger Jahrbuch, XLIV/XLV, 1940- 1941, pp. 102-114.

Jantz, Harokd, et Yorck Alexander Haase, Die Neue Welt in den Schätzen einer aiten europäischen Bibliothek, Ausstellungskatalog der Herzog August Bibliothek, Nr. Vorwort von H. Jantz, Braunschweig, 1976.

Jones, Charles Henry, *History of the Campaign for the Conquest of Canada in 1776. From the Death of Montgomery to Retreat of the British Army under Sir Guy Carleton*, Philadelphia 1882. 234 pp.

Jones, Kenneth S., *Johannes Schwalm, the Hessian*, Lyndhurst, Ohio, Johannes Schwalm Historical Association, 1976.

Kapp, Friedrich, *Der Soldatenhandel Deutscher Fürsten nach Amerika*, 2 vol., Aufl. Berlin, Julius Springer, 1874.

—, *The Life of Frederick William von Steuben, Major General in the Revolutionary Army*, Introduction by George Bancroft, New York, Mason Brothers, 1859.

Kipping, Ernst, *The Hessian View of America, 1776-1783*, M. Beach N.J. 1971, 49 pp. From a series of 14 volumes on the American Revolution, based on 17 unpublished Hessian officers journals.

—, *Die Truppen von Hessen-Cassel im Amerikanischen Unabhängigkeitskrieg*, 1776-1783, Darmstadt, Wehr und Wissen Verlagsgesellschaft, 1965.

Kipping, Ernst, et Samuel Stelle Smith, trad. et annotJ, At *General Howes Side, 1776-1778: The Diary qf General William Howes Aide-de-Camp, Captain Friedrich von Münchhausen*, Monmouth Beach, N.J., Philip Freneau Press, 1974.

Krafft, John Charles Philip von, *Journal of Lieutenant John Charles Philip von Kraffi of the Regiment von Bose, 17761784*, Collections of the New York Historical Society, XV, 1882, pp. 1-202.

Kröger, Alfred, *Geburt der U.S.A.: German Newspaper Accounts of the American Revolution, 1763-1783*, Madison, Wisc., 1962.

Kümmel, Heinrich, *Aus dem Tagebuch eines Hessischen Feldpredigers lm amerikanischen Krieg*, Hessenland VIII, 1894, pp. 72-76 et 87-91.

Lafue, Pierre, *La vie quotidienne des Cours allemandes au XVIIIᵉ siècle*, Hachette 1963. Chapter X entitled "Les Cours du milieu du siècle".

Lanctot, Gustave, *Le Canada et la Révolution américaine*, Montréal 1965, 330 p.

—, *Le Québec et les colonies américaines, 1760-1820*, third chapter entitled "Les Canadiens français et leurs voisins du sud". Montreal, Toronto and New Haven, 1941, IX, 322 pp.

Lapalice, Ovide-M.H., *Histoire de la seigneurie Massue et de la paroisse de Saint-Aimé*, 1930, pp. 120-123.

Larter, Col. Harry C., *The German Troops wilh Burgoyne, 1776-1777,* The Bulletin of the Fort Ticonderoga Museum, IX, no.1, 1952, pp. 13-24.

Learned, Marin Dexter, *Gesang nach Amerika Anno 1777,* Americana Germanica, I, 1897, pp. 84-89.

—, *Guide to the Manuscript Maierials Relating to A merican History in the German Stale Archives,* Publications of the Carnegie Institution, no.150, Washington, Carnegie Institution, 1912 (1965).

Learned, Marion D., et C. *Grosse, Tagebuch des Capitains Wiederholdt,* Americana Germanica, IV, 1902, pp. 1-93.

Lith, Friedrich, Freiherr von der, *Wilhelm, Freiherr von* Knyphausen, Hessische Denkwürdigkeiten, III, 1802, pp. 442-446.

Loewe, Victor, *Bibliographie der Hannoverischen und Braunschweigischen Geschichte,* Posen 1908.

Losch, Philip, *Soldatenhandel,* Kassel, Bärenreiter Verlag, 1933, Neudruck, Kassel, Horst Hamecher, 1974.

Lowell, Edward Jackson, *The Hessians and the Other German Auxiliaries of Great Britain in th Revolutionary War,* New York, 1884. Reissued Williamstown Mass. 1975, 328 p.

Lutz, Henry F., *The Germans, Hessians and Pennsylvania* Germans, Pennsylvania-German, X, 1909, pp. 435-443.

Lübbing, Herman, Deutsche Soldaten unter anhalt-zerbstischer Fahne lm englischen Solde, Oldenburger Jahrbücher, XLIV/XLV, 1940-1941, pp. 82-101.

Mander, Eric, I., *The Battle of Long Island, Monmouth Bay,* Philip Freneau Press, 1978. May, Robin, *The British Army in North America, 1775-1783,* Norwich 1974, 40 pp.

Melsheimer, Friedrich Valentin, *Journal of the Voyage of the Brunswick Auxiliaries from Wolfenbüttel to Quebec,* Translated by William Wood and William L. Stone, Quebec, in Transactions of the Literary and Historical Society of Quebec, 1891, no. 2, pp. 133-178. Reissued by Le Soleil in 1927.

Meyer, Christian, *Soldatenhandel deutscher Frsten nach Amerika,* Meyer, "Biographische und Kulturgeschichtliche Essays", Leipzig, 1901, pp. 381-394.

Mirabeau, Honoré Gabriel, *Avis aux Hessois et Autres Peuples de l'Allemagne vendus par leurs Princes à l'Angleterre,*Hrsg. von J.G. Rosengarten, Proceedings of the American Philosophical Society, XXXIX, April 1900, p 154.

Mockler, Anthony, *Histoire des mercenaires,* Stock, 1969, 284 p.

Mollo, John, et Malcolm Mac Gregor, *Uniformen des Amerikanischen Unabhängigkeits Kriegs, Übersetzt von Egbert von Kleist,* München, Heyne Verlag, 1975.

Monarque, Georges, *Un général allemand au Canada: le baron Friedrich Adolphus von Riedesel,* Montréal, E. Garand, 1927, 151 pp.

Münchausen, Friedrich von. *At General Howes Side, 1776-1778: The Diary of General Howes Aide-de-Camp, Captain Friedrich von Münchhausen*, übers. v. Ernst Kipping, u.m. Anmerkungen v. Samuel Smith, Monmouth Beach, N.J., 1974.

Nadeau, Gabriel, *L'apport germanique dans la formation du Canada français*, in Mémoires de la Société généalogique canadienne française, June 1945, Volume I, no. 4, 274-277.

Nickerson, Hoffman, *The Turning Point of the Revolution or Burgoyne in America*, Boston 1928, X, 500 p.

Pausch, Georg, *Journal of Captain Pausch, Chief of the Hanau Artillery during the Burgoyne Campaign*, übers. u. Hrsg. von William L. Stone, mit ein Einführung v.Edward J.Lowell, Albany, N.Y., 1886, 185 p.

Pettengill, Ray W., trad., *Letters from America, 1776-1779: Being Letters of Brunswick, Hessian, and Waldeck Officers with the British Armies During the Revolution*, Boston and New York, Houghton Mifflin Co., 1924.

Popp, Stephan, *A Hessian Soldier in the American Revolution: The Diary of Stephen Popp*, trans. Reinhart J. Pope, Racine, Wisc., private printing, 1953. Preser, Carl, *Der Soldatenhandel in Hessen. Versuch einer Abrechnung*, Marburg, N.G. Elwertsche Verlagsbuchhandlung, 1900.

Radloff, Herman et Alexander Coyle, *Hessians in the Revolution, 1776-1783*, Members of the St. Louis Genealogical Society, June 1975.

Rainsford, Charles, *Transactions as Commissary for Embarking Foreign Troops in the English Service from Germany wilh Copies of Letters Relative to it. For the Years 1776-1777*, Collections of the New York Historical Society, XII, 1879, pp. 313-543.

Reinhardt, Max, *Aus dem Tagebuch eines hessischen Feldpredigers im amerikanischen Freiheitskrieg, 1776-1783*, Nachrichten der Gesellschaft für Famillenkunde in Kurhessen und Waldeck, XVI, 1941, Nr. 1, pp. 1-16.

Reuber, Johannes, *Tagebuch des Grenadiers Johannes Reuber aus Niedervellmar vom Amerikanischen* Feldzug, hrsg. v. R.W. Junghaus, Hessenland, VIII, 1894, pp. 155-157, 167-168 et 183-186.

Riedesel, Friederike Charlotte Louise, Freifrau von, *Die Berufsreise nach Amerika*, Berlin, Haude und Spener, 1800.

—, *Baroness von Riedesel and the American Revolution: Journal and Correspondence of a Tour of Duty, 1776-1783*, edited and translated by M.L. Brown Jr.and Martha Huth, Chapel Hill, University of North Carolina, 1965.

—, *Letters and journals Relating to the War of the American Revolution and the Capture of the German Troops at Saratoga*, translated by William L. Stone, Albany, Joel Munsell, 1867; reprint by Arno Press, New York, 1968.

Rosengarten, Joseph G., *A Defence of the Hessians*, Pennsylvania Magazine of History and Biography, XXIII, 1899, pp. 157-183.

—, *American History from German Archives, with Reference to the German Soldiers in the Revolution and Franklin=s Visit to Germany*, Lancaster, Press of the New Era Printing Company, 1904.

—, Popp's Journal, 1777-1783, *Pennsylvania Magazine of History and Biography*, XXVI, 1902, pp. 25-41 et 245-254.

Roy, Joseph Edmond, *Histoire de la Seigneurie de Lauzon*, Lévis, 1900, Vol. 111, 65-75 et Vol. III, 159-164.

Roy, Pierre Georges, *Toutes petites choses du régime anglais*, Quebec 1946. First series volume I, 57-58 et 72-73.

Roy, Raoul, *Les Canadiens français et les indépendantistes américains, 1774-1783*, Une occasion manquée. Montréal, Franc Canada, Les Cahiers de la décolonisation du franc-canada, No. 7, 1977, 64 pp.

Sachse, Julius F., *Extracts from the Letter-Book of Captain Johan Heinrichs of the Hessian*

Jäger Corps, 1778-1780, The Pennsylvania Magazine of History and Biography, XXII, no. 2, 1898, pp. 137-170 hrsg. v. R.W. Junghaus, Hessenland, VIII, 1894, pp. 155-157, 167-168 et 183-186.

Savory, Sir Reginald, *His Britannic Majesty's Army in Germany during the Seven Years War*, Oxford, 1966.

Schlözer, August Ludwig, *Briefwechsel meist historischen undpolitischen Inhalts*, G-6ttingen, Verlag der Vandenhoekschen Buchhandlung, 1777-1782.

—, Vertrauliche Briefe aus Kanada und Neu England vom J., 1777 und 1778, Göttingen Verlag der Wittwe Vandenhoeck, 1779.

Schmidt, H.D., *The Hessian Mercenaries: The Career of a Polilical Cliché*, History, XLIII, 1958, pp. 207-212.

Seguin, Robert Lionel, *L'apport germanique dans le peuplement de Vaudreuil et Soulanges*, In the Bulletin des recherches historiques, Vol.63, No.I, Jan., Feb, Mar., 1957, pp 42-58.

Seume, Johann Gottfried, *Schreibenaus Amerika nach Deutschland* (Halifax, 1782). Neue Literatur und Völkerkunde. Für das Jahr 1789, 2 vol., June -December Herausgegeben von J.W. v. Archenholtz, S. 362, 381. Leipzig, 1789. Prosaschriften, Darmstadt, Melzer Verlag, 1974, pp. 51-154.

Singer, Ernst, *Der Soldatenhandel deutscher Fürsten im 18. Jahrhundert in der schönen Literatur*, Unveröffenlitche Dissertation, Universität Wien, 1935.

Sintenis, Friedrich Wilhelm, *Sinteni=s Chronik der Stadt Zerbst, 1758-1817, Mitgeteilt von Reinhold Specht*. In Zebster Jahrbuch. Jg. XV. Zerbst 1930. S.92ff (über den amerikanischen Subsidienvertrag und den Feldzug des Zerbster Regiments S. 115ff.).

Slage, Robert Oakley, *The Von Lossberg Regiment: A Chronicle of Hessian Participation in the American Revolution*, Ph. D. Dissertation, American University, Washington, D.C.

Smith, Samuel S., *The Battle of Trenton*, Monmouth Beach, N.J., Philip Freneau Press, 1965.

Smith, Clifford Neal, et Anna Piszczanczaja-Smith, German American Genealogical Research, New York and London, 1976.

1- Monograph no.1: *Brunswick Deserter: Immigrants of the American Revolution*, Thomson II., Heritage House, 1973.

2- Monograph no.2: *Mercenaries from Ansbach and Bayreuth, Germans who Remained in America after the Revolution*, Thomson II., Heritage House, 1974. Reprinted by McNeal, Ag., Westland Publicatios, 1979.

3- Monograph no.3: *Muster Rolls and Prisoner-of-War List in American Archival Colletions Pertaining to the German Mercenary Troops who served with the British Forces during the American Revolution*, De Kalb, II., Westland Publications, 1974, 1976 (En trois parties).

4- Monograph no.5: *Mercenaries from Hessen-Hanau who Remained in Canada and the United States after the American Revolution*, De Kalb, II., Westland Publications, 1976.

Stanley, George F.G., *Canada Invaded, 1775-1776*. Hakkert, Toronto, 1973.

Städler, Erhard, *Die Ansbach-Bayreuther Truppen im Amerikanischen Unabhängigkeitskrieg, 1777-1783*,Neustadt/Aisch, Schmidt-Druck, 1955.

Stevens, Benjamin F., HRSG., *Facsimiles of Manuscripts in European Archives relating to America, 1773-1783*. With Descriptions, Editorial Notes, Collations, References and Translations,4 Bde., London, 1889-1895.

Stone, William L., trad., *Letters of Brunswick and Hessian Officers during the American Revolution*, Albany, N.Y., Joel Munsell's Sons, 1891. Reprinted., New York, Da Capo Press, 1970.

—, *Journal of Cpt. Pausch, Chief of the Hanau Artillery during the Burgoyne Campaign*, Albany, N.Y., Joe Munsell's Sons, 1886. Reprint ed., New York, Arno Press, 1971.

Sutherland, Maxwell, *Case History of a Settlement*, Dalhousie Review, XLI, no. 1, Spring 1961, pp. 65-74.

Tharp, Louise Hall, *The Baroness and the General*, Boston, Little, Brown & Co., 1962.

Trudel, Marcel, *La Révolution américaine. Pourquoi la France refuse le Canada, 1775-1783*, Québec, Le Boréal Express, 1976, 291 p. Édition remaniée de *Louis XVI, le Congrès américain et le Canada*, 1949, 259 p.

Uhlendorf, Bernhard A., trad., *Revolution in America: Confidentia Letters and Journals, 1776-1784, of Adjutant General Major Baurmeister of the Hessian Forces*, New Brunswick, N.J., Rutgers University Press, 1957.

—, *The Siege of Charleston. With an Account of the Province of South Carolina. Diaries and Letters of Hessian Officers* from the von Jungken=Papers in the William L. Clements Library, Ann Arbor, University of Michigan Press, 1938.

Voisine, Nive, *Histoire de l'Église catholique au Québec, 1608-1970*.

Waldeck, Philipp, *Philipp Waldeck's Diary of the American Revolution*. With Introduction and Photographic Reproduction of the List of Officers by Marion Dexter Learned, Philadelphia, Americana Germanica Press, 1907.

Walz, John A., *The American Revolution and German Literature*, Modern Language Notes, XVI, 1901, pp. 336-351, 411-418 et 449-462.

Wertheim, Ursula, *Der amerikanische Unabhängigkeilskampf im Spiegel der zeitgenössischen deutschen Literatur*, Weimarer Beiträge, III, 1957, pp. 429-470.

Wiederholdt, Andreas, *Tagebuch des Capi.Wiederholdt vom 7.Oktober 1776 bis 7. Dezember 1780*, Hrsg. v. M. D. Learned und C. Grosse, Americana Germanica Press, IV, 1901, pp. 1-93.

Woelfel, Margarete, et al., *Memoirs of a Hessian Conscript: J.G. Seume's Reluctant Voyage to America*, William and Mary Quarterly, 3rd series, V, 1948, pp. 553-670.

Woringer, August, *Zwei Briefe Hessischer Offiziere (Johann Heinrich Henkelmann und Philipp Schirmer)*, Hessenland, XX, 1906, pp. 349-341.

—, Auszüge aus Tagebhchern undaufzeichnungen hessischer Offiziere und Regiments- Chroniken im Amerikanischen Befreiungskrieg, Deutsch-Amerikanische Geschichtsblätter/German-American Historical Review, XX-XXI, 1920-1921, pp. 251-280.

Wright, J, et W. Cobbet, *The Parliamentary History of England from the Earliest Period to the Year 1803*, London, 1806. (The parliamentary debates are in vol. XVIII.)

Zimmermann, Lothar, Hrsg., Vertrauliche Briefe aus Kanada und Neu England vom J. 1777 und 1778. Aus Herm Prof. Schlözers Briefwechsel, Toronto, 1981.

C – NEWSPAPERS AND JOURNALS

Bulletin des recherches historiques

01-1896   volume XXXI, 85-91.
02-1914   volume XX, 230 et 353-355.
03-1915   volume XXI, 146-147.
04-1915   volume..., 221.
05-1916   volume VII, 46.
06-1916   volume XVII, 3.
07-1916   volume XIX, 3-23.
08-1916   volume XXII, 195-205.
09-1916   volume XXIII, 30-31 et 316-318.
10-1916   volume XXX, 213-217.
11-1923   volume XXIX, 134-136.
12-1924   volume XXX, 182-183.
13-1928   volume XXXIV, 690.

14-1939 volume XLV, 287.
15-1939 volume XLVII, 95.
16-1942 volume XLVIII, 99.
17-1943 volume XLIX, 14 et 44.
18-1945 volume I, 274-277.
19-1950 volume LVI, 78-89.
20-1951 volume LVII, 50-60.
21-1951 volume LXIII, 42-58.
22-1961 volume LXVII, 82-83.

Gazette de Québec

1- Reel No. 2, 4 Oct. 1770 - 1776.
2- Reel No. 3, 2 Jan. 1777- Ist Aug. 1782.
3- Reel No. 4, 1st Aug. 1782-1787.

Historical Society of Mecklenburg Upper Canada Inc.German-Canadian Yearbook, ed. by Hartmuth Froeschle, Toronto

1- Vol. 1, 131-139, Anna K. Hess, 1973.
2- Vol. 11, 34-49, Herbert Wilhelm Debor, 1975.
3- Vol. 111, 71-93, Herbert Wilhelm Debor, 1976.
4- Vol. IV, 129-139, Dr. Karl J.R. Arndt, 1976.
5- Vol. V, 57-63, John Irwin Cooper, 1978.

Journal of the Society for Army Historical Research

1- Haarman, A.W.; Notes on the Brunswick Troops in British Service during the American War of Independence, 1776-1783. Volume XLVIII, No. 195, 140-143.
2- Haarman, A.W.; The 3rd Waldeck Regiment in British Service, 1776-1783, Volume XLVIII, No 195, 182-185.

La Presse

1- Article by Pierette Champoux on Christmas trees, Sat. 21 December 1974.
2- Article by Jean-Pierre Wilhelmy, 30 Nov. 1981, "L'origine du sapin de Noël, un mystère qu'il reste à éclaircir".
3- Article by Cyrille Felteau, Centennial edition, Montreal, Thurs. 20 October 1983/100th year/Nos. 1,3.

Quebec Literary and Historical Society

1- Haar Some Notes from Revington's North America List for 1783. Volume XIV, 113-120.
2- Haarman, A.W. et Holst, D.W.; *The Hesse-Hanau Free Corps of Light Infantry, 1781-1785.* Volume XV, 40-42.
3- Haarman, A.W. et Holst, D.W.; *The Friedrich von German Drawing of Troops in American Revolution.* Volume XVI, 1-9.

4- Haarman, A.W.; *The Army of Brunswick and the Corps in North America, 1776-1777.* Volume XVI, 76-78.
5- Haarman, A.W.; *The Ansbach-Bayreuth Troops in North America, 1777-1783.* Volume XIX, 48-49.
6- Knötel, H. et Tood, F.-P.; *Hesse-Cassel Field Jaeger Corps, 1776-1783.* Volume VII, 46.
7- Knötel, H. et Elting, J.R.; *Hesse-Cassel Fusilier Regiment (1780 Musketier Regt.) Erbprinz.* Volume XII, 42-44.
8- Ray, F.E. et Elting J.R.; *The Brunswick Infantry Regiment von Rhetz.* Volume XVII, 49.

Les Cahiers de la décolonisation du franc-Canada

1- Cahier No 7, 1977, 64 p. VIII-Le Boréal Express.

Journal d'histoire du Canada, volume 2, 1760-1810, 301, 326-327. X-Le Soleil.

Article by Monique Duval entitled: "10 000 Canadiens français descendent d'Allemands", Sat. 9 May 1964, 19 p.

Les Cahiers des Dix

1- Volume 4, 119-120.
2- Volume 20,220.
3- Volume 22, 137-162.

Mémoires de la Société généalogique canadienne-française

01-1945   volume I, No 4, 274-280.
02-1946   volume II, No 1, 58-62.
03-1952   volume V, 30-35 et 59-62.
04-1964   volume XV, 169.
05-1965   volume XVI, 269-270.
06-1966   volume XIII, 66.
07-1966   volume XVII, 156-161.
08-1980   volume.... 286.
09-1980   volume.... 150, 199.
10-1981   volume XXXII, No. 4, 302.
11-1981   volume.... 238.

Mémoires de la Société Royale du Canada
1- 1941 section I, 91-11 1.
2- 1950 section I, 33-53.

Military Collector & Historian

1- Chapman, F.T. et Elting, J. R.; *The Brunswick Regiment of Dragoons, 1776-1783.* Volume XII, 17.
2- Chartrand, René; *Uniforms of the Hesse-Cassel Troops Sent to America in 1776.* Volume XXIII, 90-91.
3- Haarmann, A.W.; *The Hessian Army and the Corps in North Carolina, 1776-1783.*Volume XIV, 70-75.
4- Haarmann, A.W. et Peter F. Copeland, *The Provisional Chasseur Companles of Hesse-Cassel During the Revolutionary War,* XVIII, 11-13.

Nos Racines

1- Volume 36, 170-175.
2- Volume 37, 730-731, 739.
3- Volume 38, 753.
4- Volume 39, 767.

Proceeding and Transactions of the Royal Society of Canada

1- 1888, Ist series, 100.
2- 1892, Ist series, 22.
3- 1906, Ist series, 20.
4- 1900, 2nd series, 55.
5- 1930, 3rd series, 189-210

Revue d'histoire de l'Amérique française

1- June 1948, volume 2, 133-134.
2- September 1962, volume 16, 278 -281.
3- March 1972, volume 25, 581.

Revue trimestrielle canadienne

1- June 1925, 190-213.
2- September 1936, 287-299.

Royal Nova Scotia Historical Society

1- Publication No 4, 1980.

The American Historical Review

1- Avril 1920, volume 25, 551-552.
The Archival Publications of the Literary and Historical Society of Quebec

1- Melsheimer's Journal No.20.
2- Brunswick Letters D.11,135.
3- Riedesel Memoirs of Madame D. 1 1, 135.

The Bulletin of the Fort Ticonderoga Museum

1- Volume 1, 1927-1929, No 2, July 1927, 2-5.
2- Volume 3, 1933-1935, No 4, July 1934, 171-188.
3- Volume 8, 1948-1951, No 1, Jan. 1948, 16-22.
4- Volume 9, 1952-1956, No 1, Winter 1952, 13-24.
5- Volume 11, 1962 - 1965, No 5, December 1964, 234-269.
6- Volume 12, 1966-1968, No 1, Mar. 1966, 4-62.

The Canadian Antiquarian and Numismatic Journal

1- April 1877, volume 5, 165-168.
2- April 1962, volume 2, 54-60.

The Canadian Historical Review

A- Volumes 1 à 10, 1920-1929:
   1- Volume 1, 339.
   2- Volume 5, 77.
   3- Volume 6, 164 et 277.
   4- Volume 8, 364.
   5- Volume 10, 352-355.
B- Volume 11 à 20, 1930-1939:
   1- Volume 11, 371.
   2- Volume 14, 189-198.
   3- Volume 16, 476.
   4- Volume 17, 360 et 472.
   5- Volume 19, 101.
C- Volumes 21 à 30 1940-1949:
   1- Volume 21, 229 et 459.
   2- Volume 24, 331-332.
   3- Volume 27, 1-18.
   4- Volume 30, 88.

The Canadian Magazine of Polilics, Arts and Literature

A- April 1914, 229-238. B-April 1920, 290-296.

The Dalhousie Review

A- Volume XLI, spring 1961, 65 - 74. XXIX-The Ontario Historical Society.
A- Volume XX, 159-261.

The Pennsylvania Magazine of History and Biography

A- Papet, Frederick Julius von, *The Brunswick Contingent in America, 1776-1783*, The Pennsylvania Magazine of History and Biography, XV, 1891, pp. 218-224.

D- FILM

Film on the American Revolution, produced by Time Life Film for the B.B.C. London, presented by Radio-Québec (Télé-Québec) during the programme, "America, America", Jan. 31, 1981.

E- ICONOGRAPHY

All maps are reproductions of the author.

F- USEFUL INFORMATION

a) Johannes Schwalm 127, Scotland, PA 17254-0127 USA
b) Public Record Office
    Richmond, London TW9 4
    England
c) Dominique Ritchot
    German troops in Canada, 1776-1783, to be published by of the North
    Email: ritchotd@hotmail.com
d) The Association of Families of Germanic origin (The AFOGQ)
    5-861, avenue Calixa-Lavallée
    Québec (Québec)
    GIS 3H2 Tél.:418454-1776

1- Brunswick

a) Niedersâchsisches Staatsarchiv Forstweg 2
    38302 Wolfenbùttel, Germany
b) Westland Publications Post Office,
    Box 117
    McNeal, Arizona 85617-0117, États-Unis c/o Clifford Neal Smith.
    Monograph n° 1: Brunswick Déserter - Immigrants of the American Révolution.
    Monograph n° 3: Muster Rolls and Prisoner-of-War List in American Archival Collections Pertaining to the German Mercenary Troops who served with the British Forces during the American Revolution, three volumes.

2- Hesse-Cassel

a) Hessisches Staatsarchiv
    Friedrichsplatz 15, 35037 Marburg, Germany
    At this place, one can see the program HETRINA: (Hessische Truppen I Amerikanischen unabhaengigkeitskrieg). This is a list (published by the archives of Marburg) in 6 volumes of the soldiers enlisted to fight the American rebels (1776-1783). It is possible to buy theses books.

c)   Bibliothèque et Archives nationales du Québec
     Montreal Archives Center
     Gilles-Hocquart Building 535 Viger Avenue East
     Montreal (Quebec) H2I 2P3
     Tel.: 514 873-1100 option 4 Email: @ anq.montreal banq.qc.ca
d)   You can see the volumes at the Canadian genealogical research that has the
     6 volumes. For more information, write to:
     Acadian Genealogical Review
     Haute-Ville
     Québec (Québec) GIR 4S7

3- Hesse-Hanau

a)   Hessisches Staatsarchiv Friedrichsplatz 15, 35037 Marburg, Germany
b)   Westland Publications
     (See Brunswick No. 1b for address)
     Monograph n° 5: "Mercenaries from Hessen-Hanau Who Remained in
     Canada and the United States after the American Révolution."

4- Waldeck

a)   Hessisches Staatsarchiv
     (See Hesse-Cassel No. 2a for address) Volume V
b)   St. Louis Genealogical Society
     (See Hesse-Cassel No. 2b for address) Volume V

5- Ansbach-Bayreuth

a)   Ges. f. Familienforschung in Franken e. V
     Archivstrasse 17 90408 Nuremberg. Germany
     Erhard Staedtler, *Die Ansbach-Bayreuth Truppen in Amerikannischen
     Unabhaenigkeitskrieg, 1777-1783.*
     Schriftenfolge des Gesellsschaft fuer Familienforschung in Franken
     Band 8.
b)   Westland Publications same address.
     Monograph n° 2: "Mercenaries from Ansbach and Bayreuth, Germany who
     Remained in America after the Revolution."

6- Anhalt-Zerbst

a)   Stadtarchiv
     Poststrasse 2, 38350
     Helmstedt, Germany
     05351 40 568

b)   Virginia Easley DeMarce, *The Anhalt-Zerbst Régiment in the American Revolution*, September 1982.

c)   Landesarchiv Oranienbaum
     Anhalt
     Germany
     Cote: F 135/1 et F 136/1.

d)   Archives of Canada holds some lists like MG 13, WO 28, volume 10 (B-2867) Riviere-Quelle, January 22, 1782.

e)   Max von Eelking, *The German Allied Troops...*, p. 236-239 and 350-351.

G-   INFORMATION ON THE GERMAN UNIFORM

a)   Lefferts, Charles M., *Uniforms of the 1775-1783. American, British, French and German Armies in the War of the American Révolution*, publié par W.E. Inc. Old Greenwich, Conn.

b)   May, Robin, *The British Army in North America, 1775-1783*, publié chez Osprey Publishing Limited dans Men-at-Arms Séries.

c)   Katcher, Philip, *Armies of the American Wars 1753-1815*, Hastings House Publishers, New York.

d)   Funcken, Liliane et Fred, *Les costumes et les armes des soldats de tous les temps*, Casterman, vol. 2, de Frédéric II à nos jours.

e)   Chalmann G.F., *Fahnen and Uniformen der Landgraflich Hessen; Kassel'schen Truppen in Amerikanischen Wuabhangigfeitsfrieg*, 1776-1783.

f)   Mollo, John, *Uniforms of the American Révolution* (in color), Macmillan Publishing Co. Inc., New York.

g)   Lezius, Martin, *Das Chrenfleid des Soldaten, 1m Deutschen Verlag*, Berlin.

MORE NONFICTION FROM BARAKA BOOKS

INUIT AND WHALERS ON BAFFIN ISLAND THROUGH GERMAN EYES
Wilhelm Weike's Arctic Journal and Letters (1883-84)
Ludger Müller-Wille & Bernd Gieseking
(Translated from the German by William Barr)

JOSEPH-ELZÉAR BERNIER
Champion of Canadian Arctic Sovereignty
Marjolaine Saint-Pierre (translated by William Barr)

A PEOPLE'S HISTORY OF QUEBEC
Jacques Lacoursière & Robin Philpot

AN INDEPENDENT QUEBEC
The past, the present and the future
Jacques Parizeau, former Premier of Quebec (1994-96)

TRUDEAU'S DARKEST HOUR
War Measures in Time of Peace, October 1970
Edited by Guy Bouthillier & Édouard Cloutier

THE RIOT THAT NEVER WAS
*The military shooting of three Montrealers in 1832
and the official cover-up*
James Jackson

THE FIRST JEWS OF NORTH AMERICA (Spring 2012)
The Extraordinary Hart Family (1760-1860)
Denis Vaugeois & Käthe Roth

THE QUESTION OF SEPARATISM
Quebec and the Struggle over Sovereignty
Jane Jacobs

Printed in Canada
on Enviro 100% recycled
at Lebonfon Printing.